Nancy Porter Stork

Through a Gloss Darkly
Aldhelm's Riddles in the British Library ms Royal 12.C.xxiii

This edition makes available for the first time the full set of scholia, or glosses, to Aldhelm's *Enigmata*, a popular school text in the early middle ages both in England and on the Continent. The complete glosses survive only in this early eleventh-century Canterbury manuscript (British Library Royal 12.C.xxiii), although tantalizing bits and pieces of the text have made their way into other manuscripts from St. Gall, Fleury and Lorsch, suggesting a wide provenance for the glosses.

Aldhelm's *Enigmata* is a collection of a hundred riddles used for teaching the principles of Latin verse composition to advanced students. The first Latin verses to be written by an Anglo-Saxon (Aldhelm was bishop of Sherbourne and a contemporary of Bede), these riddles also inspired the well-known Old English examples of the genre found in the Exeter Book.

The glosses to the riddles range from symbols that guide the inexperienced reader through Aldhelm's convoluted Latin syntax to grammatical comments on the text and long extracts quoted from works such as Isidore's *Etymologiae* and Bede's *De Arte Metrica*. Although mainly in Latin, a significant number of the glosses are in Old English, which are here read accurately for the first time (an "incomplete" gloss on Scilla, for example, is in fact complete and perfectly legible).

The work of the medieval glossator is complemented by an translation of the riddles into modern English as well as a detailed discussion of the surviving manuscripts and a taxonomy of the types of glosses to be found.

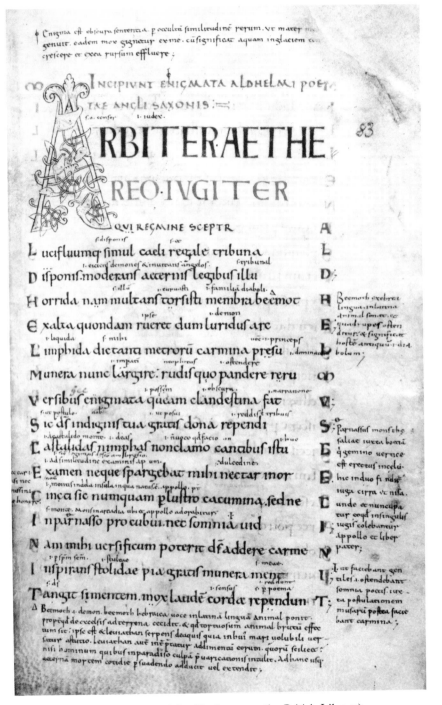

Royal 12.C.xxiii, folio 83r (courtesy the British Library)

STUDIES AND TEXTS 98

THROUGH A GLOSS DARKLY

Aldhelm's Riddles
in the British Library
MS Royal 12.C.xxiii

NANCY PORTER STORK

PONTIFICAL INSTITUTE OF MEDIAEVAL STUDIES

Acknowledgment

This book has been published with the help of a grant
from the Canadian Federation for the Humanities, using
Funds provided by the Social Sciences and Humanities
Research Council of Canada.

CANADIAN CATALOGUING IN PUBLICATION DATA

Stork, Nancy Porter, 1955-
   Through a gloss darkly

(Studies and texts, ISSN 0082-5328 ; 98)
"A diplomatic edition of Royal 12.C.xxiii."
Text of the ms. in Latin, with an English translation of each riddle, the prose
prologue, and verse preface ; commentary and notes in English.
Bibliography: p.
Includes index.
ISBN 0-88844-098-7

1. Aldhelm, Saint, 640?-709 – Translations, English.   2. Latin language,
Medieval and modern – Glossaries, vocabularies, etc.   3. Riddles, Latin –
Translations into English.   4. Riddles – Translations from Latin.   5. British
Library. Manuscript. Royal 12 C XXIII.   I. British Library. Manuscript. Royal
12 C XXIII.   II. Pontifical Institute of Mediaeval Studies.   III. Aldhelm, Saint,
640?-709. Aldhelm's riddles in Royal 12.C.xxiii.   IV. Title.   V. Series: Studies
and texts (Pontifical Institute of Mediaeval Studies) ; 98.

PA8246.A43S86 1989   871'.02   C89-093981-0

© 1990 by

Pontifical Institute of Mediaeval Studies
59 Queen's Park Crescent East
Toronto, Ontario, Canada M5S 2C4

PRINTED BY UNIVERSA, WETTEREN, BELGIUM

Contents

Acknowledgments

Many people have helped me in the course of the research for my doctoral dissertation and the writing of this book. First, I would like to thank the members of my committee, who read the dissertation for my defense in January 1985: Ashley Amos, Colin Chase, Roberta Frank, Michael Herren, Chris McDonough, and George Rigg. Many thanks also to the community of Anglo-Saxonists, smaller and poorer for those no longer among us, who have responded to my various queries and requests over the years, especially Sharon Butler, Christopher Bright, Angus Cameron, Elizabeth Stevens Girsch, Helmut Gneuss, Louis Goossens, Toni Healey, Sarah Higley, Joan Holland, Seth Lerer, David McDougall, Ian McDougall, Katherine O'Brien O'Keeffe, Raymond Page, Phillip Pulsiano, Jane Roberts, James Rosier, Paul Beekman Taylor, Pauline Thompson, and Craig Williamson, and readers for the Pontifical Institute of Mediaeval Studies and the Canadian Federation for the Humanities. Special thanks to Michael Lapidge for sharing his notes on Aldhelm manuscripts with me and to Fred Unwalla, for his meticulous editing of a recalcitrant text.

I am also indebted to the many libraries that provided me access to either their microfilm or manuscript collections: Cambridge University Library, the Bibliothèque Royale in Brussels, Bibliothèque Nationale in Paris, Biblioteca Vaticana, St. Gall Stiftsbibliothek, university libraries in Karlsruhe, Leipzig, Bremen, Wolfenbüttel, Munich and Leiden, the Institut de Recherche et d'Histoire des Textes in Paris and the incomparable collections at the Dictionary of Old English and Pontifical Institute at Toronto. I am especially grateful to the trustees of the British Library, London for permission to edit manuscript Royal 12.C.xxiiii and reproduce folio 83r.

Thanks as well to family and friends. This book, at long last (and too late to win a bet), is dedicated to David Stork.

Introduction

Aldhelm's *Enigmata*, or Riddles, were widely studied in Anglo-Saxon England and on the Continent in the early Middle Ages, and the thirty-two manuscripts and fragments that survive are testimony to the text's popularity. The work is part of his treatise *De metris et enigmatibus ac pedum regulis*, a textbook on Latin prosody aimed at teaching the subtleties of verse composition. The text thus provides evidence of how the English learned and taught Latin, and how the more proficient among them learned not only the intricacies of verse composition, but an entire corpus of Latin writings that were influential in Anglo-Saxon literary culture.

Aldhelm was one of the first English clerics to learn both Latin and Greek. Evidence for his mastery of Greek is scarce; however, he certainly was a leading exponent of the so-called Hisperic style of Latin composition, a style characterized by its use of arcane vocabulary, much of it derived from Greek. The Abstrusa-Abolita glossaries were the source for much of Aldhelm's vocabulary and several of his works (the *De virginitate, De laudibus virgini-tatis*, and the *Enigmata*) helped further to disseminate this esoteric vocabulary in the Latin-speaking world. In addition, many Latin-Old English glossaries are derived from Aldhelm's works. Some of them have many hundreds of items that can be traced to Aldhelm's works and frequently the words follow the same order in the glossary as they do in the original text. Aldhelm's influence and the influence of his *Enigmata* will be considered in more detail later, but for now it should be enough to note that for an understanding of the Latin learning in England (and, indirectly, on the Continent) it is important that we understand the use of Aldhelm's works in monastic schools.

The most important witnesses to the scope and nature of Latin education in the Middle Ages are the surviving manuscripts. Often this evidence is partial and incomplete, but careful study can bring fresh insights. Glossed manuscripts, in particular, provide evidence of how works were received or read, though earlier scholars of Aldhelm were not interested in looking at this evidence. This should come as no surprise; studies of glossing and glosses cannot properly be made until a good stable edition of the work has been completed. It was not until Rudolf Ehwald edited the complete works of

Aldhelm for the *Monumenta Germaniae Historica* series, that a firm foundation for all future studies of Aldhelm was laid. Ehwald, however, could not feasibly take into account the particular character of each manuscript and its glosses. These glosses are themselves significant witness to how a manuscript was read and used, but because they are often incomplete, illegible, incomprehensible or otherwise faulty, they must be considered with caution.

The main purpose of this study is to present an edition of the scholia to the *Enigmata* found in the tenth-century manuscript in the British Library, Royal 12.C.xxiii. The scholia, which are in Old English and Latin, are interesting in their own right; they were probably composed in England (perhaps even deriving from the school of Aldhelm himself) and have found their way only in part to a few Continental manuscripts.

The first chapter is a discussion of the surviving manuscripts, which are currently held in libraries ranging from Leningrad to St. Gallen. The glosses in British Library MS Royal 12.C.xxiii are the subject of the second chapter of the work; their grammatical, historical and paleographical significance is considered in detail. New glosses are added to the corpus of Old English glosses and previous textual difficulties are resolved. The Latin glosses, never before studied or published, provide new evidence for the ways manuscripts were used and texts were read in Anglo-Saxon England. The conclusion is a discussion of the significance of the manuscript and of Aldhelm's Riddles in the monastic culture of Anglo-Saxon England.

The text that follows is a diplomatic edition of Royal 12.C.xxiii (henceforth called L). I have preserved manuscript spelling, punctuation, and line endings and have emended the text only where there is a mistake or real difficulty in comprehending the text. Emendations are marked by angle brackets and the manuscript readings are given in the notes. Abbreviations have been expanded silently. Marking the numerous standard Latin abbreviations would be of no real interest for this study and would present nearly insuperable problems with typography, since Italic script is already being used to distinguish gloss from text. Where a form is of interest, on account of its Insular character or relevance for a specific manuscript, it is noted.

My aim is to present a readable text that is as close to the original as possible, but the peculiar nature of the glosses presents some problems. The glosses are much smaller than the text and this difference in size is preserved as well as possible. The glosses are italicized only for the convenience of this edition, and are *not* italicized in the manuscript. Occasionally, it has been necessary to reproduce a gloss as if it were two lines of text, when in fact, in the manuscript it comprises only one. Again, this convention is adopted for the convenience of the reader; a slavish reproduction of the manuscript folio would account for little.

Many of the Old English glosses are written in the margins, before or after the verse line. Where the Old English consists of one or two words and clearly belongs with a Latin lemma, I have placed it directly over its lemma; this has been made necessary by the present layout of the page. Some readings are visible only under ultraviolet light; these are marked off by square brackets. Damaged portions of the text of certain glosses (not visible even under ultraviolet light) are marked with square brackets and a series of dots [...]. The dots indicate the approximate amount of text that has been lost.

Many of the longer glosses appear in the margins of the manuscript, either to the right or left, above or below the riddles they gloss. Some of the glosses are separated from their lemma(ta) by an intervening riddle, for example when the riddle is in the middle of the folio (lines 10-15) and the gloss is in the upper or lower margin. These glosses are usually linked to their lemma(ta) by a *signe de renvoi*. There are 52 occurrences of 28 distinct *signes de renvoi* in the manuscript, but because the labour of reproducing them would have been great, they have not been printed on any of the shorter riddles. On the longer sections (Prose Prologue, Verse Preface and Riddle 101), where they are useful for linking a gloss to its lemma, they have been replaced with the modern symbols *, †, §, #, ||.

It is impossible to replicate exactly the configuration of each manuscript folio, but, as an aid to the reader, I have labelled each riddle and gloss according to its position on the folio. There are twenty-two lines per folio, so a riddle labelled "fol 84r1-8" occupies the first eight lines of folio 84 recto. To indicate the placement of glosses, I have used the following abbreviations:

upmarg = upper margin
botmarg = bottom margin
rmarg = right margin
lmarg = left margin

Thus, a gloss labelled "botmarg82r" occupies the space at the bottom of folio 82r, one labelled "rmarg90v8-10" the space to the right of lines 8-10 of folio 90v. I have also included the line number of the gloss's lemma: thus, "3 (upmarg90r)" means that the lemma for the gloss is in line 3 of the riddle. The riddles are numbered according to their appearance in the manuscript, with short titles assigned to the Prologue and Verse Preface, as follows:

(48:3) refers to line 3 of Riddle 48.
T (48:T) refers to the title of the riddle.
Prol stands for the Prose Prologue.
VP stands for the Verse Preface.

When a gloss is discussed in Chapters 1 or 2 I have not always presented it in italics over its lemma (as it appears in the printed text), but have sometimes separated lemma and gloss by a colon, for example,

subrigit: s. monstrum   (98:5),

where "s. monstrum" is a gloss to "subrigit," which occurs in line 5 of riddle 98.

The notes to each riddle provide references for all clearly identifiable sources for the glosses. Probable or indirect sources are introduced by "cf", and all but several very long sources are cited, so that readers may decide for themselves the degree of influence.

In all but two of the complete manuscripts of Aldhelm's Riddles "De trutina" is Riddle 23. In G and L, this riddle is placed after the riddle "De mirifolio" and, thus, is number 50 in this edition of L. In B, B°, U⁴, O and L "De fama" is a separate riddle appearing after "De nocte." There are thus 101 riddles in these manuscripts as opposed to 100 in the others. I have followed the order of L in this edition, but the numbers as found in Ehwald's edition are indicated at the beginning of each riddle.

The following abbreviations for texts or series are referred to frequently:

CCSL	Corpus Christianorum. Series Latina. Turnhout: Brepols, 1953-
CSEL	Corpus Scriptorum Ecclesiasticorum Latinorum. Vienna: C. Geroldi, 1866-
EETS	Early English Text Society
Keil	Heinrich Keil, ed., *Grammatici Latini*. 8 vols. 1857-1880; repr. Hildesheim: Olms, 1961
MGH	Monumenta Germaniae Historica
Auct.Ant.	Auctores Antiquissimi. 15 vols. Berlin: Weidmann, 1877-1919
Epis.Sel.	Epistolae Selectae. Berlin: Weidmann, 1916-
Poet.Lat.	Poetarum Latinorum Medii Aevi. Berlin: Weidmann, 1884-
PL	Patrologiae cursus completus. Series Latina, ed. J.P. Migne. Paris, 1844-1864.

I have provided a translation for each Riddle as well as the Prose Prologue and Verse Preface. The translations are not in English verse, but each line of the translation corresponds to a single line of poetry.

1

Manuscripts

This chapter focuses on British Library MS Royal 12.C.xxiii, the most important witness to the history of Aldhelm's riddles in England. After a detailed description of the manuscript, the other manuscripts and their relationships to Royal 12.C.xxiii will be considered. Since the manuscripts themselves are the best evidence for how Aldhelm's works were read and used in the Middle Ages, it is important to examine them carefully. Before discussing the significance of the text and glosses in Royal 12.C.xxiii, we should first describe the physical characteristics of the manuscript and outline its surviving ancestors and descendants in both England and on the Continent.

A. Physical Description of L (Royal 12.C.xxiii)

L is a manuscript of 138 folios of fine vellum with (post-medieval) gilt edges. The folios measure 245 × 150 mm; the area of written text is 174 × 98 mm; the area of the text and glosses on a fully glossed folio is 215 × 140 mm. The entire manuscript has ample space for marginal glosses, but Aldhelm's *Enigmata* is the only text that has marginal glosses (except for one short marginal gloss to Julian of Toledo's *Prognosticon*, f. 4v). All the works, except the *Opus monitorium* and the *Versus cuiusdam Scoti de alfabeto*, contain interlinear Latin glosses.

The folios were ruled with a dry point before folding (prickmarks occur in outer edges only). There are 22 lines per folio and each line is double-ruled. This double-ruling regulates the height of the body of each letter. Folios 1-98v contain double-ruling 2 mm in height; beginning with folio 99r the double-ruling is 1.5 mm in height. There is a noticeable decrease in the height of the letters, concomitant with the decrease in the distance between the ruled lines.

The left side of each folio is double-ruled vertically; this regulates the placement of the capital letters at the beginning of each line. The verse is written out in one column per folio with each verse line beginning a new manuscript line. The title of each riddle is written on a separate manuscript line.

The folios are gathered in 17 gatherings of 8 leaves each (except 12^{10}, 15^{10}, 17^{6}). The gatherings are sewn onto paper and bound in a modern binding of brown leather. The arrangement of leaves is HFHF. There are no single leaves; all gatherings consist of folded pairs. On folio 1r are written the number "109," the numbers "12.C.xxiii p. 205," and "12Cxxiii XVIC." Also on folio 1r are found two different bookmarks of the British Museum: one a rectangle with trimmed corners that reads MUSEUM BRITTANICUM, the other a crown surrounded by the words BRITISH MUSEUM. Folio 2r contains the numbers "12.Cxxiii p. 205," another rectangular stamp (as found on 1r) and a raised seal of a ship. A modern paper page has been inserted between folios 1 and 2. It has a raised annulus around a hole cut to correspond to the ship seal; this is to prevent the raised seal from damaging folio 1.

The latter part of the manuscript has suffered damage (probably by water or damp) around the edges. The damage begins with the loss of a small piece of the upper right corner of folio 81 and grows progressively worse. Folio 127 has lost two separate pieces of its upper right corner. The damage continues and creeps around to the bottom of folio 136. More than half of folio 138 is missing. The folios were consecutively numbered in the upper right hand corner in pencil after this damage occurred. The pages have all been restored to their original size by the addition of modern vellum which was then gilded. The modern restored areas are much cleaner than the original manuscript and it is easy to see where old and new meet. Some of the glosses to Aldhelm have been damaged. Beginning with folio 132, portions of the text have been lost.

B. CONTENTS

The following works are contained in L and are listed under the rubrics found in the manuscript. I give here only recent editions not listed in the British Library Catalogue. This catalogue should be consulted for further details.[1]

1. Ff. 1v-79v8: *Liber prognosticorum futuri saeculi* of St. Julian of Toledo *Sancti Iuliani Toletanae Sedis Episcopi Opera*, ed. J.N. Hillgarth. CCSL 115: 11-126. 1976.

---

[1] G.F. Warner and J.P. Gilson, *Catalogue of Western Manuscripts in the Royal and King's Collections in the British Museum*, vol. 2 (London, 1921), pp. 35-36.

2. Ff. 79v9-103v: *Enigmata Aldhelmi*
Aldhelmi Opera Omnia, ed. Rudolph Ehwald. MGH: Auct. Ant. 15: 59-149. 1919.

The Riddles of Aldhelm, trans. and comm. James H. Pitman. Yale Studies in English 67 (New Haven: Yale University Press, 1925).

Aldhelmi Enigmata, ed. Fr. Glorie. CCSL 133: 359-540. 1968.

Aldhelm: The Poetic Works, trans. Michael Lapidge and James L. Rosier, with an appendix by Neil Wright (Cambridge: D.S. Brewer, 1985), pp. 70-94.

The Old English glosses to the Riddles appear in: *Old English Glosses Chiefly Unpublished*, ed. Arthur S. Napier. Anecdota Oxoniensia 11 (Oxford: Clarendon Press, 1900), pp. 194-195.

3. Ff. 104r-113v8: *Enigmata Simphosii*
The Enigmas of Symphosius, ed. and trans. Raymond T. Ohl (Philadelphia: University of Pennsylvania, 1928).

Aenigmata Symphosii, ed. Fr. Glorie. CCSL 133A: 611-723. 1968.

4. Ff. 113v9-121v2: *Enigmata Eusebii.*
Aenigmata Eusebii, ed. Fr. Glorie. CCSL 133: 209-271. 1968.

The Riddles of Tatwine and Eusebius, ed. and trans. Mary Jane M. Williams, PhD dissertation (Ann Arbor: University of Michigan, 1974).

5. Ff. 121v3-127r16: *Enigmata Tatvini.*
Aenigmata Tatvini, ed. Fr. Glorie. CCSL 133: 165-208. 1968.

The Riddles of Tatwine and Eusebius, ed. and trans. Mary Jane M. Williams. PhD Dissertation (Ann Arbor: University of Michigan, 1974).

6. Ff. 127r17-132r17: *Opus monitorium* addressed to a youthful king, one of the grandsons of Charles the Great (Lothair, Pepin, Louis, or Charles the Bald)

E. Dümmler, ed. "Ermahnungsschreiben an einen Karolinger," *Neues Archiv der Gesellschaft für altere deutsche Geschichtskunde* [Hannover] 13 (1886): 191-196.

Wilhelm Meyer, "Smaragd's Mahnbüchlein für einen Karolinger," *Nachrichten von der königlichen Gesellschaft der Wissenschaft* (Göttingen, 1907).

Fidel Rädle, ed., *Studien zu Smaragd von Saint-Mihiel*, Medium Aevum, Philologische Studien 29 (Munich: W. Fink, 1974), pp. 28-39.

7. Ff. 132r18-134r18. *Dogmata Albini ad Carolum imperatorem* [Meyer attributes these verses to Smaragdus]
E. Dümmler, ed., "Gedichte Alcuins an Karl den Grossen," *Zeitschrift für deutsches Altertum und deutsche Literatur,* 21 (1877): 68-76.

Friedrich Vollmer, ed., "De dilectione." MGH: Auct. Ant. 14: 271. 1905.

Paul de Winterfeld, ed., "De dilectione." MGH: Poet. Lat. 4: 918. 1899.

8. Ff. 134r19-137r. *Disticha ad eundem regem* [Meyer says these are addressed to Louis the Pious]
Ernst Dümmler. *Zeitschrift für deutsches Altertum und deutsche Literatur* 21 (1877): 67.

Paul de Winterfeld, ed., "Versus cuiusdam ad Lodovicum pium." MGH: Poet. Lat. 4: 924. 1899.

9. Ff. 137v-138v: *Versus cuiusdam Scoti de alfabeto*
"Versus cuiusdam Scoti de alfabeto," ed. Fr. Glorie, in *Variae Collectiones Aenigmatum Merovingicae Aetatis.* CCSL 133A: 729-741. 1968.

C. PALEOGRAPHIC DESCRIPTION

The Latin text and glosses are written by one hand in a fine, clear Caroline script. The Old English glosses are in a mixed Caroline and Insular script. Thirty-two of the Old English glosses are by the same hand that wrote the Latin. A second, smaller hand has added forty-four of the total seventy-seven Old English glosses. The ink of the text and glosses varies from dark to light brown.

The manuscript contains seven large initials decorated in red, green and orange. Folio 1v is entirely in capitals, red and green in alternate lines. The large decorated capitals of interwoven, biting beasts occur on the following folios:

     1v   I(ncipit)
     2r   D(ie)
     6v   P(eccato)
     23v   U(nus)
     49r   I(udicii)
     83r   A(rbiter)
     84r   A(ltrix)

Large, but unadorned, capitals (alternately red, orange and green) mark the beginning of each new riddle (or each new paragraph of Julian of Toledo's *Prognosticon*). Smaller capitals (in the same brown ink as the text) begin each new poetic line (or sentence in the *Prognosticon*).

Each riddle is preceded by its title written with orange ink in Rustic Capital Display Script. The *De* of each title is alternately written as a Rustic Capital *D* or as an Uncial (Insular) *ð*. In Aldhelm's Riddles, each riddle begins with a large capital (alternately red, orange or green). All successive lines begin with a smaller orange capital. On folios 83r-v, the Verse Preface is written with orange capitals at the beginning and end of each verse line. This is to highlight the acrostic device, which reads *Aldhelmus cecinit millenis uersibus odas* at the beginning and end of the verse line.

There are four punctuation marks used throughout the manuscript:

- . punctum
- ⁊ punctus eleuatus
- ; punctus uersus
- ⁊ punctus interrogatiuus

These symbols are placed at the end of the written line, not in the margin.

The scribe uses standard Caroline abbreviations, except Insular ꟁ for *autem* found on the following folios:

85v gloss, lower margin   (18:T)
90r gloss, right margin   (45:T)
91v gloss, line 16   (53:2)
103r gloss, right margin   (101:65)

Note that this symbol occurs only in glosses.

An *NT* ligature is used ten times to save space; it is found in long verse lines which threaten to intrude into the margin and in one gloss. See Prol:11, 1:2 gloss, 52:5, 52:8, 63:1, 66:6, 67:T, 75:9, 76:7, 81:9.

Spelling in certain compounds varies between *con-* and *com-*. *Con-* is used sixteen times (twelve times before *p*) and *com-* nine times (seven times before *p*). This raises the question of how to expand "cóplendam" (Prol:17 gloss), "cóponitur" (Prol:29), cóprendere" (80:6) and "cóplector" (101:8). Since *n* is more commonly used before *p*, I have chosen to expand the above examples as *con-*.

Unlike the text, the Old English glosses use a mixture of Insular and Caroline letter forms. Sometimes both a Caroline and Insular form of one letter will be used in the same word or in different words of a long gloss. We find different forms for *d, f, g, r, s*, and *y*. We also find three standard Latin abbreviation signs used in the Old English glosses. (These signs appear regularly in the Latin text, as well.) In the Old English, the slash which usually indicates a missing nasal consonant is used four times to indicate a missing nasal consonant is used four times to indicate a missing *e*:

> ġþoht (VP:28)
> ġcyrnode (25:5)
> ġryflodre (39:1)
> ġþu (44:1)

It is used five times to indicate a missing *m*:

> finnú (16:2)
> cinú (21:2)
> cábas (25:5)
> wábe (54:3)
> gewalcudú (101:47)

The abbreviation for *uel* ƚ is found once:

> denn ƚ fereldu (65:6)

The abbreviation for *et* 7 is used in the gloss on Scilla to represent "and." This is a common orthographic practice in Old English manuscripts:

> sæ 7 wurdon (95:T gloss)

D. The Manuscripts and Their Glosses

The following list shows the relationships between the manuscripts of Aldhelm's Riddles and the amount of glossing found in each manuscript. Though it is often difficult to quantify glosses or to say that a manuscript has exactly 168 glosses, I have tried to give an idea of how heavily each manuscript is glossed. To determine the number of glosses, I counted each grammatical, lexical, interpretative and encyclopedic gloss as one complete gloss, even if it contained more than one word. For syntactical dot glosses, I counted each pair of correlating dots as one gloss. I did not count textual emendations (spelling corrections, expunction marks, dots to indicate a change in word order), pentrials, neums or drawings as glosses. The organization of this list is based on the recensions established by Ehwald. I have chosen to follow Ehwald, although the evidence of the glosses and a recent study by O'Keeffe and Journet shows that the manuscript tradition of the Riddles is very complicated and certain manuscripts can be placed in more than one group.[2] Since most of their results affect Ehwald's first

---

[2] Katherine O'Brien O'Keeffe and Alan R.P. Journet, "Numerical Taxonomy and the

recension, which consists of three lightly glossed manuscripts, and neither they nor Ehwald propose a stemma for the manuscript tradition, I have decided to leave the groups as they were divided by Ehwald. I have, however, added five manuscripts (M, V^2, U^5, S^5, U^4) not included in Ehwald's edition.

An asterisk indicates that the manuscript is in some way incomplete; either the manuscript itself is a fragment, it omits some of the Riddles but is not physically damaged, or it has lost some of its original folios. Group 6 is a set of anthologies; each of these manuscripts contains a selection of Aldhelm's Riddles mixed with other riddles or poems. Linked manuscripts share a set of common glosses.

MANUSCRIPT		NUMBER OF GLOSSES
First Recension		
T	Leningrad Q.v.I.15	30
B	Brussels 10615-729	1
B°	Brussels 9799-809	0
Second Recension		
Group 1		
K	Karlsruhe, Aug. LXXXV	24
* M	Miskolc fragment	1
P^2	Paris, lat. 2339	246
V^1	Leiden, Voss. lat. oct. 15.xii	32
V^2	Leiden, Voss. lat. Q.106	33
* R	Leipzig, Rep. I.74	2
[P^1	Paris, lat. 16700	451
[P^4	Paris, lat. 8440	531
Group 2		
U	Vatican, Pal. lat. 1753	19
* U^5	Vatican, Pal. lat. 1719	0
B^1	Brussels, 4433-38	39
Group 3		
* S	St. Gallen 1394	0
[S^2	Bremen 651	69
[* S^5	St. Gallen 273	1

Analysis of Manuscript Relationships," *Manuscripta* 27 (1983): 140. They have studied the manuscripts of Aldhelm's *Enigmata* using a statistical system of numerical taxonomy and have challenged Ehwald's division (in his edition *Aldhelmi Opera Omnia*, MGH 15 [Berlin, 1919]) of the manuscripts into two recensions, in part because T turns out to have no close connection to B and B° and to be a "highly individual manuscript which groups with other manuscripts at a very low level of similarity."

MANUSCRIPT			NUMBER OF GLOSSES
Group 4			
* P5	Paris, lat. 2773		262
* S¹	St. Gallen 242		1249
* M°	Munich, lat. 23486		20
U¹	Vatican, Reg. lat. 2078		231
* P³	Paris, lat. 7540		4
Group 5			
E	Einsiedeln 302		13
Group 6: "Anthologies"			
* T¹	Leningrad F.v.XIV.1		0
* U⁴	Vatican, Reg. lat. 1553		0
* J	Wolfenbüttel, Gud. lat. 331		0
* U²	Vatican, Pal. lat. 591		0
Group 7: The "English" Manuscripts			
L¹	London, Royal 15.A.xvi		57
O	Oxford, Rawlinson C.697		85
G	Cambridge, Gg.v.35		575
L	London, Royal 12.C.xxiii		1286

Since the main concern of this work is with the glosses to Aldhelm's Riddles, I will concentrate on the most heavily glossed manuscripts, groups 1, 2, 3, 4, and 7 of the second recension. The first recension, as well as groups 5 and 6 of the second recension, contain too few glosses to allow any significant conclusions to be drawn.

E. The Second Recension

Boyer, describing the second recension, says: "The second recension [is] characterized by emendation of the more difficult readings and the introduction of glosses."[3] This is, of course, precisely when the manuscripts begin to be of interest for the present study.

Group 1

K	Karlsruhe, Aug. LXXXV	24
* M	Miskolc fragment	1

---

[3] Blanche B. Boyer, "Insular Contributions to Medieval Literary Tradition on the Continent," [Part 1] *Classical Philology* 42 (1947): 217.

P²	Paris, lat. 2339	246
V¹	Leiden, Voss. lat. oct. 15.xii	32
V²	Leiden, Voss. lat. Q.106	33
* R	Leipzig, Rep. I.74	2
P¹	Paris, lat. 16700	451
P⁴	Paris, lat. 8440	531

K is an early manuscript, of the late eighth or early ninth century and once at the monastery of Reichenau. It is written in a graceful Caroline hand, and lightly glossed by the same hand; in seven folios (16r-23r) it contains only 24 glosses. These are variant readings or lexical glosses, e.g. "tyrannum: gigantem" (20r); "fateor: constat" (22r).

M, according to Mady and O'Keeffe and Journet,[4] is closely related textually to K. It was written in Insular minuscule, in the eighth century, by an Anglo-Saxon scribe, probably at Canterbury. Mady suggests that it came to the Continent with the missionary activities of Boniface in the eighth century. Its close relationship to K is evident from the one surviving gloss on Riddle 101 where "sermone" is written in the margin after line 64:

> Ni rerum genitor mundum sub lege coherces.

This variant reading gloss shows that the manuscript was compared to a manuscript with the later reading:

> Ni rerum genitor mundum sermone coercens.

This same gloss is found in K and, thus, Mady suggests that M may be the exemplar from which K was copied.

P², written in the late ninth to early tenth century and once the property of the monastery at Limoges, is a heavily glossed manuscript; in 11 folios (47r-58v) it contains 246 glosses. The text is written in a Caroline hand and there are two distinct medieval glossating hands in addition to the hand of the text. Most of the medieval glosses are synonym glosses, but there are scattered grammatical and syntactical dot glosses and seven short interpretative/encyclopedic glosses (5 to 10 words long).

In V¹, a manuscript of the late tenth to early eleventh century and also once at the monastery of Limoges, the glosses and text are written by the same Caroline hand. There are two verse lines contained in each manuscript line of text. Of its 32 glosses 31 are synonym or interpretative glosses, most of which are also found in P² and very likely copied from this manuscript.

---

[4] Z. Mady, "An viiith Century Aldhelm Fragment in Hungary," *Acta Antiqua Academiae Scientiarum Hungaricae* 13 (1965): 445; O'Keeffe and Journet, "Numerical Taxonomy," 140.

V^2, the "Leiden Riddle" manuscript, was written in western France, in the ninth century, very likely at Fleury. It contains numerous pentrials of neums, which are characteristic of other Fleury manuscripts.[5] The manuscript was written in Caroline script by one scribe. In addition to the hand that wrote the text, we find three medieval glossating hands, one of which wrote titles to Riddles 1-19 in the margin, and one which wrote several short glosses that are faded or erased and now almost totally illegible. Though the manuscript has received attention from three medieval scribes/glossators (and one post-medieval hand), the glosses are haphazard, much like the pentrials and neums sprinkled over the folios.

In V^2, there are eight glosses of 5 to 20 words each; the remaining medieval glosses are single word synonym glosses. There are two Old English additions to the text, which are written by the text hand. On folio 10r at the end of the Table of Contents for the Riddles we find a list of types of nymphs in Old English. This gloss is found nowhere else. On folio 25v we find an Old English translation in Northumbrian dialect of Riddle 32 "De Lorica," commonly known as the "Leiden Riddle." Both the "Leiden Riddle" and the Old English list of nymphs are added in folio space that was not filled by the preceding Latin texts. The addition of Old English suggests that the scribe, though writing at Fleury, was an English speaker.[6] Because V^2 contains Old English, it might be considered an "English" manuscript, but there is no evidence that it ever was in England. Textual similarities between V^2 and the other manuscripts of Group 1 suggest that it should be included here.

R, a Continental manuscript from the Loire region (perhaps Orleans), of the late ninth to early tenth century, once contained a complete copy of the Riddles, but it has lost folios containing Riddles 52:8 to 92:9. It is written in a Caroline hand and is virtually unglossed.

P^1 (ninth-tenth century) and P^4 (tenth-eleventh century) are two heavily glossed manuscripts, which share a common set of over 400 lexical glosses along with five interpretative and three encyclopedic glosses. In addition to

[5] M.B. Parkes, "The Manuscript of the Leiden Riddle," *Anglo-Saxon England* 1 (1972): 213.

[6] A.H. Smith, ed., *Three Northumbrian Poems*, 2nd ed. (London, 1968), p. 25. There was considerable contact between English monasteries and the monastery at Fleury, beginning in the tenth century. Wulfstan, in his life of St. Ethelwold says "Adeluuoldus autem misit Osgarum monachum trans mare ad monasterium sancti patris Benedicti Floriacense, ut regularis obseruantiae mores illic disceret ac domi fratribus docendo ostenderet. ..." (Michael Winterbottom, *Three Lives of English Saints* [Toronto, 1972], p. 42). Abbo of Fleury spent two years (985-987) at the abbey of Ramsey and wrote a life of St. Edmund. For further information on interaction between Fleury and Anglo-Saxon monasteries, see Winterbottom's introduction, pp. 4-6, and David Knowles, *The Monastic Order in England* (Cambridge, 1963).

this common set of glosses, P^4 contains other lexical and variant reading glosses as well as glosses (mainly to titles) in Tironian notes.

P^1 (ff. 103v-104r) contains a list of types of metrical feet with scansion markings underneath,

ia   troch   etc.,

which suggests that it was used to scan Latin poetry. Since these are Continental manuscripts, we can see that the active study of Aldhelm's text as a primer of Latin poetry was not limited to England.

Both the text and glosses of P^4 are written in the same Caroline hand. The text and glosses of P^1 are written in a Caroline hand in black ink; a small number of glosses are added by a similar hand in brown ink. P^1 and P^4 each inherited a large set of common glosses, but P^4 contains 80 glosses in addition to those found in P^1. P^4 may have been copied from P^1, but it has also received attention from another glossator. The glosses in P^4 show some Insular features not found in P^1, e.g. Insular ∂ in the glosses "inuisa: odiosa" (f. 30v); "algida: frigida" (f. 30r). This, together with the Tironian notes, suggests that a scribe from the British Isles may have added the extra glosses.

Group 2

U	Vatican, Pal. lat. 1753	19
* U^5	Vatican, Pal. lat. 1719	0
B^1	Brussels, 4433-38	39

U and U^5 were both written at Lorsch, U^5 in the late eighth to early ninth century and U in the ninth century, and they both contain the text in continuously written lines which the scribe has filled without regard to the endings of verse lines. This is a space-saving device which leaves little room for glosses. Both these are written in "typical Lorsch script, with Insular graphemes for 'r' and 's.'"[7] Neither of the Lorsch manuscripts is heavily glossed. U contains 16 synonym and three variant reading glosses. These glosses occur in the margin and are written in black or brown ink, in each case by a hand very similar to the hand of the text. U^5 is entirely unglossed.

The text of B^1 is written in a tenth-century Caroline hand and the glosses are by the same hand. In addition to its 25 synonym and 14 variant reading glosses, B^1 contains 45 neums added at the ends of poetic lines (especially f. 58r and 70v), a characteristic of Fleury manuscripts that suggests this manuscript had its origins at Fleury or that a Fleury scribe worked on it.

---

[7] Valerie M. Lagorio, "Aldhelm's *Aenigmata* in Codex Vaticanus Palatinus latinus 1719," *Manuscripta* 15 (1971): 24.

Group 3

* S	St. Gallen 1394	0
S²	Bremen 651	69
* S⁵	St. Gallen 273	1

"From the Anglo-Saxon manuscript of which only fragments exist (S) is derived Bremensis 651, olim Sangallensis."[8] As early as the ninth century, there were copies of Aldhelm's works at both St. Gall and Reichenau. "The patristic collections in Reichenau's and St. Gall's libraries were very similar. Even less common treatises point to a liberal exchange between the two monasteries. Aldhelm's works, which were quite rare, were available in several copies at both St. Gall and Reichenau."[9] The presence of these manuscripts can be attributed to the extensive contacts between Anglo-Saxons and various Continental monasteries and missions during the eighth century.

S is written in Anglo-Saxon Majuscule. There are two scratched Old English glosses on one folio of S: "lucis: monan" and "cocinia: storg (p. 127)."[10] The corresponding portion of the surviving text of S is more fully glossed in S². The same hand, a coarse Caroline with some Insular features, has written both the text and glosses and while there are only 69 glosses to a complete text of the Riddles in S², these glosses show a surprising range of type and are, for the most part, unique to this manuscript.

Four glosses are in Old High German: "cicada: snegezerz" (f. 22r); "ebulus: i. atuh" (f. 29r); "Brattea: glodfama" (f. 29v); "eleuorus: i. alada" (f. 31r). The rest are in Latin. The range of glosses is as wide as that of heavily glossed manuscripts such as P¹ and P⁴. S² contains lexical, interpretative and encyclopedic glosses, but no variant reading glosses. Many of these glosses are also found in manuscripts of Group 4. S² also shows some similarities to the glosses of the "English" manuscripts. It contains glosses in a vernacular language and has two interpretative glosses of the "nomen" and "genus" type. While glosses of this type do occur in heavily glossed manuscripts (one is found in P¹–"Populus: genus arboris" [f. 110r]; one in P⁴–"nardi: genus floris" [f. 34v]), the occurrence of two glosses out of a total of only 69 glosses in S² is remarkable. The two glosses are found in S² as well as in P⁵ and S¹ (Group 4 manuscripts):

---

[8] Boyer, "Insular Contributions," p. 219; see also Ehwald, ed., *Aldhelmi opera omnia* pp. 52-53.

[9] John J. Butt, "The Ninth-Century Library at St. Gall," *St. Gall and the Middle Ages, Cuyahoga Review* 1 (1983): 75.

[10] Herbert Dean Meritt, "Old English Glosses, Mostly Dry Point," *Journal of English and Germanic Philology* 60 (1961): 441.

> cauri: nomen uenti   (f. 22r)
> sistri: genus tubae   (f. 29v)

S^2 also contains two encyclopedic glosses (to "Coloseus" [f. 23r] and to "eumenides" [f. 29v]) and several other interpretative glosses (especially to Riddle 101 "De creatura"), which are closely related to glosses found in Group 4, such as:

> Peruigil excubiis numquam dormire ualebo: i. sicut angeli   (f. 32r)
> Sed tamen extimplo clauduntur lumina somno: ut pigri   (f. 32r)

Twenty-nine of the glosses in this manuscript are to the final riddle "De creatura." We will see that this interest in "De creatura" is a special feature of two "English" manuscripts, G and L. S^2 is thus a manuscript with glosses that are drawn from both Anglo-Saxon and Continental traditions. This makes sense when we consider that St. Gall had strong links to the Insular tradition and yet was firmly established as a Continental scriptorium.

S^5 is the smallest fragment of Aldhelm's Riddles that survives today. It consists of one line on a folio which contains the end of Aldhelm's Riddles and the beginning of Symphosius' Riddles. The entire surviving text and gloss read:

> Sciscitor inflatos fungar quo nomine sophos: ignota res quo nisi creatura uocatur.   (f. 13r)

The text is black and the gloss is dark brown, but seem to be written in the same ninth-century Caroline hand. This exact gloss is also found in S^2. We can postulate from this that the complete text of S^5 shared all or many of the glosses in S^2.

Group 4

* P^5	Paris, lat. 2773	262
* S^1	St. Gallen 242	1249
* $M°$	Munich, lat. 23486	20
U^1	Vatican, Reg. lat. 2078	231
* P^3	Paris, lat. 7540	4

P^5, a ninth-century manuscript from Rheims, is written in a tall, thin Caroline script. This hand seems to have written the glosses as well as the text, though the glosses are, in general, a lighter shade of brown than the text. The text is nearly complete; only the last 47 lines of "De creatura" are missing. The text is heavily glossed, with many synonym and variant reading glosses, as well as long interpretative and encyclopedic glosses. The glosses to P^5 have been incorporated, perhaps copied directly, into the manuscript S^1, which is one of the more curious of the Aldhelm Riddle manuscripts.

S^1 is one of three manuscripts (L and U^1 being the others) expressly designed as glossed texts. The folios of S^1 are ruled with a dry point into two main sections, one for the text and one for the glosses. Approximately one-fourth of the folio space (along the outer side margin) is reserved for glosses. There is, in addition to this marginal space, plenty of space between the lines for interlinear glosses. The same glosses found in P^5 have been added to the outer side margins of S^1. These glosses are set apart from the text and it is easy to see how a glossary could have been compiled from such a manuscript.

In addition to Latin glosses, there are Old High German glosses to the titles of most of the Riddles, e.g. "De vento: i. vuint" (f. 22v), "De nube: i. uuolchan" (f. 22v). These were probably added at the monastery at St. Gall. Unfortunately, the manuscript has lost the latter part of the Riddles and the last surviving title is "De Elephanto." There were very likely more Old High German glosses on the lost folios.

Not only does this manuscript contain the Latin glosses it received from P^5 and Old High German glosses; it also has an astonishing number of other glosses. Above nearly each line of text we find lexical glosses, grammatical glosses and syntactical dot glosses. The grammatical glosses on nouns reveal an unusual interest in the ablative case. For example, on folio 22v, there are thirteen glosses indicating the ablative case (e.g., "uersu: s. cum"), and this is indicative of what is found throughout the manuscript. On the same folio, we find 26 pairs of syntactical dot glosses using the following symbols:

Along with L, S^1 is the manuscript that is most thorough in its use of syntactical dot glosses. S^1 is an earlier manuscript than L and as there are connections between St. Gall and England, the evidence of these two manuscripts might suggest that the glosses travelled from the Continent to the British Isles, though one would hesitate to draw a firm conclusion from such meager evidence.

With such an embarassment of glossatorial riches, one would expect a nearly illegible text, but S^1 is surprisingly clear. Because it was intended to be glossed, there is sufficient room for all the glosses and the folios, though full of writing, are not cluttered. The same hand wrote both the text and glosses in this manuscript, another fact which suggests that the manuscript was planned as a glossed text and that at least some of the glosses were copied along with the text and not added as part of a learning or teaching process.

M^o is an eleventh-century manuscript containing a complete copy of Aldhelm's *Carmen de Virginitate*, but only the Verse Preface to the Riddles, which occurs on a badly stained folio and is lacking its last three lines. There was probably at one time a complete copy of the Riddles in this manuscript. The glosses to the Verse Preface in M° are identical to the common set of glosses to the Verse Preface in P⁵ and S¹. There is also an Old High German gloss, "Examen: suarm." The *Carmen de Virginitate* in M° is heavily glossed and contains many encyclopedic glosses from Isidore which are similar to those found on the Riddles in U¹ and L (e.g. Castalidas, Salamandra).

U¹ is a manuscript from Rheims with textual links to the other manuscripts in Group 4 and with some encyclopedic glosses similar to those found in M° and L. It does not share the glosses common to P⁵, S¹ and M°, and on the evidence of glosses alone could be considered along with the "English" manuscripts, but I decided here (as with V²) that similarities in text are more important than similarities in glossing for placing a manuscript in a group of related manuscripts.

The text of U¹ is written in a tenth-century Caroline script; there are two glossating hands, each different from the hand of the text. The first glossator has written the glosses on folios 123r-126v; the second takes over for folios 126v-135r. In U¹ we notice a style of glossing that we have not encountered before. In the previous heavily glossed manuscripts the glosses are evenly distributed throughout the text. In U¹ we find a large number of glosses on folios 123r-128r (Riddles 1 to 56) and an almost total cessation of glosses on the rest of the text. Glossator 1 adds lexical glosses to the text of the Riddles and supplies an explanatory gloss (often an etymological gloss) to the title of most of the Riddles from 1 to 38. The second hand continues glossing the titles of Riddles 39 to 56. These glosses can be very short lexical glosses, e.g. "De moloso: id est cane" (f. 124r), etymological glosses, e.g. "De urtica: Urtica ex eo uocata quod tactus eius urat" (f. 127r) or long, encyclopedic extracts from Isidore, Gregory or other sources (e.g. "De pliadibus," "De salamandra"). These glosses are similar (in some cases nearly identical) to those found in L. There is ample marginal space to accommodate these long glosses, which suggests that the manuscript was planned as a glossed text.

P³, a tenth-century manuscript, is written in a small, delicate hand; it has been damaged and Riddles 64 to 101 have been lost. There are four glosses by a different hand than the hand of the text; even under ultraviolet light these glosses are illegible. The verse lines are written continuously, thus leaving little room for glossing. It does not share in the glossing tradition of the other manuscripts of this group.

Group 7   The English Manuscripts

    L¹   London, Royal 15.A.xvi   57

O	Oxford, Rawlinson C.697	85
G	Cambridge, Gg.v.35	575
L	London, Royal 12.C.xxiii	1286

All of the English manuscripts are in Caroline script. Boyer says that "the four English codices are collections of Aenigmata." [11] This is not accurate; only G and L contain any riddles other than those by Aldhelm. L^1 contains Juvencus' *Libri iiii euangeliorum*, Aldhelm's *Enigmata*, an extract from Bede's *De arte metrica* and a *Scolica glosarum* (glossary of Greek words). O contains Aldhelm's *Enigmata, Versus de nominibus litterarum, Carmen de Virginitate, De octo uitiis principalibus* and Prudentius' *Psychomachia*. G and L are "collections of Aenigmata" and other works in Latin (the exact contents are discussed below).

Boyer gives the following description of the four English manuscripts:

> The oldest is London B.M. Reg. 15.A.xvi *olim* Cantuariensis, *saec. IX* [L^1], written, according to Thompson, not in England but in France. To it supplements were added in the tenth century, and in England there were bound with it some eleventh-century folios. MS B.M. Reg. 12.C.xxiii, *saec. XI in.* [L], is remarkable on two counts: It is the first collection of Anglo-Saxon *aenigmata* with Symphosius, and it is the sole manuscript in England which contains any portion of the tract *De Metris*. In it the *Aenigmata* and metrical Preface of Aldhelm are immediately preceded by that part of the tract which pertains to the *Aenigmata* (=75.21-77.5, 77.9-81.8). Like [L^1], it formerly belonged to Canterbury. The two are similar in titles but differ in text. An Oxford manuscript, Rawlinson C.697 *olim* Bury St. Edmunds, *saec. IX/X* [O] whose origin is in dispute (Germany?), agrees with [L] in the *Incipit*, with [P^2] in some places of text, with [four] French manuscripts of the same stock as [P^2] in a transposition of lines, and in its corrections with [L] and another Canterbury manuscript, Cambridge 1567 Gg.v.35 [G], *saec. XI*. The latter, a *Corpus poetarum christianorum*, the most extensive collection of its kind, was written by an Englishman, but whether at home or abroad is not known. The text, though much emended, appears to be from the same exemplar as [L]; the two agree in titles and in the misplacement of *Aen.* 23 before *Aen.* 50.[12]

Helmut Gneuss gives the following origin and provenance of each of the "English" manuscripts:

L^1 origin: possibly on the Continent
     provenance: St. Augustine's, Canterbury
O   origin: northeast France
     provenance: Bury St. Edmunds

[11] Boyer, p. 219.

[12] Ibid., p. 219-220. See also Edward Thompson, *Catalogue of Ancient Manuscripts in the British Museum* (London, 1884) 2: 74.

G   provenance: St. Augustine's, Canterbury
L   provenance: Christ Church, Canterbury.[13]

Though M.R. James first defined the Canterbury style of Caroline
Minuscule script, it was T.A.M. Bishop who identified the scribal hands in
many surviving manuscripts from the St. Augustine's and Christ Church
scriptoria.[14] Bishop was the first to attribute L to Christ Church on the basis
of its script. Because its folio arrangement is HFHF, Bishop dated it before the
beginning of the eleventh century. At this time, the scriptorium of Christ
Church switched from HFHF to HFFH arrangement of manuscript leaves.
Temple, in her survey of Anglo-Saxon illuminated manuscripts from 900 to
1066, attributes L to Canterbury by virtue of its decorated capitals. She
follows Bishop in attributing it specifically to Christ Church and dates it
"second half of the 10th century." [15]
    M.J. Williams says that L originated in Canterbury, but may have spent
some time in Glastonbury. She cites a remark by John Leland on his visit to
Glastonbury Library about 1536:

> Inveni librum Aenigmaton quem Tatvinus hexametris versibus scripserat.
> Neque hic lectorem celabo, quod ibidem repererim libellos Symposii, Ald-
> helmi, et Eusebii, qui de eadem materia scripserunt carmine non omnino
> improbando.[16]

She adds that L "was not apparently in the Royal collection when the
catalogue of 1666 was compiled and that it probably belonged to Thomas
Howard, Earl of Arundel in the early 17 c." [17] Considering the heavy losses
sustained by the Glastonbury library during the Dissolution, it is possible that
Leland saw a now-lost manuscript related to L and G.
    L[1] is glossed by a medieval hand (not the hand of the text) and by a
post-medieval hand, identified as that of Patrick Young, who collated this

---

[13] Helmut Gneuss, "A Preliminary List of Manuscripts Written or Owned in England up
to 1100," *Anglo-Saxon England* 9 (1981): 1-60. Neil R. Ker, *Medieval Libraries of Great
Britain*, 2nd ed. (London, 1964) also gives the same provenances for L[1] (p. 367), O (p. 385)
and G (p. 336). He does not ascribe a provenance to L.

[14] T.A.M. Bishop, *Transactions of the Cambridge Bibliographic Society* (1949-1953)
432-440.

[15] Elzbieta Temple, *Anglo-Saxon Manuscripts 900-1066* (London, 1976), p. 56. Temple
also ascribes L[1] to St. Augustine's, Canterbury (p. 102).

[16] "I found a book of Aenigmas which Tatwine had written in hexameter verses. Nor will
I conceal from my reader that I found there books of Symposius, Aldhelm, and Eusebius, who
wrote on the same matter in verse not at all to be despised" (Text and translation are cited
from Mary Jane Williams, *The Riddles of Tatwine and Eusebius*, PhD dissertation [Ann Arbor:
University of Michigan, 1974], pp. 93-94).

[17] Ibid. p. 94.

manuscript with a codex of the Earl of Arundel, probably L.[18] The glosses to folios 59v and 60r are in the same hand as the text; beginning with folio 60v another medieval hand glosses the text. Despite a small number of glosses, L[1] shows a wide range of Latin glosses – grammatical, lexical, variant reading, syntactical, interpretative and encyclopedic. It contains only one Old English gloss:

> uerme: hondworm   (f. 73r, 101:66)[19]

The text of O is written by two hands, which provide a few of the glosses.[20] Most of the glosses, however, are written by another, unruly hand, larger than either of the text hands. This glossating hand alternates between Caroline and Insular letter forms and has added the Old English glosses to the manuscript. The titles are each given a separate manuscript line and often the second glossator simply rewrites the title in the margin. The first glossator adds sporadic grammatical, variant reading, lexical and interpretative glosses to the text. In addition, the second text hand provides some Latin synonyms and five Old English glosses, three of which are on Riddle 84 "Scrofa pregnans." We will notice this clustering phenomenon in our next two manuscripts as well.

G and L are both connected with Canterbury. Of all the Aldhelm manuscripts, they are the most extensive collections of Latin riddles. They both contain Riddles of Aldhelm, Symphosius, the *Dogmata Albini ad Carolum Imperatorem* (ascribed to Smaragdus), the *Disticha eiusdem ad eundem regem* and the *Versus cuiusdam Scoti de Alfabeto*. In addition, they are the only two manuscripts that contain copies of the Riddles of the English writers Tatwine and Eusebius. L contains, in addition to the above texts, the *Prognosticon* of Julian of Toledo. G, a huge manuscript of 447 folios, contains numerous other Latin poetic and prose works.[21]

G's version of Aldhelm's Riddles is particularly interesting because it shares many of L's Latin glosses. The Riddles were written and glossed by

---

[18] Warner and Gilson, *Manuscripts in the Royal and King's Collections* 2: 35.

[19] Printed in Arthur S. Napier, ed., *Old English Glosses: Chiefly Unpublished* (Oxford, 1900), p. 193.

[20] One of the more interesting results of O'Keeffe and Journet's research is that O, when grouped by numerical taxonomy, shifts between two families of manuscripts. I have grouped it with the English manuscripts on the basis of its glosses, but it also exhibits the transposition of lines 61-67 after line 43 in Riddle 101 that is characteristic of Group 1 manuscripts. O'Keeffe and Journet have discovered that it shifts from this group to show affinity with T. They say that "this shift of families suggests a switch in exemplars, a suspicion supported by a clear change in scribal hand in [O] after l. 20 of f. 14v" (O'Keeffe and Journet, "Numerical Taxonomy," p. 140).

[21] A. George Rigg and G.R. Wieland, "A Canterbury Classbook of the Mid-Eleventh Century (the 'Cambridge Songs' Manuscript)," *Anglo-Saxon England* 4 (1975): 113-130.

one hand. The Verse Preface and Riddles 1 to 46 occupy folios 394v-398v. On these folios, G contains a set of interlinear Latin glosses virtually identical to those found in L. G does not have margins large enough to accommodate marginal glosses the length of those found in L. While G may have been intended to be a glossed text, its layout does not allow for the marginal glossing found in S¹, L and U¹. With only a few omissions and misspellings, the Latin interlinear glosses on the Verse Preface and Riddles 1 to 46 in G are identical to those found in L. On Riddles 47 to 69 (ff. 399r-401v24), we find only two Latin glosses (and no Old English glosses) in G:

fortunatus: s. essem (f. 400r, 58:6)
lumen: s. meum (f. 400r, 58:7)

These are also found in L.

Riddles 70 through 80 (ff. 401v25-403r24) contain occasional Latin glosses (33 to be exact) and these are not found in L. Riddles 81 to 100 (ff. 403r25-406r7) are unglossed. Riddle 101 (ff. 406r8-407r27) is heavily glossed in both Latin and Old English. Some of the glosses are written cryptically, in a code where each letter of a word is replaced by the letter immediately following it in the alphabet. Thus, we find:

Setigero rursus constans audacior apro: ut mfp (f. 406r17, 101:10)

where "mfp" is decoded "leo." We also find Latin and Old English glosses in standard orthography. The Latin glosses are in Caroline script and the Old English are Insular, though occasionally the scripts are mixed.

One further point should be made about the Old English glosses. L and G share only one common Old English gloss:

Sic: swa (f. 395r31, 6:4)

With this exception, even where L and G share the same Latin glosses, they do not share the same Old English glosses.

G is the most striking example of a phenomenon noticed in S². Riddle 101 "De creatura" contains most of the Old English and all of the encoded glosses in G. These glosses occur after a long stretch of unglossed or lightly glossed Riddles (47-100) and are concentrated on this long, final riddle. It is a shame that "De creatura" has not been preserved in S¹; it is possible that the Old High German glossator of St. Gall also expressed unusual interest in this last riddle, but without the lost folios there is no way for us to know.

G and L are closely related by a set of common Latin glosses and they each received individual attention from Anglo-Saxon glossators writing in Old English. Their texts are closely related; the major differences are that in G the titles are found in the margin and in L the titles are given a separate manuscript line. There is no Riddle 98 "De fama" in G; this section of the text is contained in Riddle 97 "De nocte," where it originally belonged. Thus, neither G nor L is an apograph of the other, yet they both received a common set of glosses and a similar text from the same ultimate source.

L contains part of the Prose Treatise *De metris.* The full treatise is entitled *De metris et enigmatibus ac pedum regulis* and contains within it the Riddles of Aldhelm. K, P^2, M, U, B^1, and S are the only other manuscripts containing all or part of this treatise.

Appendix

The Manuscripts of Aldhelm's Riddles

The Riddles of Aldhelm appear in the following manuscripts:

First Recension

T: Leningrad, Saltykov-Shchedrin Public Library, Q.v.I.15, ff. 72r-79v (*saeculum VIII*)

B: Brussels, Bibliothèque Royale, 10615-729, ff. 191v-194r (*saeculum XII*)

B°: Brussels, Bibliothèque Royale 9799-809, ff. 134v[137v]-137v[140v] (*saeculum XII Apograph of B*)

Second Recension

K: Karlsruhe, Badische Landesbibliothek, Aug. LXXXV, ff. 1r-2r; 2v-15r; 15v-23r (*saeculum VIII/IX*)

M: Miskolc, Hungary, Zrinyi Ilona Secondary School ff. 1r-1v (*saeculum VIII*)

P²: Paris, Bibliothèque Nationale, lat. 2339, ff. 47r-58v; 74; 74v-98r (*saeculum IX/X*)

V¹: Leiden, Bibliotheek der Rijksuniversiteit, Voss. lat. oct. 15.XII, ff. 148r-153v (*saeculum X/XI Apograph of P²*)

V²: Leiden, Bibliotheek der Rijksuniversiteit, Voss. lat. Q.106, ff. 9r-10r; 10v-25v (*saeculum IX*)

R: Leipzig, Karl-Marx-Universitätsbibliothek, Rep. I.74, ff. 1r-13r (*saeculum IX/X*)

P¹: Paris, Bibliothèque Nationale, lat. 16700, ff. 96v-98r; 99r-114r (*saeculum IX/X*)

P⁴: Paris, Bibliothèque Nationale, lat. 8440, ff. 11v-13r; 13v-36v (*saeculum X/XI*)

U: Vatican City, Biblioteca Apostolica, Pal. lat. 1753, ff. 87r-97v (*saeculum IX*)

U⁵: Vatican City, Biblioteca Apostolica, Pal. lat. 1719, ff. 1v-14v (*saeculum VIII/IX*)

B¹: Brussels, Bibliothèque Royale, 4433-38, ff. 1-2v; 2v-54v; 55r-57r; 57r-72r (*saeculum X*)

S: St. Gallen, Stifsbibliothek, 1394, pp. 121-122; 125-128 and Zofignen, Stadt-bibliothek p. 32 (fly-leaf) (membrum disiectum) (*saeculum VIII* ex.)

S^2: Bremen, Staats- und Universitätsbibliothek, 651 (4°.11.52), ff. 7r-34v (*saeculum IX/X*)

S^5: St. Gallen, Stifsbibliothek, 273, p. 13 (*saeculum IX*)

P^5: Paris, Bibliothèque Nationale, lat. 2773, ff. 95r; 95v-106v; 107 (*saeculum IX*)

S^1: St. Gallen, Stifsbibliothek, 242, pp. 21-48 (*saeculum IX/X*)

M°: Munich, Bayerische Staatsbibliothek, lat. 23486, ff. 343 (*saeculum XI*)

U^1: Vatican City, Biblioteca Apostolica, Reg. lat. 2078, ff. 123r-135r (*saeculum X*)

P^3: Paris, Bibliothèque Nationale, lat. 7540, ff. 69r-74v (*saeculum X*)

E: Einsiedeln, Stifsbibliothek, 302, ff. 125; 132-144 (*saeculum X*)

T^1: Leningrad, Saltykov-Shchedrin Public Library, F.v.XIV.1, ff. 133r-138v (*saeculum VIII/IX*)

U^4: Vatican City, Biblioteca Apostolica, Reg. lat. 1553, ff. 8v-21v (passim) (*saeculum IX* in.)

J: Wolfenbüttel, Herzog-August Bibliothek, Gud. lat. 331, ff. 67r-69v (*saeculum X/XI*)

U^2: Vatican city, Biblioteca Apostolica, Pal. lat. 591, ff. 139v-141v (*saeculum XV:* 1472)

L^1: London, British Library, Royal 15.A.xvi, ff. 59v-73v (*saeculum IX*)

O: Oxford, Bodleian Library, Rawlinson C.697, ff. 1r-13v; 14v-16r (*saeculum IX/X*)

G: Cambridge, University Library, Gg.v.35, ff. 394r-407r (*saeculum XI*)

L: London, British Library, Royal 12.C.xxiii, ff. 79v-103v (*saeculum X/XI*)

2

The Glosses

Aldhelm, in *De metris et enigmatibus ac pedum regulis,* says "Prosodia est signum sermonis iter rectum faciens legenti."[1] Though this section of his treatise does not survive in L or any English manuscripts, we can assume that at some time the full treatise was available in Anglo-Saxon England. For Aldhelm, prosody consists in the actual signs made to indicate accent, length of syllables, aspiration and proper word division. The *Oxford English Dictionary* defines prosody as "the science of versification, that part of the study of language which deals with the forms of metrical composition."[1] I am using the modern sense of the word to encompass all the glosses on prosody in L.

1. *Accent Marks*

Returning to Aldhelm, we find that he borrows from Donatus the following comments on accent (*prosodia*) and includes them in his own work on metre:

> Tonus autem aut pertrahitur aut attrahitur aut medietas sillabae bonam vocem habens ... toni sunt tres: acutus, gravis, circumflexus. Acutus tonus est nota per obliquum ascendens in dexteram partem ut est páx níx núx.[2]

He goes on to say that the acute accent falls on two possible syllables in Latin, the penultimate and the antepenultimate. He makes no further mention of monosyllables, though his initial examples *pax, nix, nux* are monosyllables. Twenty-seven of the 30 accent marks on Latin words in L appear over monosyllables.

---

[1] *Aldhelmi opera omnia,* ed. R. Ehwald, MGH: Auct. Ant. 15: 199.
[2] Ibid., 200. See also Donatus, *Ars grammatica,* in Keil 4: 371.

Three accent marks are found in the Prose Prologue, all occurring on folio 81v:

> Rursus ídem dicit líricus libro quarto   (Prol:92)
> uersu libro nono bís elisit dicens   (Prol:96)

In each case, these glosses indicate the stress of the word, on the penultimate (*idem*), antepenultimate (*liricus*) and only (*bis*) syllable. Note that these 3 marks occur over the letter *i*. Earlier in the Prologue, the glossator[3] has marked the letter *i* with a mark smaller than the acute accent mark found elsewhere (folio 80r):

> quínis íam senís uel etíam septenís   (Prol:20)

These marks are clearly orthographic, intended only to distinguish the *i* from among the other letters. They "dot" the *i* and cannot be construed as marking the stress, yet the glossator may have been influenced in the glossing of *idem, liricus* and *bis* by the previous "dotting" of *i*.

Accent Marks on Glosses (Latin and Old English)

The greatest number of accent marks in the manuscript is found, surprisingly, on the glosses. These accent marks may serve to emphasize the monosyllable and prevent it from being slurred onto the word before or after, but there are no instances where the monosyllable could easily be conflated with another word, and the script itself is quite clear. These marks, then, may be simply an aid to reading aloud. If so, it is interesting that the glosses are marked more often than the text and that one gloss, concerning the crab, has 7 accent marks.

Only 2 accent marks occur on Old English glosses:

> híndergenga   (36:3)
> sǽhund (95:T[lmarg100v3-6])

The vowels of *hindergenga* are all short; the *æ* of *sæ* is long and the *u* of *hund* is short. The syllables *hind-* and *-hund* are both metrically long since the short vowel is followed by two consonants. This evidence suggests that the Old English as well as the Latin is being marked for stress rather than vowel or syllable (metrical) length.

---

[3] I use the term "glossator" in the singular, though it is not necessarily true that the glosses were written by one person. There are two distinct glossating hands in L and many of the glosses copied by the hand of the text may have accumulated over a period of years.

There are 10 accent marks found on the poetry, all occurring in the last 9 riddles.[4] When we scan the poetic line containing each of these words, we see that the acute accent coincides with the long syllable of a dactyl or one of the long syllables of a spondee in each case. Most of the accented words are monosyllables, with the exception of *cacumine* (101:44). Since *cacumine* takes its stress on the antepenultimate syllable (which is glossed), it is impossible to tell from these examples whether the glossator is marking word stress (as in the prose and glosses) or has begun to mark verse quantity. Since the acute accent mark is defined by Aldhelm and Pompeius as a stress mark (and not for length of poetic feet) and the manuscript offers no evidence to the contrary, it seems reasonable to assume that the glossator was marking for stress.

2. *Glosses on Metre and Poetic Technique*

Since Aldhelm's Prologue is concerned with teaching Latin versification and glosses are often closely related to the subject matter of their lemmata, it is natural that we find glosses on metre and poetic technique in the Prologue. We also find them, but in far fewer numbers, on the Riddles themselves.

Aldhelm addresses the problem of elision (*sinalifa* or *iactalemsis*) in his Prologue and gives examples from earlier poets to illustrate his points. The elision and scanning of the examples are sometimes explained in the text (e.g. Prol: 89-91). Where the elision is not explained in the text, the glossator has written *sinalifa* over the elided syllables.[5]

Another instance where the glossator comments on the metre of an actual line of poetry occurs on folio 82r:

   maior: pro duabus consonantibus   (Prol:117)

Here, the *i* is effectively doubled as *mai-ior* for purposes of scansion. Isidore discusses this in the *Etymologiae* 1.4.7:

   I vero propterea interdum duplex dicitur, quia quotienscumque inter duas vocales invenitur, pro duabus consonantibus habetur, ut 'Troia'.

Elision is not the only poetic technique glossed in L. Many other glosses, some of which are drawn from independent sources, occur in the margins.[6]

---

[4] They occur on the following lines: 93:1, 94:8, 96:14, 101:4, 101:27, 101:39, 101:40, 101:44, 101:47, 101:70.

[5] Prol:96, 98, 99, 109, 123, 126.

[6] The glosses deal with such topics as cola, commata, pentimemeris, eptimeris, dactylic metre, and the eight types of metre. They occur at Prol:15, 23, 24, 58, 59, 60, 62, 71, 77, 85.

One final gloss on prosody occurs in Riddle 57, where Aldhelm is describing the sound of cranes:

> Arsantesque: i. uociferantes arsis. i. eleuatio   (57:5)

Arsis is a metrical term which indicates "the raising of the voice on an emphatic syllable," according to *The Oxford Latin Dictionary*. The glossator, seeing the participle *arsantes*, was no doubt reminded of the more technical word *arsis* and took the opportunity to point out the relation between the two. *Arsis* occurs 8 times in Aldhelm's *De pedum regulis*[7] and would have been known to anyone familiar with that work. A similar gloss occurs in P^5 (f. 100v) and S^1 (p. 35):

> Arsantesque: i. colla uel uoces eleuantes.
> arsis enim eleuatio interpretatur

As Peter D. Scott points out, Isidore also uses the verb *arsare* to describe the noise cranes make in his *Liber differentiarum*: "... rana coaxat, coruus crocitat, grus arsat ... ."[8]

The glosses on prosody in L show an awareness of the variety of metres, feet and poetic techniques, which is appropriate for a text designed to teach Latin prosody. Wieland's conclusions from his study of the glosses to Arator and Prudentius in G are worth comparing:

> The almost total absence of glosses on poetic technique implies that A[rator] and P[rudentius] of Gg.5.35 were not used for the teaching of prosody. Possibly the knowledge of the art of versification was not regarded as important in late Anglo-Saxon times as it appears to have been in the seventh and eighth centuries. This suspicion is supported by the fact that Aldhelm's Riddles, which form only part of the *Epistola ad Acircium*, appear without the theoretical observations on prosody later in Gg.5.35.[9]

Although the Riddles in G occur without any of Aldhelm's "theoretical observations on prosody," they occur in L after a heavily glossed Prologue on versification, drawn from these same "theoretical observations." The evidence of L (especially the long gloss from Bede's *De arte metrica*, which is found in no other manuscript) shows some active interest in prosody in late Anglo-Saxon England. Most of the glosses on prosody occur on the Prologue (not found in G) and not on the Riddles themselves.

---

[7] *Aldhelmi opera*, ed. Ehwald, pp. 150 (twice), 162, 168, 170, 174, 175, 182.

[8] Peter Dale Scott, "Rhetorical and Symbolic Ambiguity: The Riddles of Symphosius and Aldhelm," in *Saints, Scholars and Heroes*, ed. M.H. King and W.M. Stevens (Collegeville, 1979), 1: 140.

[9] Gernot R. Wieland, *The Latin Glosses on Arator and Prudentius in Cambridge University Library MS Gg.5.35* (Toronto, 1983), p. 24.

B. Grammatical Glosses

Ælfric, in his *Grammar,* gives 30 "divisiones grammaticae artis":

> vox, littera, sillaba, nomen, pronomen, participium, verbum, adverbium, coniunctio, praepositio, interiectio, pedes, accentus, positurae, nota, orthographia, analogia, ethimologia, glossa, differentia, barbarismus, solocismus, vitia, metaplasmus, scemata, tropi, prosa, metra, fabulae, historiae.[10]

Today we consider many of these divisions to belong more to the realm of literature than grammar. For the purposes of this discussion, I shall adopt a modern definition of grammar, as a discipline concerned with the morphology and function of words, rather than the more inclusive medieval definition.

1. *Glosses Using Grammatical Forms*

Two glosses clarify the form or gender of a noun by providing its nominative form. The first of these glosses uses *haec* to show that *incus* is feminine and *dis* to show that it is a third declension noun:

> incus: haec incus.dis   (54:7)

One gloss provides the first person singular present of a verb and then offers a synonym:

> tricent: trico i.soluo   (47:9)

In Latin grammars (ancient, Anglo-Saxon and modern) a noun is often memorized with a demonstrative pronoun and the first part of a verb to be learned is always the first person singular present tense form. This bespeaks a familiarity with the Latin grammatical tradition.

2. *Glosses Using Grammatical Terms*

Other grammatical glosses use grammatical terms to specify the case and/or number of nouns or the mood of verbs. For example:

> guttis: ablatiuus   (3:4)

The majority of these glosses occur over nouns and they show the glossator's ready knowledge of Latin grammatical terminology.[11]

---

[10] *Aelfrics Grammatik und Glossar,* ed. Julius Zupitza (Berlin, 1966), 289-296.

[11] Although I have expanded these terms for the purposes of this list, all of these glosses occur in abbreviated form, e.g. abl, dat, nom, etc. This argues further for the glossator's familiarity with Latin grammatical terminology: *ablatiuus* 3:4, 12:2, 28:6, 42:6, 52:4, 54:2,

3. *Glosses Using Prepositions*

The glossator uses prepositions and interjections, in addition to grammatical terms, for specifying the case of nouns.

Vocative

To indicate the vocative case, the glossator will often write *o* over the word in question. Four glosses of this type appear in the manuscript:

> arbiter: s. o censor   (VP:1)
> deus: o   (VP:9)
> genitor: s. o   (VP:35)
> credentes: s. o   (101:80)

While the interjection *o* is not a grammatical term like *ablatiuus, uocatiuus,* etc. above, it is commonly used in medieval grammars to indicate the vocative case. We find it used by Ælfric[12] and also by Alcuin, who writes:

> Tum vocativus, qui et salutativus vocatur, ut *o Ænea,* et *salue Ænea!*[13]

In one other instance, a vocative phrase is used to indicate the imperative mood:

> crede: s. o lector   (4:1)

Ablative

The most commonly glossed case is the ablative: this is true when the glossator uses the term *ablatiuus* or the prepositions *cum, de, in,* or *ex.* Four Old English glosses (written by the same scribe who wrote the text and the other grammatical glosses) use *of* or *on* to indicate the ablative case.[14] Wieland discusses in detail the difficulty the ablative case presented for the Anglo-Saxons, whose native tongue had an instrumental case often identical

---

57:6, 58:2, 77:5, 79:9, 82:4, 89:4, 91:11, 94:7, 101:74; *genitiuus singularis* Prol:108; *genitiuus* 101:39; *accussatiuus* 47:6; *accussatiuus grecus* 16:3, 34:5; *proprium (nomen)* 81:4; *nominatiuus* 101:58; *nominatiuus singularis* 9:4; *unum nomen compositum* 18:2 (gloss); *pluralis* 84:6; *datiuus* 31:6; *uocatiuus* VP:6.

Two more glosses of this sort appear over verbs, in both cases specifying the imperative mood: *imperatiuus* VP:7, 18:5. Four adverbs are labelled *aduerbium:* VP:19, 7:3, 15:2, 100:4. In one instance, the glossator indicates a comparative adjective with *comparatiuus* 40:3.

[12] See Wieland, *The Latin Glosses,* pp. 51-52. He gives Ælfric's definition of the vocative, which includes the phrase "o homo."

[13] Alcuin, De grammatica, PL 101: 869.

[14] *Latin* (VP:10, VP:25, VP:35, 1:4, 3:2, 27:4, 34:3, 34:7, 36:5, 36:6, 73:5, 78:3, 78:4, 86:4, 91:7, 99:3, 99:5, 101:81). *Old English* (5:3, 94:1, 94:2, 101:39).

in form with the dative (much as the ablative and dative are often identical in Latin), but had no ablative.[15]

In L, many third declension nouns (whose dative and ablative forms cannot be confused) are glossed to indicate that they are ablative. Strangely, parisyllabic i-stem nouns and adjectives, whose ablative and dative singular forms are the same, are not glossed this way. This suggests that the glossator is interested in more than simply recognizing an ambiguous form, but also in the function and meaning of the ablative in context. Most ablative glosses occur over nouns and adjectives expressing means, manner, accompaniment, place or time.

It is difficult to make an absolute distinction between a gloss with a grammatical function and a gloss with a syntactic function. Wieland also mentions this difficulty — of determining where morphology ends and syntax begins.[16] In a basic Latin grammar such as Donatus', the words are divided according to their class and we know that Anglo-Saxon students learned nouns, verbs, adverbs, etc. according to these grammars. However, the glossing of Aldhelm's Riddles reflects a more advanced stage of learning and is intended to clarify an obscure text and not simply to review noun or verb forms. My classification of syntactical and grammatical glosses is different from Wieland's because many of the glosses I found in Aldhelm's Riddles reveal a concern with syntax in addition to grammar. (These are discussed in the section on syntactical glosses.)

4. *Glosses on Numerals*

Glosses on numerals occur 11 times in L; in 10 instances the glossator adds a Roman numeral over a numerical adjective or adverb. Since the common Roman symbols *i, v, x, l* and *c* stand for the cardinal numbers 1, 5, 10, 50 and 100, the addition of *XII* (duodecim) over *bisseni* is simply clarifying the adjectival (or distributive) form by relating it to the ordinal number. In one instance, the glossator writes out the numeral:

Terni: i. tres digiti scriptoris   (29:5)

In all other instances, the Roman numeral is used.[17] The glossator is mainly concerned with distributive numerals, as is evident in the list above. Riddles 84 "De scropha pregnante" and 90 "De puerpera geminos enixa" seem to have been written as exercises in the use of distributive numerals.

---

[15] Wieland, *The Latin Glosses*, pp. 53-58.
[16] Ibid., p. 97.
[17] Prol:23 (gloss, botmarg80r), Prol:58, 8:2, 36:5, 84:1, 84:3, 84:4, 90:2, 90:3, 90:4.

C. SYNTACTICAL GLOSSES

Wieland defines syntactical glosses as those "glosses which create a relationship between various words of a sentence."[18] Although many syntactical glosses consist of a single word gloss to a single word lemma, these glosses are concerned with a linguistic structure larger than a single word and its morphology (grammatical glosses) or meaning (lexical glosses). In L, the glossed syntactical units are both prose sentences and hexameter verse lines.

1. *Syntactical Glosses Using Symbols (Syntactical Dot Glosses)*

The symbols used in Anglo-Saxon manuscripts to guide the reader through the intricacies of Latin syntax were first studied by Fred Robinson. He cautions, as does Wieland, that these marks may not have originated in Anglo-Saxon England.[19] The evidence of the other Aldhelm manuscripts (P^2, P^4, B^1 and especially S^1) shows that these marks were also used on the Continent.

The ten symbols used in L are the following combinations of dots and dashes:

$$. \quad .. \quad ... \quad : \quad \cdot\cdot \quad \cdot- \quad \cdot\sim \quad ; \quad ...- \quad :-$$

These marks occur above or beneath words and in groups of one, two, three or more. They are found in the Prose Prologue, Verse Preface and 65 of the 101 Riddles. There are approximately 180 syntactical glosses using symbols in L. These glosses are designed to clarify Latin syntax by linking words that belong together in a sentence.

Syntactical glosses are closely linked to punctuation; both are systems for marking intelligible sections that structure a text. The manuscript punctuation in L divides the text into sentences and clauses, usually with a finite verb for each clause. The syntactical dot glosses then specify the relationship of certain words within the sentence. Riddle 1 is a good example of this.

One can imagine that, then as now, the key to unlocking Latin syntax was to define the limits of a sentence and isolate the main verb. Punctuation and syntactical dot glosses are both useful for this. As examples of the way these glosses were used, consider the following three glosses:

---

[18] Wieland, *The Latin Glosses*, p. 98.

[19] Fred C. Robinson, "Syntactical Glosses in Latin Manuscripts of Anglo-Saxon Provenance," *Speculum* 48 (1973): 443-475. See also: Michael Korhammer, "Mittelalterliche Konstruktionshilfen und Altenglische Wortstellung," *Scriptorium* 34 (1980): 18-58 and Wieland, *The Latin Glosses*, p. 98.

Et psalmista canens metrorum carmina uoce

Natum diuino promit generamine numen   (VP:21,22)

Sed nouem decies sunt et sex corporis ungues   (84:4)

Pignora nunc pauidi referunt ululantia nautae   (95:7)

The Significance and Use of Syntactical Dot Glosses

The syntactical dot glosses clarify Latin syntax, but they are unlike other syntactical glosses, which consist of a word or words written over a lemma. One syntactical dot gloss will cause a reader to seek the other. These glosses, thus, work very well as *visual* clues to the structure of Aldhelm's Latin. They are not simply marks of stress, for reading aloud; there would be no need for such a variety of visually distinct symbols – a simple accent mark would suffice. One can imagine a nun or monk reading Aldhelm's Riddles as part of a course of private reading and using the glosses to weave through the convoluted syntax or a teacher using the glosses to clarify Latin syntax for a pupil or class. Since it is unlikely that each pupil would have access to a full copy of the text, these glosses would be most useful for reminding a teacher to discuss a syntactical point (such as agreement of nouns and adjectives). The visual aspect of these glosses is of prime importance and, unless the class were small enough so that everyone could see the text, the syntactical dot glosses were most useful for someone (private reader or teacher) who actually had the manuscript in hand.

2. *Syntactical Glosses Using Words*

All of the remaining syntactical glosses use words instead of symbols, yet they serve to clarify the Latin syntax in much the same way, by correlating words that are closely related within a sentence.

Glosses Giving Alternate Forms of Verbs, Adjectives or Nouns

Fourteen syntactical glosses give alternate forms of words; twelve of these are glosses to verbs, one is a gloss to a noun, one a gloss to an adjective. All occur in the verse.

The poetic form *uirum* for *uirorum* is glossed:

> *pro*
> *uirorum*
Per me fata uirum dicunt decerpere parcas   (44:5)

This gloss prevents the reader from misinterpreting *uirum* as the singular accusative object of *decerpere*. The remaining twelve glosses are all to verbs.

In each case they give an alternate verb form of the same number and person, but of a different tense.[20] In each of these instances, the glossator has commented on a change in tense within the text and seems to be "correcting" Aldhelm's syntax. For example, Riddle 32 begins with the perfect tenses "Roscida me genuit," "non sum ... facta," then continues in the present tense. After five verbs in the present tense (*trahunt, resultant, texunt, carpor, pulsor*), we come to *uocabor*. The glossator noticed that *uocabor* was in the future tense and glossed it with the present to make it "agree" with the others.

In Riddle 95, an extended grammatical structure has confused the glossator. The Scilla's description of what sailors hear begins in line 7 and continues through line 11. The infinitive *auscultare* (line 11) is dependent on *referunt* (line 7). The glossator does not realize this and tries to recast line 11 by substituting *audiere* (the syncopated third person plural preterite) for *auscultare*. In doing so, a lexically equivalent verb is given, but the purpose of the gloss is to make a sentence out of line 11.

In all of the above instances, Aldhelm's choice of tense may be determined by metrical considerations (note that eight of these glosses have a different number of syllables from their lemmata). In four of the glosses, the word *pro* is used to introduce the gloss. Wieland found in G that *pro* was often used to introduce glosses dealing with metrical questions.[21] This would be a nice explanation for the four *pro* glosses above, but the others are introduced by *i.*, so the results are not conclusive.

Correlative Glosses

Wieland discusses the use of antecedents in his section on "Grammatical Glosses on the Pronoun." He finds that many of the glosses in G reveal an interest in the morphology of pronouns and this leads him to conclude that the glosses may have been used by a teacher for testing students' knowledge of the declension of pronouns.[22] There is a section of Arator in G where, within a few lines, several cases of a relative pronoun occur and are glossed:

> qui: deus
> quem: deum
> cuius: dei
> cuius: dei
> quo: deo[23]

---

[20] vp:28, vp:34, 15:2, 25:4, 30:3, 32:6, 42:4, 49:3, 50:5, 62:6, 95:11, 96:9.
[21] Wieland, *The Latin Glosses*, pp. 31, 81, 82, 83, 86, 89, 97, 110.
[22] Ibid., pp. 61-76.
[23] Ibid., p. 66.

We find no such proliferation of glosses in L; instead the glosses providing antecedents to relative pronouns in L serve a syntactical rather than grammatical function. Wieland's own definition suggests as much: "the glosses clarify and ascertain that the correct antecedents are joined with their respective relative pronouns."[24]

Correlative Glosses Using a Noun

These twenty-two glosses consist of antecedent nouns added to pronouns. They occur in both prose and verse. A typical example is:

Sed semen segeti de caelo ducitur almum

s. semen
Quod largos generat millena fruge maniplos   (31:6,7)

Correlative Glosses Using a Verb

These glosses are not as numerous as those giving nouns; only 9 occur (1 in the prose, 8 in the verse). They also correlate 2 clauses by showing that one clause is dependent on a verb appearing previously (or subsequently) in the text[25]. For example:

Nec natura sinit celeres ⟨natare⟩ per amnes

s. nec sinit
Pontibus aut ratibus fluuios transire feroces.   (37:4,5)

As Wieland says: "One of the main difficulties facing Anglo-Saxons seems to have consisted in recognizing that a certain verb continues to influence a sentence beyond a coordinating conjunction."[26]

Suppletive Glosses

Wieland begins his section on suppletive glosses with a discussion of ellipsis, "the concept which necessitates and shapes them." [27] It is common in Latin for a syntactical unit to be omitted from a sentence or poetic line; the glossator emends or "fills in" an ellipsis with a suppletive gloss.

In Aldhelm's Riddles we find suppletive glosses to both the prose and verse. A suppletive gloss usually consists of one word (noun, verb, conjunction, adjective or adverb) added to a word of another grammatical

---

[24] Ibid., p. 65.
[25] Prol:99, vp:2, 37:5, 87:5, 91:4, 91:7, 98:3, 101:58.
[26] Wieland, *The Latin Glosses*, p. 139.
[27] Ibid., p. 109.

class, i.e. nouns are added to adjectives, verbs to adjectives or nouns, conjunctions to verbs, etc. The most common suppletive glosses consist of the addition of some form of *esse* or some form of *ego* (including forms of *nos* and *meus*) to the text. Aldhelm frequently leaves *esse* out of his Latin and the glossator has supplied 48 glosses indicating where it would appear syntactically in the text. Of these, 42 are a form of *esse* in the first person, e.g. *sum, sumus, fui, fueram, essem.* This is not surprising when one considers the nature of the Riddles. They all use the rhetorical device of *prosopopoeia,* in which an object, plant or animal speaks in the first person. Thus we find:

> *s. sum*   *s. ego*   *s. sum*
> Pulcher et excellens specie mirandus in orbe   (14:1)

The glosses make it more than clear that *Pulcher, excellens,* and *mirandus* all modify the speaker.

Twenty-two of the glosses providing *esse* in a first person form occur in the last riddle "De creatura." This riddle is unique in that it employs a series of speakers in rapid succession:

> *s. sum*
> Grandior in glaucis ballena fluctibus atra
>
> *s. sum*
> Et minor exiguo sulcat qui corpora uerme   (101:65,66)

In one instance, the glossator has not read the riddle carefully enough. The speaker of Riddle 7 is Fate — a pagan deity who quotes Virgil's description of fate. In the last lines of the Riddle, Aldhelm says that while the ancients believed fate to rule the world, it was in fact the grace of Christ that ruled.

> *s. sum*   *uel a*
> Sceptra regens mundi dum Christi gratia regnet;   (7:4)

Since *gratia* is the subject of this line, modified by *regens,* the *sum* does not belong here. Either the glossator fell into the trap of simply reading *regens* and not joining it with *regnet* or this gloss has slipped in from another manuscript with an alternate reading.

In addition to first person forms, *esse* also occurs as: *sunt, fuerint, esse, est.*[28] For example:

---

[28] Suppletive *esse* glosses occur at Prol:19, vp:27, 1:4, 7:4, 14:1, 15:2, 20:1, 26:1, 27:2, 27:3, 27:4, 29:1, 33:6, 35:6, 41:2, 48:1, 48:3, 57:3, 58:6, 65:1, 66:3, 70:3, 81:6, 88:1, 92:9, 93:9; 101:10, 13, 25, 26, 29, 31, 32, 35, 36, 42, 43, 54, 55, 56, 65, 66, 73, 74, 77, 82.

Denique predicta enigmatum capi
                                        i. narranda
tula primitus quaternis uersiculorum lineis di
s. sunt
gesta⸴   (Prol:17-19)

Amidst these occurrences of *esse*, we find two occurrences of Old English
beon:

conspicimur: beoð   (8:4)
replentur: sint   (12:2)

In these two glosses, the Old English gloss indicates that the Latin lemma
is in the passive voice. *Beon* is necessary to express the passive in Old
English, but *esse* is not always needed for the Latin passive (as in the
instances above). This grammatical difference no doubt presented some
problems to Anglo-Saxons learning Latin, and these glosses would have
helped them recognize the passive voice.

Ego, nos and *meus* in various forms are also added to the text. The
glossator uses the first person pronouns and adjectives 45 times in the
glosses. Once again, Aldhelm's use of *prosopopoeia* explains the appearance
of so many glosses in this form.

             s. me
Licia nulla trahunt. nec garrula fila resultant.
                   s. me
Nec crocea seres texunt lanugine uermes   (32:3,4)

Note that only one gloss of this type appears in "De creatura," in the last line,
and that this gloss, in effect, "solves" the riddle.

s. ego creatura
Sciscitor inflatos fungor quo nomine sophos   (101:83)[29]

Suppletive Conjunctions or Adverbs

These glosses are very like correlative glosses using prepositions, conjunc-
tions or adverbs, because they not only "fill in" an ellipsis, but also clarify the
relationship between two successive phrases or clauses. The only difference
between these and the correlative glosses is that suppletive glosses use a word
that has not previously appeared in the text. *Et* is the most common gloss,

---

[29] Suppletive *ego* glosses occur at vp:6, vp:9, vp:15, vp:31, 3:3, 8:2, 10:2, 10:3, 12:2, 14:1,
15:4, 19:4, 24:5, 29:2, 29:6, 32:3, 32:4, 37:4, 38:5, 39:6, 41:2, 41:5, 42:6, 44:6, 45:1, 49:4,
51:4, 53:8, 57:7, 58:7, 60:8, 60:9, 76:5, 79:5, 81:1, 82:1, 85:5, 87:3, 93:5, 93:10, 94:4,
96:13, 97:4, 99:4, 101:83.

occuring seven times, *sed* appears twice, and *ut, ante, si* and *eo* each appear once. All of these glosses occur in the poetry. For example:

s. et
Erro caput circa tenues extendor in auras   (74:9)

Since there is no punctuation to indicate that this line consists of two independent clauses, the gloss serves this function.

Suppletive Pronouns

Nine glosses occur in which a suppletive pronoun refers back to a preceding noun. In five of these glosses, the pronoun *ipse* is used:

Materia trucibus processit caetera tauris
ipsa
Aut potius putidis constat fabricata capellis   (61:2,3)

Here, *ipsa* refers back to *Materia.*
We also find an Old English gloss in this category:

on   *hit*
Sambucus in silua. botris dum fronde rubescit   (94:1)

Here, *hit* refers back to *Sambucus.* Note that the Old English glossator (who is *not* the scribe of the Latin text and glosses) writes *hit* instead of *he,* assigning to *Sambucus* a natural, rather than grammatical, gender. In all these instances, the gloss shows the syntactical relation between two words of a sentence or clause.[30]

One final point should be made about correlative and suppletive syntactical glosses. Most of them are introduced with *s.* (scilicet), though occasionally *i.* (id est) is used. Wieland found a higher incidence of *s.* than *i.* introducing suppletive glosses in G, but he says that "suppletive glosses are not clearly distinguished formally from their lexical or grammatical counterparts by any introductory words."[31] In L, a distinction is made in the use of *s.* for syntactical glosses, *uel* for variant readings, and *i.* for lexical glosses. While there are exceptions to this rule, the glossator usually makes the distinction between the various types of glosses.

D. Textual Glosses

Textual glosses are concerned with the actual text of the Riddles and the variant readings that inevitably arise over centuries of textual transmission.

---

[30] Others occur at vp:4, vp:5, 61:3, 63:2, 77:6, 94:1, 95:6, 97:3.
[31] Wieland, *The Latin Glosses*, p. 110.

Wieland does not use the term "textual gloss" or include textual glosses as a separate type of gloss. He does address the question of textual variants in his discussion of lexical glosses. In G, Wieland finds that a gloss beginning with *uel* often introduces a word which is a variant reading in another manuscript.[32] We find this to be also true in L; most textual glosses introduce a variant reading with *uel*. The existence of these glosses shows that at some point the glossator had access to more than one manuscript and noted the discrepancies between the alternate texts. Many textual glosses consist of an entire word that is metrically equivalent to its lemma. For example:

> munera: uel munia   (72:2)

These glosses can be considered a type of lexical gloss, but other textual glosses provide only part of a word, indicating a change of conjunction, tense and mood, person or spelling.[33] Many of the textual variants noted in L are, in fact, the reading preferred by Ehwald in his critical edition of the Riddles.[34] Some of the glosses in L indicate a reading not found in Ehwald's text, but included in his notes.[35] I found two other textual variants Ehwald does not mention in his critical apparatus. These variants are indicated by the following glosses in L:

> bulla: uel gemma uel bula   (55:5)
> mei: uel mihi   (101:80)

Mihi actually occurs in the texts of P[1] and P[4], while *gemma* appears as a gloss to *bulla* in P[2] and V[1].

There are seven puzzling glosses that seem to indicate variant readings but do not occur in any of the surviving manuscripts:

---

[32] Ibid., pp. 31, 84, 195.

[33] Et: U (12:4); glescunt: i (46:3); flagrat: r l (55:7); uulnere: uel a (60:5); flamina: uel flu (69:3); carebunt: uel rent (70:6); gubernat: uel nant (84:2); quadripedante: uel u (100:6).

Thus, we would read *Ut, gliscunt, fraglat, uulnera, flumina, carerent, gubernant, quadrupedante*. All of these variants occur in at least one other manuscript and since they cannot be read as lexical glosses, I have created the category of textual gloss to accommodate them.

[34] 3:1, 9:4, 12:4, 14:1, 18:4, 44:5, 54:1, 54:2, 67:9, 70:2, 70:6, 72:2, 84:2, 90:4, 94:2, 95:5, 96:5, 96:9, 98:1, 99:3, 100:3, 101:5.

The gloss "profundam: s. relinquo" (3:1) is particularly interesting because it seems to be a suppletive gloss, giving a finite verb to a line which has only a present participle: "Versicolor fugiens caelum terramque profundam" (3:1). This gloss probably slipped into the text, supplanting *profundam* and becoming an alternate reading in later manuscripts. Likewise with the other *s.* glosses in this section: "Pulcher: s. sum" (14:1). This looks like a suppletive *sum* that has entered the text in other manuscripts. In one other case, we find *in-* added to *durescit*: "durescit: s. in" (67:9). Primarily a lexical gloss, this, too, has created an alternate reading.

[35] 7:4, 23:4, 23:5, 60:3, 69:3, 100:6. These glosses, unlike textual emendations, do not include an expunction mark to indicate a change in the text, and should not be confused with them.

Cum: uel qui   (16:2)
Qui: uel cum   (29:6)
turmis: uel bis   (53:1)
Culmine tecta: uel na templi   (55:9)
et: ni   (62:5)
miseros: uel a   (96:2)
quos: uel quas   (96:2)

Perhaps these readings were once present in a now-lost manuscript.
   One textual gloss is simply a mistake:

                    uel tantis   uel rerum   uel causis
   Credere quis poterit tantarum   foedera   rerum.
                    uel rerum
   Temperet et fatis. morum contraria fata   (54:1,2)

The gloss *uel rerum* belongs properly over *morum*, but it is accidentally
repeated in the first line over *foedera*. Michael Herren has suggested that the
glossator may be thinking of the famous line from Virgil's *Georgics* 2.490:
"Felix qui potuit rerum cognoscere causas." Certainly there are enough other
references to Virgil in the text and glosses to support this conjecture.

E. Lexical Glosses

Ælfric defines "Glossa" in his Grammar as follows:

> Sum ðæra is GLOSSA, þæt is glesing, þonne man glesð þa earfoðan word mid
> eðran ledene. faustus is on oðrum ledene beatus, þæt is eadig. fatuus is on
> oðrum ledene stultus þæt is stunt; and swa gehwylce oðre.[36]

This is a good working definition of a lexical gloss — a gloss that provides
an easy Latin word for a difficult Latin word. Ælfric gives his example,
glossing the difficult *faustus* with the easier *beatus*, which he then translates
(glosses) as Old English *eadig*. He thus demonstrates for us two types of
lexical glossing: Latin-Latin and Latin-Old English. We find both of these
types in L.
   Wieland has a long and interesting discussion of the nature and use of
lexical glosses, especially those found in G.[37] He defines a lexical gloss as "a
lexical unit (usually a word, sometimes more) which explains another lexical
unit in such a way that both lemma and gloss have approximately equivalent

---

[36] *Aelfrics Grammatik*, J. Zupitza, ed., p. 293.
[37] Wieland, *The Latin Glosses*, pp. 26-46.

meaning." [38] This definition covers all types of lexical glosses found in L. In both L and G, the vast majority of lexical glosses consist of a Latin lemma glossed by a Latin equivalent (synonym), but other types of lexical glosses are also found. In L, we find "differentiae" glosses, glossed titles, paraphrase glosses, Old English glosses, "genus" glosses and "nomen" glosses.

1. *Latin Glosses*

Synonym Glosses

There are 443 Latin synonym glosses to Aldhelm's Riddles in L. They are found in Appendix A, alphabetized as a Latin-Latin glossary. These glosses are by far the most common in all the surviving manuscripts of Aldhelm's Riddles.

The most typical form of synonym gloss is one word glossing another word of the same grammatical class. Usually the case, gender and number or mood, tense and voice agree. For example:

> apicibus: i. litteris   (Prol:3)
> frutescit: i. germinat   (49:4)

We find *i.* introducing most of the lexical glosses in L. Wieland found that it appeared "rather arbitrarily in connection with lexical glosses," i.e. that it could be used or not, at the discretion of the glossator/scribe, because the gloss itself "already constitutes an *id est.*" [39] We find in L that *i.* is included more often than not, though some lexical glosses are not introduced with any words at all, and a few others are introduced with *s., pro*, or *uel.* I have included these introductory words in the Glossary.

Most of the lexical glosses consist of a single word, but sometimes they are longer:

> prestantiorem: i. ad alias partes perfectiores uel grandiores   (Prol:13)
> Examen: ad similitudinem examinis apum   (VP:11)
> ornamenta: s. quae ornantur gemmis   (11:3)
> cessit: i. locum dedit uel se subdidit   (19:2)
> salpix: i. tuba bellandi   (96:4)

In several instances the glossator supplies words that are nearly identical to their lemmata:

> cretus: i. pro creatus sum   (14:2)
> creta: pro creata nata uel formata   (20:1)

[38] Ibid., p. 26.
[39] Ibid., p. 30.

> nantesque: pro natantes   (28:4)
> uolitantis: i. uolantis   (29:4)

In these examples, *creta* may be glossed to avoid confusion with the island Crete, which itself is glossed in Riddle 27 "De Minotauro":

> creta: nomen insulae   (27:4)

In these longer glosses, the glossator not only offers a lexical equivalent, but suggests that the shorter form may have been chosen by Aldhelm for metrical reasons. The use of *pro* may substantiate this.

Wieland notes that the glossator of G sometimes uses a negated antonym rather than a synonym to define the lemma.[40] Only one gloss of this type appears in L and it seems to have been miscopied:

> erro: i. maneo   (101:76)

The original gloss may have read *non maneo* and somehow the *non* has been lost in transmission or perhaps, it is a mistake for *meo, meare*.

"Differentiae" Glosses

Glosses of this sort distinguish "homographs or near homographs" and derive from works such as Alcuin's or Bede's *De orthographia* and Isidore's *Etymologiae*. Only three such glosses occur in L:

> Pignus pignoris .i. filius uel soboles
> Pignus pigneris .i. uadimonium   (1:2)
>   [cf. Bede *De orthographia*, CCSL 123: 42]

> Tergus. tergoris .i. cutis
> Tergum. tergi. dorsum   (31:3)
>   [cf. Bede *De orthographia*, CCSL 123: 54]

> i. orbus dicitur qui filios numquam genuit
> orbatus qui filios genuit et amisit   (63:10)
>   [cf. Isidore *Etymologiae* 10.200]

The Glossed Titles

An unusual group of glosses occurs in L, though at first sight, they do not appear to be glosses at all. I refer to the titles of some of the riddles, which contain phrases that were originally glosses. For example, Riddle 5 is entitled "De Iri uel Arcu Celesti." The phrase *uel Arcu Celesti* was originally a gloss,

----

[40] Ibid., p. 27.

but over the course of many years and many scribes the gloss has become part
of the title. Thirty-one of the Riddles in L have titles "glossed" in this way.[41]
What is especially interesting here is that 16 other Aldhelm manuscripts
share some or all of these same glossed titles. Some of the manuscripts have
titles in the nominative, e.g. *LULIGO*, others have them in the ablative, e.g. *DE
LULIGINE*. The following manuscripts share some or all of the "glossed titles"
found in L:

nominative: T, P^2, P^5, O
ablative: K, V^2, R, P^1, P^4, U^5, B^1, S^1, U^1, P^3, L^1, G

In P^5, a heavily-glossed manuscript, the titles to the Riddles are still distinct
from their glosses. For example:

LULIGO: i. pisce uolante   (f. 96v)

LULIGO is written in a display script, *i. pisce uolante* in the Caroline script of
the text. In other manuscripts, especially those with titles in the ablative, the
gloss has become part of the title and is written in the same display script
as the titles. This is true of L.

An unusual feature of L is that it contains 101 Riddles, as opposed to the
100 found in Ehwald's edition and most manuscripts. This "extra" riddle was
created by a gloss that became a title. The Riddle "De fama" (98) was
originally part of the Riddle "De nocte" (97). This is how Ehwald prints it,
and also how it appears in 12 manuscripts (T, K, P^2, V^1, R, P^1, B^1, U^1, P^3,
E, L^1, G). In four manuscripts there is a gloss identifying the sister of night
as fame:

P^5 Ingrediturque: i. fama   (f. 106r)
P^4 sororem: fama   (f. 33v)
V^2 sororem: i. fama   (f. 23v)
S^2 sororem: i. famam   (f. 31r)

In transmission, this gloss eventually became a title and *FAMA* emerged as a
separate riddle in the following manuscripts: B, B^o, U^4, O, L. In L, we have
not only a separate riddle entitled "De fama," but a gloss like the ones above:

sororem: i. famam filiam terrae   (98:1)

Paraphrase Glosses

Paraphrase glosses are lexical glosses on a larger scale; instead of providing
a semantically equivalent word for a lemma containing only a single word,

---

[41] See the titles of Riddles 5, 7, 11, 12, 13, 15, 16, 17, 21, 22, 23, 29, 36, 37, 40, 44,
48, 49, 50, 51, 56, 60, 61, 62, 65, 67, 72, 76, 88, 92, 95.

they provide a semantically equivalent phrase (or sentence) for a lemma of
more than one word (another phrase or sentence). Wieland says that
paraphrase was elevated to an "art form" among Anglo-Latin writers; he cites
Aldhelm's *De laude virginitatis* in both prose and verse and Bede's *Life of
Cuthbert*, also in prose and verse. Wieland also says that paraphrasing verse
into prose was part of "the curriculum for the Anglo-Saxon student." [42] This
is the sort of exercise that could easily have been done on wax tablets. The
scant number of paraphrase glosses in L suggests that paraphrasing was
either done on wax tablets (and hence has not survived) or that Aldhelm's
Riddles was not a popular text for paraphrasing. Only seven paraphrase
glosses occur in L.[43] For example:

> Versicolor fugiens caelum terramque profundam: s.non teneo locum
> certum in caelo uel in terra   (3:1)

2. *Old English Lexical Glosses*

Old English lexical glosses to Latin lemmata have been the subject of much
research in the past, although most of it has concentrated only on Old
English glosses, to the exclusion of the Latin glosses in the same manuscript.
The works of Aldhelm, especially the prose and poetic *De laude virginitatis*,
are well-represented in earlier gloss studies because they are heavily glossed
in many manuscripts. This extensive glossing arose in large part because of
Aldhelm's use of unusual and arcane vocabulary. There is still debate over
how much of his vocabulary and syntax is derived from such "Hisperic"
works and authors as the *Hisperica Famina*, Virgil the Grammarian, and
Gildas, and how much is derived from Continental sources.[44] Another
subject of research is his dependence on and knowledge of early Latin-Greek
glossaries such as the Hermeneumeta, the Abolita and Abstrusa.[45] Aldhelm
certainly knew and used abstruse vocabulary and some later glossaries of

---

[42] Wieland, *The Latin Glosses*, p. 44.

[43] The others occur at 3:1, 9:4, 14:4, 46:2, 57:1-3, 82:7-8, 9:T.

[44] For a good discussion of this problem see Michael Lapidge, Introduction to *Aldhelm:
The Prose Works*, trans. Lapidge and Michael Herren (Cambridge, 1979), p. 7. The argument
for Aldhelm's indebtedness to the *Hisperica Famina* is put forward by Paul Grosjean,
"Confusa Caligo," *Celtica* 3 (1956): 64-67, and contested by John Marenbon, "Les Sources
du Vocabulaire d'Aldhelm," *Archivum Latinistatis Medii Aevi* 41 (1977-1978): 75-90, who
attributes Aldhelm's style and vocabulary to Continental sources; see also Michael Winterbot-
tom, "Aldhelm's Prose Style and Its Origins," *Anglo-Saxon England* 6 (1977): 39-76. The
influence of Old English poetic technique on Aldhelm is described by Michael Lapidge,
"Aldhelm's Latin Poetry and Old English Verse," *Comparative Literature* 31 (1979): 209-231.

[45] For Aldhelm's knowledge of Greek see Lapidge's comments in *Aldhelm: The Prose
Works*, p. 8. On the Latin-Greek glossaries see: J.D. Pheifer, *Old English Glosses in the
Epinal-Erfurt Glossary* (Oxford, 1974), pp. xliv, li-liii.

Latin-Old English are derived in part from earlier glosses to his works.[46] The interdependence of Aldhelm's vocabulary and glossaries is beyond question, but is seems impossible to determine accurately the ultimate sources of his vocabulary.

More recent scholarship has concentrated on Latin glossaries or on the interrelationship of Latin and Old English glosses.[47] The newest debate is not over glosses and glossaries, but over school texts. Wieland and Rigg contend that G was a classroom text, an anthology of Christian Latin poetry, used in a school for teaching Latin,[48] and that the glosses and layout of the manuscript are evidence of how the text was taught and read.[49] Lapidge argues that because many of the glosses in a text are copied along with the text and may be handed down over many years, they are not necessarily indicative of classroom practice at the time a manuscript was written.[50] He contends that manuscripts may have been read privately during the daily private reading or the Lenten reading prescribed by the Benedictine Rule.[51] It is possible that a manuscript may have served both functions, though as Lapidge and Wieland both point out, in a classroom, a manuscript was most likely to have been the teacher's copy.[52] Students would write on wax tablets, like those described in Riddle 31, "De pugillaribus".

What does all this tell us about the relationship of Old English and Latin glosses in an Anglo-Saxon manuscript? The evidence of Aldhelm's Riddles in G and L suggests that Latin interlinear glosses were perceived and copied as part of the text (G copies large sections of Latin glosses directly from L or a close exemplar), whereas Old English glosses were added by individual Anglo-Saxon readers. (G and L share only one Old English gloss and each has a wide range of unique Old English glosses.) The evidence of other manuscripts also suggests a difference between the treatment of Latin and

---

[46] See Goossens, *The Old English Glosses of MS Brussels 1650*, pp. 14-16; and Pheifer, *Old English Glosses*, pp. xxviii-xli, lv-lvii. See also: William G. Stryker, *The Latin-Old English Glossary in Ms. Cotton Cleopatra AIII*, PhD dissertation (Stanford, 1951), pp. 11-14.

[47] See the complementary discussions of "The Study of Latin Texts in Late Anglo-Saxon England" by Michael Lapidge "(1) The Evidence of Latin Glosses," and of R.I. Page, "(2) The Evidence of English Glosses," both in *Latin and the Vernacular Languages in Early Medieval Britain*, ed. N.P. Brooks (Leicester, 1982), pp. 99-140 and 141-165.

[48] A.G. Rigg and G.R. Wieland, "A Canterbury Classbook of the Mid-Eleventh Century (the 'Cambridge Songs' Manuscript," *Anglo-Saxon England* 4 (1975): 113-130. Wieland, *The Latin Glosses*, passim, but especially in the conclusion, pp. 191-198. See also his "The Glossed Manuscript: Classbook or Library Book?" *Anglo-Saxon England* 14 (1985): 153-174.

[49] Wieland, *The Latin Glosses*, pp. 2-3.

[50] Lapidge, "The Evidence of the Latin Glosses," p. 125.

[51] Ibid., pp. 126-127.

[52] Ibid., p. 101; Wieland, *The Latin Glosses*, p. 192.

vernacular glosses. In the two manuscripts containing Old High German glosses (S^1 and S^2) we find that the Latin glosses outnumber the Old High German glosses and that the vernacular glosses are chiefly on difficult words with no readily available Latin synonyms (especially on the titles of the Riddles). None of the Old High German glosses are common to these manuscripts, though this may be due in part to the vagaries of manuscript survival. Three pairs of manuscripts share significant groups of common Latin lexical glosses (P^1 and P^4; P^5 and S^1; G and L); one pair shares a common set of Latin encyclopedic glosses (L and U^1). All of this suggests that Latin glosses are much more likely to be transmitted as part of an exemplar than are vernacular glosses.

The Old English Glosses

Napier prints the Old English glosses of L in his collection of Old English glosses.[53] This work is a catalogue of all the glosses he found in various manuscripts. He provides notes and suggests alternate readings or interpretations for puzzling glosses, but he only rarely takes into account the paleographic features of a manuscript. With regard to L, this is a serious omission; there are two glossating hands in L, one that wrote the text, Latin glosses and 33 Old English glosses, another that added 44 Old English glosses to the text. This second hand almost always adds glosses in the margin rather than directly above the lemma (39 of the 44 glosses by the second hand are in the margin; 7 of the 33 by the first hand are in the margin). The second hand has added three glosses to the text that are not included in Napier's edition. He, no doubt, considered them to be Latin, but the fact that they are written in the margin by a hand that glosses elsewhere exclusively in Old English, suggests that they may be Old English. They are the following:

> Romuleis scribor biblis sed uoce pelasga: i. Nycticorax   (34:6)
> Raucaque clangenti rebohant dum classica sistro:
>   genus tubae: tuba   (96:5)
> Necnon accipitre properantior et tamen horrens: hor   (101:36)

Is there any evidence that *Nycticorax, tuba,* or *hor-* are Old English words?

The form *nocticoraces* occurs in the Old English version of *Alexander's Letter to Aristotle.*[54] While this suggests that the word was known to

[53] Arthur S. Napier, *Old English Glosses: Chiefly Unpublished,* Anecdota Oxoniensa, Medieval and Modern Series 11 (Oxford, 1900), pp. 194-195.

[54] *Three Old English Prose Texts,* ed. Stanley Rypins, EETS, Original Series, 161 (London, 1924), repr. 1971, p. 69. "... þa cwoman þær þa fugelas, nocticoraces hatton, wæron in wealhhafoces gelicnesse. ..."

Anglo-Saxons (or at least to the translator of this work), it is not proof that it ever entered the language as more than a nonce-borrowing. In this case, the word has been borrowed twice into the language, but both times it is specifically referred to as a name, thus drawing attention to the fact that it is not an Old English word. Alexander says that these birds are called *nocticoraces* and the glossator of L writes the name *Nycticorax* in the margin, after the phrase *uoce pelasga*, i.e. this is the name of the bird in the Greek tongue. In Latin-Old English glossaries we find the following:

Nocticorax: nihtræfn
nocticorax: nihtræm
Nicticorax: nihtremn[55]

This shows that there was a native Old English word for the night raven, as well as the borrowed *Nycticorax* and *nocticoraces*.

The gloss *tuba* may belong with either *classica* or *sistro*. The Latin *tubae* appears on this same line, in the gloss "sistro: genus tubae." It is possible that *tuba* in the margin is an Old English borrowing of Latin *tuba*, but it is more likely to be a repetition of the previous Latin gloss. Clark Hall gives one occurrence of Old English *tuban* glossing Latin *classicum* in glosses to Prudentius, but Meritt deletes this. Though he does not articulate his reasons for the deletion he no doubt thought that *tuban* was simply a Latin gloss (with *n* for *m*) and not an otherwise unattested OE *tube*. Also, an indisputably Old English *scypbyman* occurs on this same instance of *classicum*.[56]

Finally, *hor* may be a shortened form of an Old English word or it may simply be a repetition of the first three letters of *horrens*. If it is Old English, the most likely word it could be is *horsc*, which Bosworth-Toller define as "Quick, ready, active, valiant." This meaning would fit well, if *hor⟨sc⟩* is glossing *properantior*. (Bosworth-Toller also give an Old High German cognate, *horsc*.) If this is an occurrence of Old English *horsc* it would be the only instance of *horsc* glossing Latin *properantior*. We find in the Old English corpus only three related glosses:

---

[55] These examples are taken from: A.diP. Healey and R.L. Venezky, *A Microfiche Concordance to Old English* (Toronto, 1980). They occur in the following texts, respectively: T. Wright and R.P. Wülcker, eds, *Anglo-Saxon and Old English Vocabularies*, 2nd ed. (London [Trüber], 1884) 1: 287; J. Zupitza, "Altenglische Glossen," *Zeitschrift für deutsches Altertum und deutsche Literatur* 33 (1889): 237-242, entry 30; L. Kindschi, *The Latin-Old English Glossaries in Plantin-Moretus MS. 32 and BM MS. Add. 32246*, PhD dissertation (Stanford, 1955), Glossary 2, entry 1016.

[56] See J.R. Clark Hall and H.D. Meritt, eds, *A Concise Anglo-Saxon Dictionary*, 1960; H.D. Meritt, ed., *The Old English Prudentius Glosses at Boulogne-sur-Mer* (Stanford, 1959), p. 27; and Alfred Holder, ed., "Die Bouloneser Angelsächsischen Glossen zu Prudentius," *Germania. Vierteljahrsschrift für deutsche Altertumskunde* (Wien, 1878), p. 391.

nauiter: horsclicae
nauiter: horsclicae
Nauiter: horsclice[57]

One other gloss, though written by the first hand (the hand of the text and
Latin glosses) may have been confused with an Old English word. The word
botraca is a form of Latin *botrax*, which is ultimately derived from the Greek
βάτραχος, "toad." The form *botraca* is attested in the Glossary of Ælfric:

botrax uel botraca: yce[58]

If *botrax* or *botraca* means "toad," why is *botraca* used to gloss *testudo* in L?

Lumbricus et limax et tarda testudo palustris   (101:37)

Latin *testudo* is usually glossed with Old English *bordþaca*, which also glosses
Latin *laqueariis*. The following examples are taken from the *Microfiche
Concordance to Old English*:

Testudo: bordðeaca
Testudo: brodthaca uel sceldhreða uel fænucæ
Testudo: borohaca uel sceldreda uel ifænucæ
Laqueariis: bordþacan[59]

From this evidence, the word *bordþaca* obviously refers to a covering, ceiling
or roof of some sort. *Testudo* refers to a tortoise, the shell of a tortoise, a
screen formed by the interlocking shields of troops, a wooden screen used
in the military or a roof. In the context of Aldhelm's Riddle "De creatura,"
where the slowness of the turtle is emphasized, *testudo* refers to the tortoise
(and its lack of speed) and not to its shell or to a roof or military cover. Why
then is it glossed with *botraca*, which elsewhere clearly means "toad"? Has
botraca been confused with *bordþaca* or miscopied at some point? The
glossator may have remembered seeing *testudo* glossed as *bordþaca* in
another context and wanted to indicate that *testudo* in this Riddle refers not
to a covering but to a creature living in a swamp (*palustris*). *Botraca* would
certainly indicate a swamp creature, though not a turtle. While these four
glosses are problematic and only *horsc* is an indisputable Old English word,
they are worth adding to the list of Old English glosses in L.

---

[57] The first two of these glosses are from J.D. Pheifer, ed., *The Old English Glosses*, p. 36;
the last is from W.M. Lindsay, ed., *The Corpus Glossary* (Cambridge, 1921), p. 118.

[58] Wright and Wülcker, *Anglo-Saxon and Old English Vocabularies*, 1: 122.

[59] The first of these examples is taken from Lindsay, *The Corpus Glossary*, p. 174; the
second and third from Pheifer, *Old English Glosses*, p. 52; and the last from Stryker, *The
Latin-Old English Glossary in Cotton Cleopatra AIII*, p. 268.

The "Incomplete" Old English Glosses

I suggested above that *hor* might be expanded to *horsc*, because the use of such abbreviations in Old English glosses is quite common. Goossens says that an incomplete gloss shows the glossator was interested only in the meaning of the lemma, whereas a complete gloss shows an interest in the grammatical aspects of the lemma.[60] This distinction is hard to apply here, because there are so few Old English glosses in L (compared to the 5,380 glosses that Goossens prints from MS Brussels 1650).

The following glosses in L are "incomplete" in some way, usually lacking their last few letters. All of them, except *wo*, are written by the second Old English hand. I include in square brackets the emendations suggested by Napier.[61]

> error: hi   (VP:27)
> uirescens: geþu [geþuf?]   (44:1)
> uaga: wo [woriende]   (65:6)
> hoc nectar: ða swe [swetnysse]   (78:7)
> caelestis: upli [þæs uplican]   (91:5)
> coronis: hel [helmum]   (91:6)
> ostriger: brunba [brunbasu]   (99:1)
> Pallida: æ [æblæce?]   (101:52)
> sperula: sinewea [sinewealt cliwen?]   (101:58)

Napier's suggestions are usually based on evidence of other texts or glossaries and most of them are likely solutions. I offer only the following suggestions:

> error: hi
>> [This may be short for *hiwung* "form, figure, pretence, feigning, hypocrisy, dissimulation" (Bosworth-Toller).]
> uaga: wo
>> [This may be short for *woh* "twisted, bent, crooked" (Bosworth-Toller).]

Napier expands one of the following glosses, which seemed to him "incomplete"; on the other he makes no comment:

> ciborum: w [wista]   (39:3)
> tulerunt: wa   (46:2)

One must read these glosses in relation to the verse lines they gloss and not simply to the last word of these verse lines. They both occur in the right margin; they both use the Old English rune graph ᚹ.

---

[60] Goossens, *The Old English Glosses of Brussels MS 1650*, p. 29. Goossens is contrasting complete glosses with glosses such as *-lice* to indicate a Latin adverb.

[61] Napier, *Old English Glosses Chiefly Unpublished*, pp. 194-195.

> Dilicias epulas regum luxusque ciborum: ᚹ (39:3)
> Sed sopor et somnus ieiunia longa tulerunt ᚹa (46:2)

The rune ᚹ means *wynn* "delight, pleasure" and could refer to *Dilicias* or *luxus* or to the entire line describing the joys of feasting. *Wa* means "woe" and no doubt refers to the sorrow of fasting, *ieiunia longa*. Perhaps the second Old English glossator inscribed this woeful message during Lent, when feasting was a far-off joy and fasting a daily reality! I include these glosses as lexical glosses, though the second gives the reader's opinion and not a strict lexical equivalent.

The remaining Old English lexical glosses present a few other problems.

> nothas: suderborene (29:2)

Napier rightly suggests that this should read *sunderborene*, but his suggestion that it might gloss *non ... adnumerandas* "'born apart,' hence 'not to be numbered (with the others)'" is unnecessary.[62] There is no reason not to take it as a lexical gloss for *nothas* "illegitimate, spurious, born out of wedlock" (Lewis and Short).

Napier misreads "errat: hwearft" (53:6) as *hwearfl* "hwearflað," when the manuscript actually reads *hwearft*, from *hwerfan* "to turn, revolve, move about" (Bosworth-Toller).

A List of the Old English Glosses

The following list of the Old English lexical glosses is arranged according to their appearance in the manuscript. Those entries marked with an asterisk were written by the second glossating hand. I have included the problematic entries discussed above. Except for the gloss ᚹ (*wynn*) (39:3), I have changed all ᚹ's to *w*'s. Appendix C contains an alphabetical index to these glosses.

> cola: i. lim   (Prol:23)
> commata: i. limes dæl   (Prol:23)
> * error: hi⟨wung⟩   (VP:27)
> * mentis: geþoht   (VP:28)
> Sic: swa   (6:4)
> telas: i. webb   (12:1)
> * squamis: finnum   (16:2)
> * rimis: cinum   (21:2)
> * asperrima: unsmeþust   (21:4)
> * Garrio ... rauco cum murmure: ic gyrre mid haswre hroðrunge   (21:5)

---

[62] Ibid., p. 194.

* Serratas: gecyrnode   (25:5)
* cristas: cambas   (25:5)
* nothas: su⟨n⟩derboren   (29:2)
  Calciamenta: þwancgas   (31:3)
* tergora: hyda   (31:3)
* seres: assirisce   (32:4)
* rubetae: ican   (33:5)
* Romuleis scribor biblis sed uoce pelasga: i. Nycticorax   (34:6)
* trudo: ic þy   (35:4)
  retrograda: hindergenga   (36:3)
* rugoso: geryflodre   (39:1)
* Dilicias epulas regum luxusque ciborum: ⼒ (wynn)   (39:3)
* irrita: unsoðe   (40:1)
* plumescunt: feðriað   (41:1)
* uirescens: geþu⟨f⟩   (44:1)
* uertigine: tyrninge   (44:3)
* Sed sopor et somnus ieiunia longa tulerunt: wa   (46:2)
* prolem: cnosle   (46:5)
* gentis: cynnes   (46:5)
* cataplasma: clyþan   (46:8)
  MILLEFOLIUM: ⟨g⟩earwe   (49:T)
  TRUTINA: wegan   (50:T)
  SOLSEQUIUM: goldwyrt   (51:T)
* errat: hwearft   (53:6)
* succumbere: asigan   (53:9)
* uentris: wambe   (54:3)
* pandit: undeð   (55:2)
  ripis: staðum   (56:1)
* belliger: kene   (56:2)
  pestemque: ge wole   (56:8)
* lapsu: fylle   (62:2)
  aceruos: mugan   (65:4)
  uaga: wo⟨h⟩   (65:6)
  lustra: denn *uel* fereldu   (65:6)
  ruminat: ceuwð   (66:6)
* FURFURAE: syfeda   (67:T)
  hoc nectar: ða swe⟨tnysse⟩   (78:7)
  conpressis: toaset   (80:8)
  constet: hit wunað   (85:2)
* caelestis: upli⟨can⟩   (91:5)
* coronis: hel⟨mum⟩   (91:6)
* cautes: i. næssas   (92:1)
  EBULO: wælwyrt   (94:T)
* bino: ge   (95:5)

ELLEBORO: tunsinwyrt (99:T)
* ostriger: brunba⟨su⟩ (99:1)
  Conquilio: weolcscille (99:2)
  halans: reocende (101:13)
* zephiri: suðernes (101:35)
* properantior: hor⟨sc⟩ (101:36)
  testudo: i. botraca (101:37)
  calamistratis: gewalcudum (101:47)
  calamistro: of wolcspinle (101:47)
* Pallida: æ⟨blæce⟩ (101:52)
* Sperula: sinewea⟨lt⟩ (101:58)
  ceu serica pensa: swa seolcen ðræd (101:59)
* atomo: mote (101:67)
  quae: ða (101:81)

3. *The "Genus" and "Nomen" Glosses*

The lexical glosses discussed above provide a Latin or Old English equivalent for a Latin lemma. Glosses like these are straightforward and clarify the meaning of a word, but they are limited to lemma(ta) that have Latin or Old English synonyms. Words lacking an obvious Latin synonym or Old English equivalent, are glossed by two types of lexical glosses, the "genus" and "nomen" glosses.

The "Genus" Glosses

The glossator is concerned that a reader will not recognize the word and provides the genus, the general class of things to which it belongs. The *Grammar* of Diomedes contains a useful definition of genus and species.

> Genus is a category of speech in which many species are contained, both animate and inanimate. Species is a category of speech originating from a genus, but containing a smaller number of expressions (members) than a genus, for example *man* or *tree*.[63]

Saint Augustine puts it more simply: "Every horse is an animal; not every animal is a horse."[64]

Six glosses in L use the term *genus* to define an unusual word. One other gloss, though it does not use the word *genus*, deserves to be included here:

---

[63] "Genus est dictio qua plures continentur species, animale et inanimale. Species est dictio originem trahens a genere, paucioribus confusa significationibus quam genus, ut homo arbor" (Diomedes, *Ars grammatica* 3, in Keil 1: 326).

[64] "Omnis equus animal est, non omne animal equus est" (Augustine, *De trinitate* 15.9.15, CCSL 50A: 481).

salpicae: i. genus tubae   (13:1)
perna: genus cuiusdam piscis qui [incomplete gloss]   (17:T)
DRACONTI GEMMA: genus gemmae   (23:T)
MAGNETE FERRIFERO: genus lapidis   (24:T)
adamante cypris: adamans genus lapidis in cipro   (24:5)
sistro: genus tubae   (96:5)

The "Nomen" Glosses

Another type of lexical gloss clarifies the meaning of a word that has no
immediately obvious Latin synonym or Old English equivalent. This is the
"nomen" gloss and it glosses proper nouns or other unusual nouns. The
glosses usually take the form of *nomen* plus a noun in the genitive case. By
specifying the word as a *nomen* or *proprium nomen*, the gloss serves a
grammatical as well as a lexical function.

In all but one instance, the lemma is unusual enough that it might give
trouble to a reader; in one case (*creta*) the proper noun could be mistaken
for the perfect participle of *cresco*. The "nomen" glosses follow

pedagogum: nomen artis   (Prol:119)
Cincti: i. nomen montis in dela insula in qua natus est appollo
    pater   (VP:12)
DE IRI: hiris huic proprium nomen est   (5:T)
Taumantis: nomen montis   (5:1)
athlante: nomen montis   (8:1)
Mulcifer: i. nomen est uulcani   (26:4)
creta: nomen insulae   (27:4)
ARCTURO: nomen sideris   (53:T)
letheaque: Nomen paludis inferni somnium inferens hominibus
    (53:8)
onocratulus: i. nomen auis   (59:1)
delo: i. nomen insulae   (79:3)
ambrosiae: i. dulcedinis. proprium nomen holeris   (101:14)

Though the "nomen" and "genus" glosses are used to gloss words without
synonyms, it is not always true that there is no synonym for a proper name.
Compare the following lexical glosses with those above:

poenorum: i. affricorum   (41:6)
achiuorum: i. grecorum   (49:1)
pelasga: i. greca   (60:10)
Argolicae: i. grece   (95:2)

Here, where there is a readily available synonym, the glossator provides it. The gloss and lemma are synonymous, so the gloss could replace the lemma with no change in meaning or grammatical structure. This is not the case with the "nomen" and "genus" glosses. Since they could not directly replace their lemmata, they are metaglosses: they comment upon the text, even as they provide a lexical category for their lemmata.

A similar type of glossing is found in the Old English glosses to the Lindisfarne Gospels. A.S.C. Ross says:

> In some cases the OE gloss is an explanation and not a translation of the Latin word. This is very common when the Latin word is a proper name. The following will serve as typical examples:
>
> Mt i,5   racab: ðæm wife
> Mt i,3   thamar: ðær byrig
> Mk xv,4   pilatus: se geroefa
> Mk v,41   talitha cumi: ðis is ebrisc word
> Mt x,25   beelzebub: þ is diowla foruost.[65]

In the *Salisbury Psalter*, we find another type of glossing similar to the "nomen" glosses. Here the letter *n* is used alone, and can be presumed to stand for nama:

> *audiuit et laetata est Sion, Et exultauerunt filiae Iude proper iudicia tua domine*: Gehyrde and geblissod is n and fægnodan dohtra for dome þinan hlaford.[66]

F. COMMENTARY GLOSSES

Commentary glosses, according to Wieland, "interpret the text, summarize it, and give background and source." [67] There are many such glosses in L; they go beyond the prosody, grammar and syntax of the text and offer explanations of names, figures of speech and puzzling passages in the Riddles.

1. *Etymologies*

In addition to "nomen" and "genus" glosses, which are concerned with proper or unusual nouns, there are also glosses that deal with etymologies. The popularity of Isidore's *Etymologiae* throughout the Middle Ages is evidence that word-origins were a lively concern among learned readers.

---

[65] Alan S.C. Ross, "Notes on the Method of Glossing Employed in the Lindisarne Gospels," *Transactions of the Philological Society* (1933): 108-109.

[66] Gloss to Psalm 96:8 in *The Salisbury Psalter*, ed. Celia Sisam and Kenneth Sisam, EETS 242 (London, 1959), p. 213.

[67] Wieland, *The Latin Glosses*, p. 147.

Isidore is a major influence on Aldhelm's Riddles in L: the *Etymologiae* not only serve as a source and inspiration for many of the Riddles, but are also mined for the manuscript's many encyclopedic glosses. (Appendix D is an index to the interpretative and encyclopedic glosses, many of which contain etymologies.)

Etymologies, thus, are important in the Riddles, not only as glosses, but as an integral part of the text. Many of the Riddles are based on the significance of names. For instances, Riddle 18 "De formica leone" is concerned with why the Ant-Lion has a double name; four of the five lines of the riddle refer to the name. It ends by saying, "Let the wise consider why I have a double name." The glossator has answered the riddler and comments heavily on this *conundrum*. Riddle 34 "De nicticorace" provides another example.

Etymological glosses are not found exclusively in riddles concerned with names. They can occur on any interesting word, and are usually, but not always, found on a proper noun. One interesting set of etymological glosses occurs in Riddle 14 "De pauone." The glossator shows an interest in the word *pulpa* and gives its etymology:

Pulpa: a pululando dicitur pulpa   (14:4).

Later, in an encyclopedic gloss from Isidore, we find:

Pulpa est caro sine pinguedine dicta eo quod pulpitet.
(14:4; *Etymologiae* 11.1.81).

The preferred reading here is *palpitet,* but the glossator (or scribe) has been swept up by etymological fervor and changed *palpitet* to *pulpitet* after the spelling of *pulpa.*

Another etymological gloss has either been conflated in transmission or misremembered:

Arista ab ariditate dicta   (88:3)

We find two similar passages in Isidore:

Arena ab ariditate dicta (*Etymologiae* 16.3.11)
Arista appellata quod prius ipsa arescat (ibid., 17.3.16)

Most of the short etymological glosses are interlinear and I list them here, followed by their likely source (where I have been able to trace it) in parentheses:

Castalidas: i. a castalido monte   (VP:10)
[cf. *Scholia Bernensia* at *Georgics* 3:293]
nectar: Nectar .i. quasi nectirassin .i. sine honore   (VP:11)

[Michael Herren has suggested that this may be a Latin-Greek
hybrid: Lat. *ne* plus Gr. *κτερείσειν*. The Greek means "to bury
with due honors." Nectar would be consumed by those who do not
require burial. When or why the link was made between *nectar* and
nectirassin is obscure.]

brumae: Bruma a breui motu dicitur solis   (1:4)
    [Isidore *Etymologiae* 5.35.6]
Nomina de uerno: i. uergilia   (8:5)
    [Isidore *Etymologiae* 3.71.13]
pulpa: a pululando dicitur pulpa   (14:4)
cypri: Ciprus a ciuitate quae in ea est nomen accepit   (24:5)
    [Isidore *Etymologiae* 14.6.14]
populorum nomine fungor: Galli meo nomine uocantur   (25:3)
Minotaurus: i. minois taurus   (27:5)
nilotica: dicta a nilo flumine   (33:6)
    [Isidore *Etymologiae* 13.21.7]
memphitica: i. de nomine ciuitatis quae dicitur memphis quae est
    metropolis aegypti   (35:6)
    [Isidore *Etymologiae* 15.1.31]
Nepa: i. nec petens   (36:1)
culinae: a celando   (39:4)
    [Isidore *Etymologiae* 20.10.1, "Ab igne colendo et ligna antiqui
    appellaverunt focum." Lindsay, in his footnote 24 gives the
    alternate reading *et ligna: culinam.*]
parcas: i. iii deae dictae sunt parcae eoquod minime parcant   (44:5)
    [Isidore *Etymologiae* 8.11.93]
cerula: s. a similitudine coloris caerae   (47:4)
    [Isidore *Etymologiae* 12.6.10]
cognomine: i. septentrio de septem bobus iouis. triones autem antiqui
    boues dicebant   (53:2)
    [Isidore *Etymologiae* 3.71.6]
dardana: i. de genere dardanii. Dardanus rex troianorum erat   (57:3)
    [Isidore *Etymologiae* 9.2.67 and 14.3.41]
arcister: uel arcifer.i. arcum ferens   (60:3)
Indidit ex cornu nomen mihi lingua pelasga: monoceron. i. unicor-
    nus   (60:10)
aristis: Arista ab ariditate dicta   (88:3)
    [Isidore *Etymologiae* 16.3.11 and 17.3.16]
De Camelo: Camelus humiliatus interpretatur   (100:T)
    [Gregory *Moralia in Job* 1.28.39]

One etymological gloss is in Old English:

Scilla ðet is sæhund gecweden; (95:T)

R. Page traces this etymology from the Greek σκύλαξ "puppy" and the connection between Scilla and dogs in the Riddle itself. He says it may also be related to two other Greek words for "a sea creature, σκύλιον or σκύλλα.[68]

2. *"Quia" Glosses*

Wieland defines the *quia* glosses as glosses which provide "a reason for the poet's ... choice of a particular word or words."[69] In L, we find that the *quia* glosses always explain a phrase, rather than a single word. These glosses not only give a reason for the poet's choice of words, but in the process of doing so, explain part of the riddle's mystery. There are only nine *quia* glosses in L.[70] For example

tabescens tempore brumae: i. quia non gigno fructum in hieme (1:4)

3. *Source Glosses*

These glosses serve a bibliographic function, by providing the name of an author, title of a text, a quotation from or paraphrase of a text. They refer to a source mentioned by Aldhelm in his text. For example:

psalmista: dauid (Prol:43)
[Psalm 95:12 and 97:8]
sapientissimus: i. salomon (Prol:50)
[Ecclesiastes 3:19, 6:8][71]

4. *Interpretative Glosses*

Wieland defines three types of interpretative glosses, glosses decoding metaphors, glosses decoding synecdoche and glosses decoding metonymy.

---

[68] Page, "The Evidence of English Glosses," pp. 161-162.

[69] Wieland, *The Latin Glosses*, p. 164.

[70] They occur at: Pro:71, 1:4, 3:3, 4:2, 5:4, 8:5, 28:6, 29:7, 100:1.

[71] The others are: "Examen: i. sicut legimus de sancto ambrosio" (VP:11), cf. Paulinus, *Vita S. Ambrosii*, PL 14: 30; "Metrica nam Moysen declarant: in deutoronomio" (VP:17), see Deuteronomy 32; "trophei: i. uenire filios israel per mare rubrum" (VP:18), see Exodus 15; "psalmista: i. dauid Ut est illud ante luciferum genui te" (VP:21), see Psalm 109:3; "Natum diuino promit generamine: Et illud permanebit ante solem et lunam in generationes generatum" (VP:22), see Psalm 71:5; "cecinit: Quando dixit. qui diuisit mare rubrum in diuisiones" (VP:34), cf. Psalm 135:13; "cecinisse: i. in XII libris aeneidei" (7:1), see *Aeneid* 12.677; "poetam: s. uirgilium" (7:1), see *Aeneid* 12.677; "poetam: i. sedulium" (63:6), see *Carmen Paschale* 1.75.

He says that "the basic tools for any interpretation are the tropes" and gives Bede's definition of a trope: "A trope is an expression transferred from its proper meaning to a signification not its own." [72] Metaphor, synecdoche and metonymy, the three tropes Wieland found glossed most often in Arator and Prudentius, are also used by Aldhelm in his Prologue, Verse Preface and Riddles. An enumeration of the tropes *prosopopoeia, metaphor, synecdoche* and *metonymy* might be a useful approach to understanding these glosses (and entirely appropriate to the Prologue and Verse Preface). But it would not be appropriate for the Riddles because it would overlook a far more important trope: *enigma. Enigmata* are found in the Bible as well as in Christian commentators and were classified by Bede and other writers of Latin grammatical texts. A survey of these writings can help us better understand what the term *enigma* meant in Anglo-Saxon England and how Aldhelm's Riddles were interpreted.

The word *enigma* appears nine times in the Bible, eight times in the Old Testament and once in the New.[73] When Miriam and Aaron have spoken against Moses, God descends in a cloud and reprimands them, saying that he speaks to Moses not through dreams, but "ore enim ad os" and that Moses sees him "palam, et non per aenigmata et figuras" (Numbers 12:8). Solomon, the wisest of kings, is connected with the solving of riddles. The Queen of Sheba visits him and tests him with "aenigmatibus" (3 Kings 10:1; 2 Chronicles 9:1).[74] Job speaks to his comforters in riddles (Job 13:17). In Ezechiel, God tells Ezechiel to propose a riddle to the Israelites: "Et factum est uerbum Domini ad me, dicens, Fili hominis, propone aenigma, et narra parabolam ad domum Israhel" (Ezechiel 17:1-2). *Aenigma* and *parabola* are used in apposition here,[75] and they both refer to the story that follows, the "parabola de duabus aquilis et de uinea." When the parable has been told, Ezechiel continues with a "Declaratio parabolae" (Ezechiel 17:11) in which he explains what the story means. The expounding of dreams, visions and parables is a commonplace in the Bible. Certainly this tradition of explaining mysterious stories would influence the scholars who glossed the Riddles.

---

[72] "Tropus est dictio translata a propria significatione ad non propriam similitudinem" (Beda Venerabilis, *De schematibus et tropis*, CCSL 123A: 151). Wieland, *The Latin Glosses*, pp. 147-154.

[73] All Biblical quotations are taken from: *Biblia Sacra iuxta Vulgatam Versionem*, ed. R. Weber (Stuttgart, 1969).

[74] Frederick Tupper, *The Riddles of the Exeter Book* (Boston, 1910), p. xviii. He says the Queen's actual riddles survive "in the Midrash Mishle and the Second Targum to the Book of Esther."

[75] This conjunction also occurs in Habakuk 2:6, "Numquid non omnes isti super eum parabolam sument. Et loquelam aenigmatum eius."

The last occurrence of *enigma* in the Bible is the celebrated passage in 1 Corinthians 13:12: "Videmus nunc per speculum in aenigmate; tunc autem facie ad faciem," which is reminiscent of God's words to Miriam and Aaron. This passage is significant not only in itself, but also for the commentary it has inspired. Augustine mentions it in *De trinitate* 15.9.15. He explains that allegories are figures of speech that "signify one thing by another." [76] *Enigma* is a species of allegory:

> Of this trope, that is allegory, there are many types, including the one called enigma. The definition of a generic name must, of necessity, include all the species. And because of this, just as every horse is an animal, but not every animal is a horse, so every enigma is an allegory, but not every allegory is an enigma. To explain briefly, an enigma is an obscure allegory. [77]

In this passage, Augustine defines *enigma* as a type of allegory, but in his *Commentary on Psalm 48* he defines it in terms of parable: "An enigma is an obscure parable, which is understood with difficulty." [78] In his letter *Ad Simplicianum*, he emphasizes that an enigma does not utterly conceal the truth:

> Indeed a veil entirely covers the vision; an enigma (as if through a mirror, as the apostle says: 'We see now through a glass darkly') does not uncover the most evident aspect nor does it absolutely hide the truth. [79]

One of Augustine's main objectives is to reveal the truth of scripture; this is especially evident in *De doctrina christiana*, where he outlines the duties of a Christian teacher (2.29). He is speaking here of knowledge of the natural world, which can help to clarify scripture: "We have spoken of that above and we have taught that this knowledge can be useful in solving the riddles of scripture." [80] In the labour of expounding scripture, Augustine feels, even the secrets of riddles have some value; they may help to sharpen the love of truth

---

[76] "... quae sunt aliud ex alio significantia," Augustine, *De trinitate* 15.9.15, CCSL 50A: 481.

[77] "Huius autem tropi, id est allegoriae, plures sunt species in quibus est etiam quod dicitur aenigma. Definitio autem ipsius nominis generalis omnes etiam species complectatur necesse est. Ac per hoc sicut omnis equus animal est, non omne animal equus est, ita omne aenigma allegoria est, non omnis allegoria aenigma est. ... Aenigma est autem ut breuiter explicem obscura allegoria" (ibid.).

[78] "Aenigma autem est obscura parabola, quae difficile intelligitur," Augustine, *Enarrationes in Psalmos I-L*, CCSL 38: 554.

[79] "Velamen quippe omnimodo intercludit aspectum, aenigma uero tamquam per speculum sicut idem apostolus ait: 'Videmus nunc per speculum in aenigmate,' nec euidentissimam detegit speciem nec prorsus obtegit ueritatem," Augustine, *De diuersis quaestionibus ad Simplicianum*, CCSL 44: 57.

[80] "De quo genere superius egimus eamque cognitionem ualere ad aenigmata scripturarum soluenda docuimus" (Augustine, *De doctrina christiana*, CCSL 32: 63-64).

among those who already have some knowledge of literature and who know the Bible to be full of "solidum eloquium, quia non est inflatum."[81]

Like Augustine, other early medieval writers available to the Anglo-Saxons, such as Cassiodorus, Isidore and Gregory the Great, have much to say about *enigmata*. Cassiodorus' *Commentary on the Psalms*, which is the source of two of the encyclopedic glosses in L (Riddles 13 and 34), is a study of the figures of speech found in the Psalms. In "De schematibus in Commentarium Cassiodori in Psalmos occurrentibus," he defines the figures of speech and among them is *enigma*:

> An enigma is an obscure sentence, as when someone says one thing and wishes something else to be understood. He spoke of fire, lightning, mountains, heavens and through all these the one wish was to announce the Lord Saviour.[82]

Isidore says:

> An enigma is an obscure question which is understood with difficulty unless explained, for example 'From the eater came forth meat and from the strong came forth sweetness' which signifies the honeycomb taken from the mouth of the lion. The difference between allegory and enigma is this: allegory has a double meaning and beneath certain things it indicates something else figuratively; but in an enigma only the sense is obscure and shadowed over by certain images.[83]

It is curious that Samson's riddle concerning the honeycomb and the lion is not called an *enigma* in the Bible, but a *problema*.

Gregory the Great has occasion to discuss *enigmata* in his *Moralia on Job*. Job's words, "Audite sermonem meum, et aenigmata percipite auribus uestris" (Job 13:17) are explained as follows: "This is a figurative speech of Job. Through that which he calls riddles he shows that he is using figurative utterances."[84] Like Augustine, Gregory seeks to explain or uncover the meaning of scripture. In his letter *Ad Leandrum*, which precedes the *Moralia in Job*, he describes his purpose:

---

[81] Augustine, *De catechizandis rudibus*, 9.13.3, CCSL 46: 135.

[82] "Αἴνιγμα, aenigma, id est obscura sententia, quando aliud dicit, et aliud uult intelligi. Dixit *ignem*, dixit *fulgura*, dixit *montes*, dixit *caelos*; et per haec omnia unum votum est annuntiare Dominum Salvatorem" (Cassiodorus, *Expositio in Psalterium* PL 70:1271).

[83] "Aenigma est quaestio obscura quae difficile intellegitur, nisi aperiatur, ut est illud (Iud. 14:14) 'De comedente exivit cibus, et de forte egressa est dulcedo,' significans ex ore leonis favum extractum. Inter allegoriam autem et aenigma hoc interest, quod allegoriae vis gemina est et sub res alias aliud figuraliter indicat; aenigma vero sensus tantum obscurus est, et per quasdam imagines adumbratus" (Isidore, *Etymologiae* 1.37.26).

[84] "Job figurata locutio—Per hoc quod aenigmata nominat, figuratas se habere locutiones demonstrat" (Gregory the Great, *Moralia in Job* 11.37, CCSL 143A: 614).

Since you had asked me to do it anyway and the brothers liked the idea (as you yourself remember), they asked me with importunate pleading to expound the book of the blessed Job, and according as Truth supplied my powers, that I might open mysteries of great depth to them.[85]

Augustine, Cassiodorus, Isidore and Gregory are all concerned with explaining the Bible, yet only Augustine mentions the value of riddles for sharpening the love of truth. All are concerned with *enigma* as a figure of speech, a trope. The term *enigma* (as a trope) is commonly found in the grammars of the early Middle Ages, as well as in the Biblical commentators and encyclopedists.

Donatus, in his section on tropes (in the *Ars Minor*) defines *enigma* as one of seven types of allegory: *ironia, antiphrasis, aenigma, charientismos, paroemia, sarcasmos* and *astismos.* "A riddle," he says, "is a sentence not well understood because it plays on a hidden similarity between things." [86] Pompeius, in his *Commentary on Donatus*, follows the same division of allegory into seven types, but explains each in more detail:

An enigma occurs where children play among themselves, when they ask themselves little questions that no one understands, for example "Tell me, what is it that is the daughter of its mother and whose mother is the daughter of her own daughter?" Once can interpret this as: "My mother bore me, then is born again from me." This is an enigma; it signifies that water can be created from frozen ice, then that same water can once again become solid ice. Thus, ice is made from water and water is made from that same ice. This is an enigma.[87]

Diomedes, another early grammarian who based his work closely on Donatus, also mentions this same enigma, but adds a riddle not found in the grammars of Donatus or Pompeius:

For example, you could say "There is a solid sea in clay on a wooden field where human flesh was playing with bones" when you wish to signify that salt was in a clay salt-cellar on a table on which a hand was throwing dice.[88]

---

[85] "Tunc eisdem fratribus etiam cogente te placuit, sicut ipse meministi, ut librum beati Iob exponere importuna me petitione compellerent et, prout ueritas uires infunderet, eis mysteria tantae profunditatis aperirem" (Gregory the Great, *Moralia in Job* [praefatio], CCSL 143: 2).

[86] "Aenigma est obscura sententia per occultam similitudinem rerum" (Donatus, *Ars Grammatica* 3, in Keil 4: 402).

[87] "Aenigma est, quo ludunt etiam paruuli inter se, quando sibi proponunt quaestinculas, quas nullus intellegit. dic mihi, quid est hoc, est quaedam filia matris et mater filia est filiae suae? hoc qui potest intellegere, 'Mater me genuit, eadem mox gignitur ex me?' aenigma est; hoc autem significat, aquam soluta glacie posse procreari, iterum ipsam aquam coactam glaciem posse facere. ergo et de aqua fit glacies, et de ipsa glacie fit aqua. aenigma est hoc" (Pompeius, *Commentum Artis Donati*, in Keil 5: 311).

[88] "Item ut 'mare concretum in creta ligneo in campo, ubi caro humana ossibus ludebat' cum significare vult salem in salino fictili fuisse, quod super mensam esset, in qua manus talos iactabat" (Diomedes, *Ars grammatica* 3, in Keil 1: 462).

These two Latin riddles are different from the *enigmata* and obscurities of the Bible. They were composed in a secular tradition and are preserved in Latin grammatical writings. Yet, even this grammatical tradition is absorbed into the philosophy of Christian thinkers, for example, Augustine defines *enigma* as a species of allegory in *De trinitate*. Cassiodorus takes the classical system of tropes and classifies the figures of speech found in the Psalms. Reworking the writings of earlier grammarians, Bede substitutes examples from the Bible for examples from Latin poetry in his *De schematibus et tropis*. When he comes to speak of the seven types of allegory he does not cite the popular riddle "My mother bore me ...," as Donatus, Pompeius, and Diomedes had, but quotes instead Psalm 67:14 (68:13). However, like earlier grammarians and commentators, he is careful to explain what it means.

> A riddle is a sentence not well understood because it plays on a hidden similarity between things, such as "The wings of the dove are plated with silver and the feathers of its back are gold," when this signifies the eloquence of holy scripture full of divine light, and the inner meaning of this shines with the greater grace of celestial wisdom, and is either the present life of the holy church rejoicing on the wings of virtues, or the future life in the heavens where (the faithful) will enjoy eternal light with the Lord.[89]

Aldhelm, too, drew on the classical Latin tradition and adapted it to his Christian literary purpose. His riddles are designed with a pedagogical aim and he states this quite explicitly in the Prose Prologue (10-13). Even more interesting is his justification of the riddle form. The characteristic voice it gives to "mute and insensible objects" is an acceptable literary form because it has scriptural precedent (Prol:27-47). He notes several Biblical examples, and adds the riddle we have already found in the Latin grammars, "My mother bore me ...." Aldhelm was obviously well acquainted with both Latin grammars and the Bible but it is the Prose Prologue which shows clearly that he saw these verses as a means for teaching Latin metre and the writing of Latin verse.

Not all riddle collections were composed with an educational purpose in mind. Symphosius (about whom we know little more than that he wrote his riddles in the 4th-5th century AD) wrote 100 riddles as a Saturnalian after-dinner amusement; he calls his verses "nugas," and asks the reader's

---

[89] "Enigma est obscura sententia per occultam similitudinem rerum, ut 'Pennae columbae deargentatae, et posteriora dorsi eius in specie auri' cum significet eloquia Scripturae spiritalis diuino lumine plena, sensum uero eius interiorem maiori caelestis sapientiae gratia refulgentem, uel certe uitam sanctae ecclesiae praesentem, uirtutum pennis gaudentem, futuram autem, quae in caelis est, aeterna cum Domino claritate fruituram" (Beda Venerabilis, *De schematibus et tropis*, CCSL 123A: 162-163).

indulgence for the "indiscretions of a tipsy muse" (*Da ueniam lector quod non sapit ebria musa.*)

Although he knew of Symphosius' riddles (he mentions him by name in the first line of the Prologue), Aldhelm's purpose is quite different from his predecessor's. Symphosius means to entertain, Aldhelm to teach. His riddles are a propaedeutic leading to greater work.

Explaining the Enigmata

The interpretative glosses to Aldhelm's Riddles are intended to explain the *enigmata* contained within the riddles. How is this possible? The title to each riddle is prominently displayed on the folio, so the *enigma* does not consist in guessing the speaker of the riddle, as it does in the riddle "My mother bore me ..." (Prol:47). The *enigmata* presented in Aldhelm's Riddles are of a different sort. They are riddles within riddles. Take, for instance, Riddle 29, "De elemento." The following *enigmata* are proposed: Who are the six counterfeits? Who are the three brothers? Who is the unknown mother? How do letters silently give words to one who thirsts for knowledge? The glossator, with a quotation derived from Donatus' *Ars grammatica* (Keil 4: 334, 368), explains the six counterfeit letters:

> Id est K.Q.H.X.Y.Z. Duae superuacuae .K. et .q. Duae grece .y. et .Z. X non fuit ad tempus augusti. h. autem aspirationis nota est.

The three brothers are the three fingers of the scribe and the unknown is the mind, the hand of the scribe, the parchment or wax or even the quill, which may have come from a crow or a goose or a reed. Finally, the glossator explains that the letters teach, even though they are silent. In line 6, the glossator identifies the teachers, *docentes*, as the letters in written works (or perhaps, holy works), .*i. litteras in scripturis*, who are speaking in this riddle, *s. nos*. This last gloss makes clear the use of *prosopopoeia*.

This example shows how the interpretative glosses solve the *enigmata* contained in Aldhelm's Riddles. While the glossator is attentive to the solving of such riddles, the glosses also reveal an interest in metaphor and synecdoche. In the Prologue, Aldhelm says that David speaks metaphorically in one of the Psalms:

> Ab inanimale. ad animale. metaforice retulit   (Prol:46).

The glossator then explains that the trees of the forest represent inconstant men and the rivers represent teachers:

> dauid   *i. homines instabiles*   *s. in credendo*
> Et psalmista omnia ligna   siluarum exultasse.

> *i. doctores*
> et flumina plausibus manuum lusisse⁻   (Prol:43-45)

The glossator of L is also aware of Aldhelm's use of synecdoche. Synecdoche, Isidore says, is a figure of speech in which the whole is understood by the part or the part by the whole. Therefore, the genus is represented by the species and the species by the genus.[90]

In Riddle 2, "De vento," the glossator quite specifically says that the species "oak" is representing the genus "tree":

> quercus: i. species pro genere pro omnibus lignis posuit   (2:3)

The comments on Aldhelm's use of *enigma, prosopopoeia, metaphor,* and *synecdoche,* the declaration that Aldhelm wrote the Prologue after finishing the rest of the work: — "Denique: post complendam artem prologum scribit" (Prol:17) — and the glosses themselves, all show that the glossator's voice is distinct from the author's. Elsewhere, however, the voices merge. When Aldhelm calls for inspiration, saying "Sic deus indignis tua gratis dona rependis" (VP:9), the glossator adds:

> *s. ut postulo.*
>   ó   *nobis*   *i. ut posui*
> Sic deus indignis tua gratis dona rependis   (VP:9)

In these glosses,the glossator speaks in the first person. Are these the glosses of Aldhelm explaining his text or has the glossator simply identified with the persona of the poet in this passage? The glossator knows the term *persona,* as is evident in Riddle 88, "De Aspide uel Basilisco":

> Late per mundum dispersi semina mortis: Ex persona diaboli
>   dicit   (88:2)

The use of the first person in a few glosses is not sufficient evidence to prove that Aldhelm himself wrote the glosses. If mute and insensible objects can speak to us in the riddles, then certainly a later commentator can also effectively use the first person.

There are over 200 interpretative glosses contained in L and the above discussion covers only a few. The rest are for the reader to discover in conjunction with the text.

5. *Encyclopedic Glosses*

Wieland defines encyclopedic glosses as those which "clarify primarily geographical names, medical terms, provide information about unusual

---

[90] "Synecdoche est conceptio, cum a parte totum uel a toto pars intellegitur. Eo enim et per speciem genus et per genus species demonstratur" (*Etymologiae* 1.37.13).

objects and customs of foreign cultures, comment on the seasons and ages of the world, i.e., explain to the reader of the poem anything that is unusual and foreign to him."[91] I add to this definition the proviso that encyclopedic glosses are usually drawn from another work, a source independent of the text.

The subject matter of Aldhelm's Riddles is unusual; the reader encounters many strange objects, animals, names, places and customs. There are, as a result, many encyclopedic glosses to the text. Sometimes the encyclopedic glosses add information not found in the riddle itself. For example, in Riddle 30, "De ciconia," Aldhelm makes no mention of where storks come from, but the glossator tells us: "Ciconia auis precipua est quae uenit ab affrica" (30:T). (Isidore, in the *Etymologiae* 12.7.16 says storks come from Asia. Might the gloss represent a traditional belief among the Anglo-Saxons?) At other times, the encyclopedic gloss simply repeats information already found in the riddle. In "De salamandra," both riddle and gloss tell the reader, in different words, that the salamander lives in fire. This gloss resembles a paraphrase gloss, but it should not be confused with one, because it is taken from an identifiable source, the *Etymologiae*. Indeed, Aldhelm very likely modelled his riddle on Isidore's description of the salamander. The text and encyclopedic glosses are interdependent in a way that goes beyond merely explaining unusual terms. In many instances, these glosses are drawn from the text which provided the source and inspiration for the riddle.

Not all the encyclopedic glosses draw on the direct source of Aldhelm's verses. Aldhelm's passing reference to Beemoth (VP:4) is glossed with Isidore's description of Beemoth and Leviathan. Here, the gloss adds much more information than is found in the text, which relies more on stories of the fall of Satan than Isidore's description.

The glossator is more than a slavish copier of passages from Isidore or other sources. Take, for instance, the gloss to Riddle 4, "De natura." It begins by quoting from *Etymologiae* 13.5.6: "Conuexa autem caeli extrema eius sunt a curuitate dicta." Instead of continuing with Isidore, the glossator adds a quotation from Juvencus' *Evangeliorum* 3.224: "conuexum quotiens cludit nox humida." This interpolation is followed by Isidore's description: "conuexum enim curuum est quasi eius uersum seu inclinatum ad modicum circum flexum." The glossator, copying from manuscript or memory the passages from Isidore suddenly recalls a line from Iuuencus that uses the word *conuexum*. This reveals a familiarity with other Latin poetry and not just a mechanical repetition of Isidore *verbatim*. A gloss like this would be

---

[91] Wieland, *The Latin Glosses*, p. 180.

valuable for anyone learning verse composition as it gives another example
of *conuexum* used in verse.

The glossator quotes more often from Isidore's *Etymologiae* than any other
text, but we also find encyclopedic glosses drawn from the Bible, and various
Patristic and Classical authors (see Appendix E for an index to the sources
cited by the glossator.) It is interesting to note that several of the encyclo-
pedic glosses on prosody are drawn from Aldhelm's *De metris et enigmatibus
ac pedum regulis*. These glosses are taken from parts of the treatise that do
not survive in any English manuscripts, but must have been available to the
glossator. (Appendix D contains a complete list of the encyclopedic glosses
in L, arranged by their first word or subject matter.)

There is only one encyclopedic gloss in Old English; it occurs on Riddle
95, "De Scilla." The gloss is badly damaged and only a fraction of it is visible
to the unaided eye. Under ultraviolet light, I was able to make out the
following words in the manuscript (readings visible only under the ultraviolet
lamp are in square brackets):[92]

> [.....circ]e forsceop
> [ða wif] þet hi of þem
> [æfp]rigum gewiton
> [in] sæ 7 wurdon to hun
> [d]um. ⌐̸ gecweden;
> Scilla ðet is sæhund

The spellings *þet, þem* and *ðet* for *þæt, þæm* and *ðæt* suggest a Kentish origin
for this gloss, appropriately enough for a manuscript from Canterbury. But
in other glosses by the first hand, the hand of the text and Latin glosses, we
find the more common *æ* spellings – *dæl* (Prol:23), *wælwyrt* (94:T), *ðræd*
(101:59). The second glossating hand, in the one instance where such a
choice is possible, also prefers the West-Saxon *æ* to the Kentish *e* – *næssas*
(92:1).

There are also two Latin glosses on Scilla. Again, I have supplied readings
visible only under ultraviolet light in square brackets:

> [Scilla] filia porci et cretidis nimphae pulcherrimae a glauco deo maris
> adamata est.
> [et Circe] filia solis quae glaucum amauerat cum uiderit scillam frequen-
> tare ad alium fontem
> [ad lauan]dum iecit ueneficia in fontem. et in beluam marinam transfi-
> gurata est. et fretum siculum

---

[92] Thanks to Professor Jane Roberts, University of London, who confirmed these readings.

obsedit. ibique pretereuntes naufragio afficiebat. eam neptunus percussit tridenti. et in scopulum

mutauit. et sonos undarum populi putant. Unde uirgilius. canes in inguine scillae;;

[...rg.liœ.i.] filia
[....is que c]armi
[....subm]ersit clas
[......]icis;

Page says that Michael Lapidge has found a probable source for the first of these Latin glosses in the *Scholia Bernensia* to Virgil's *Bucolics* and *Georgics*.[93] The gloss above and its source retell the story of Scilla found in Ovid's *Metamorphoses* 14.1-74.

The Old English gloss, even when read in relation to these two Latin glosses, is puzzling. It reads: "Circe transformed the women and then they went from the spring into the sea and became dogs." "ða wif" is the plural subject of *gewiton* and *wurdon*, yet the story of Circe and Scilla told in the Latin gloss says that Circe changed *one* woman into a sea monster with dogs around her waist. The Old English glossator seems to have confused Scilla and her dogs, with regard to number.

Another problem with the Old English gloss is the noun after *þem*. The letters *-rigum* are clear to the naked eye. Under ultraviolet light, three more letters are visible: *æfþ*. **æfþrigum* is not a recognizable Old English word. The most likely solution would be that the *f* is a mistake for *s* and that the macron used to indicate a nasal consonant before the *g* has not been copied. This gives us the Old English word *æspringum*, which would make sense in this context. In both the Latin gloss and the riddle, Scilla is described as going from a fountain into the sea, after being poisoned.

The second Latin gloss also presents a problem. Page says:

> With conjectural material supplied to the third and fourth lines, this seems to say, '(.....), daughter of (.....), by her songs (?spells) sank the fleet of (.....).' I do not know who this could have been. There may be a connection with Scilla in the second Vatican mythographer's sentence "Haec (i.e. Scilla now turned by Glaucus into a sea-goddess) classem Ulixis cum sociis ejus euertisse narratur."[94]

The letters in the latter half of this woman's name seem to be *rg(i)liæ* under the ultraviolet light. Is one of the Pleiades, the Virgiliae, intended or is this a reference to a story recounted by Virgil?

---

[93] Page, "The Evidence of English Glosses," p. 165.
[94] Ibid., p. 163.

G. Conclusion

I should like to conclude this survey of the glosses in the surviving manuscripts of Aldhelm's Riddles and the detailed conspectus of the glosses in one Anglo-Saxon manuscript, by discussing the glosses in a broader context. Several questions need to be asked. How are text and gloss related? Are there identifiable features peculiar to English manuscripts? Where and how were the English manuscripts read?

Louis Holtz, in an article on the typology of Latin grammatical manuscripts, points out that there is a natural hierarchy of text and gloss: "Il existe entre le texte canonique ou classique et le commentaire dont il est l'objet une hiérarchie naturelle; le second est subordonné au premier, n'existe que par le premier." [95] He says there are two traits that distinguish gloss from text, "la graphie" and "l'emplacement." The text tends to be "régulier, calligraphié ou stylisé," while the gloss is "cursif, personnel, anarchique même." (He refers here to the original glossator.) Regarding placement of the gloss he says: "La glose va donc se placer là où l'espace n'est pas rempli: ce peut être entre les lignes, ou bien en face des lignes, à gauche ou à droite du corps principal du texte, ou encore en haut ou en bas." He goes on to say that this system of glossing is rarely unified into a coherent commentary:

> Ce système de glose n'arrive que très imparfaitement à constituer un véritable commentaire. En effet, il faut que d'une glose à l'autre apparaisse une certaine unification, afin que l'on sente la présence d'un auteur, la continuité d'une méthode de lecture et d'interprétation." [96]

Certain commentaries do achieve the status of unified works; one thinks of the *Glossa Ordinaria* to the Bible and also of the Biblical commentaries by Bede, Gregory, Cassiodorus or Augustine. In the case of Aldhelm's Riddles, we do not find a glossator who has become a commentator; we have no name and no work that could stand alone, no "commentary" on Aldlhelm's Riddles. Even though the glosses do not form a discrete commentary, however, a great number of them can no longer be called "anarchique même."

Many of the glosses to Aldhelm's Riddles have been copied with the text into more than one manuscript (e.g. P^1 and P^4) or have been copied into carefully marked manuscript space (S^1 and L). These glosses are a far cry

---

[95] Louis Holtz, "La typologie des manuscrits grammaticaux latins," *Revue d'Histoire des Textes* 7 (1977): 257.

[96] Ibid., p. 258.

from the marginal notes we find squeezed into such manuscripts as E or T. At some point, the glosses were taken into account by the scribe and ample space was left for them on the folio. We can see this happening with several of the shared glosses in L and G. Certain interlinear glosses in L are squeezed into insufficient space; when these glosses were copied into G, the scribe separated the two glosses and left ample room for both.[97] For example:

> *i. sicut legimus de sancto ambrosio*
> *i. ad similitudinem examinis apum.*
> Examen   neque spargebat mihi nectar in ore   (VP:11)

In L, the gloss *i. sicut legimus de sancto ambrosio* is squeezed in between the gloss beneath and the verse line above; in G these glosses are distributed more evenly over the available space. The glosses, then, establish themselves as an integral, though still subordinate, part of the text on the manuscript folio. These glosses show quite clearly that the Latin glosses in G were copied from L.

My second question concerns the English manuscripts: are there any identifiable characteristics unique to English manuscripts of Aldhelm's Riddles? One possible feature is the appearance of Old English glosses, though even this is problematic. S^1 and S^2 have Old High German glosses, so glossing in the vernacular, though it is found only in the Germanic manuscripts, is not unique to the Anglo-Saxons. Old English glosses occur in V^2, which is from Fleury. We know that there was contact between Anglo-Saxon England and northern France, so it is no surprise that an English scholar has read and commented on Aldhelm's Riddles while in Fleury, but Old English glosses are no guarantee that a manuscript was ever in England or used in English monastic schools.

One aspect of L and G perhaps characteristic of English manuscripts is the use of grammatical term glosses, e.g. *ablatiuus*, etc. Wieland found these glosses to Arator and Prudentius in G[98] and we find two similar glosses on the Riddles of Eusebius in G (though not in L). Only one other manuscript of Aldhelm's Riddles contains glosses of this type and it contains only two:

> P^5 (f. 104v) aethrae: genetiuus
>   (f. 106v) glebae: id est genetiuus singularis

Further study is needed on Anglo-Saxon manuscripts and their glosses before we can say for certain that this is characteristic of English manuscripts, but the evidence of Aldhelm's Riddles suggests that it is.

---

[97] This occurs with glosses on the following lines: VP:11, 4:2, 5:1, 19:4, 26:4, 27:3, 27:4, 27:5, 31:5, 31:6, 36:5.

[98] Wieland, *The Latin Glosses*, pp. 49-50.

The Anglo-Saxons seem to have been particularly inspired by Aldhelm. This is natural, considering he himself was an Anglo-Saxon, bishop of Sherbourne, and renowned for his learning and poetic skill. Tatwine, archbishop of Canterbury 731-734, wrote forty Latin Riddles and Eusebius (perhaps the Eusebius-Hwætberht to whom Bede dedicated his *De natura rerum*[99]) wrote sixty Latin Riddles. Together, these Riddles make a collection similar to Aldhelm's. Tatwine and Eusebius' Riddles survive only in L and G, two manuscripts that also contain Aldhelm's Riddles. It is likely that Tatwine and Eusebius were directly inspired by Aldhelm's example.

Another versifier who clearly draws her inspiration from Aldhelm is the English nun, Leobgyda. In a letter to Boniface, she asks him to pray for her parents, then says she is sending him some verses she has written:

> Istos autem subter scriptos versiculos conponere nitebar secundum poeticae traditionis disciplinam, non audacia confidens, sed gracilis ingenioli rudimenta exercitare cupiens et tuo auxilio indigens. Istam artem ab Eadburge magisterio didici, quae indesinenter legem divinam rimare non cessat.

> Vale, uiuens aeuo longiore, uita feliciore, interpellans pro me.
> Arbiter omnipotens, solus qui cuncta creauit,
> In regno patris semper qui lumine fulget,
> Qua iugiter flagrans sic regnet gloria Christi,
> Inlesum seruet semper te iure perenni.[100]

Note her use of the phrase "ingenioli rudimenta exercitare cupiens." The identical phrase is used by Aldhelm in his Prologue (11-12). Leobgyda's poetry, as well, owes much to the Verse Preface. Here is evidence of at least two nuns who were studying Latin poetry, using Aldhelm's Riddles as a text.[101]

---

[99] Neil Wright has cast some doubt upon this commonly accepted theory, by studying the metrical practices of the Southumbrian riddlers and concluding that Eusebius was probably a Southumbrian and not a Northumbrian (as was Hwætberht, Abbot of Wearmouth-Jarrow). See Michael Lapidge, "The Present State of Anglo-Latin Studies," in *Insular Latin Studies*, ed. Michael Herren (Toronto, 1981), p. 52.

[100] "I have tried to compose the verses written below according to the discipline of poetic tradition, not trusting to valour, but wishing to exercise the rudiments of slender talent and needing your help. I learned this art from my teacher Eadburg, who never ceases to put the divine law into verse.

'Farewell, you who are living a happier life in eternity, interceding for me.
May the omnipotent judge, who alone created all things,
Who eternally spills forth light from the kingdom of the father,
Where the blazing glory of Christ reigns forever,
Keep you whole forever in the eternal law.'

(Boniface, *Epistolae*, ed. Michael Tangl, MGH: Epist. Sel. 1: 53).

[101] Lapidge, "Aldhelm's Latin Poetry and Old English Verse," pp. 209-231. Lapidge discusses the formulaic nature of Aldhelm's verse and suggests that his method of learning to

The last piece of evidence we have for how Aldhelm's Riddles were read in Anglo-Saxon England is the Exeter Book. Though damaged, it seems originally to have contained a set of 100 Riddles in the vernacular, three of which are translations/adaptations of Aldhelm's Riddles 32 "De lorica," 83 "De iuvenco" and 101 "De creatura." Another of the Exeter Book riddles (number 31 or 33, depending on the modern edition) translates the Latin riddle "Mater me genuit ..." into Old English as part of a speech given by an iceberg. Add to this the Leiden Riddle in V² (a translation in Northumbrian dialect of Aldhelm's Riddle 32 "De lorica") and we have firm evidence of Aldhelm's influence on a school of vernacular riddling. The Old English glosses clustered on "De creatura" in both G and L show that this riddle had a special fascination for the Anglo-Saxons. The "coded" glosses in G (e.g. mfp = leo) suggest an active interest in cryptography and riddling. W. Levison says that "the Fulda tradition of the ninth century also attributed to St. Boniface the importation of cryptographic puzzles, which enjoyed some popularity in the Middle Ages." [102] St. Boniface may have transplanted some of his own native tradition. The Tironian notes in P⁴ also reveal a Continental interest in secret writing.

The above evidence suggests that Aldhelm's Riddles were read, as intended, as a primer in Latin poetry, although they also provided inspiration for Old English poetry. This brings us to another question: where were the Riddles read and by whom; were they read aloud in a classroom by a teacher or were they read privately? Let us look at the evidence from Aldhelm's Riddles in both L and G, two manuscripts which can be associated with the monastic establishments at Canterbury.

First, L is in good physical condition; except for the damage caused by damp near the end of the manuscript, its folios are clean and the writing clear. Although the manuscript is not illuminated, a good deal of care was taken in the decoration of capitals and of the first folio. The Latin glosses were planned and copied as part of the text and there is ample space in the margins for the longer glosses and between the lines for interlinear glosses. Except for the Old English glosses by the second hand and a handful of Latin glosses squeezed in between the lines, the glosses were written along with the text, and ample space was left to accommodate them.

The fact that the scribe of G copies *verbatim* many of L's Latin interlinear glosses suggests that these were not the work of a teacher making notes while

---

write Latin verse included memorizing a large number of stock phrases which could be used to fill out the poetic line. He points out the similarity of Leobgyda's phrases to those found in Aldhelm's verse.

[102] W. Levison, *England and the Continent in the Eighth Century* (Oxford, 1946), p. 138.

teaching a class, but rather, the work of a scribe copying what was seen as an integral part of (or an important adjunct to) the text. One can argue that L and G were merely the last in a long series of glossed texts and the glosses were originally notes for teaching, but while this may be true, there is still no indication that the Latin glosses were used in a classroom. They could just as easily be the notes of an individual reader as those of a teacher. The Anglo-Saxon reaction to Aldhelm's Riddles can be better gauged from the Old English glosses, which are unique in L and G. Here we find evidence of a struggle with unfamiliar vocabulary, the ablative case and the passive voice — understandable concerns for someone whose native tongue is not Latin. We also find a spirit of playfulness (in the encoded glosses of G) and a spirit of impromptu commentary (in the *wynn/wa* glosses in L). Undoubtedly, G and L were written and used in a learned (and learning) environment, but it is virtually impossible to penetrate beyond the evidence of the glosses and to determine whether they were used in a classroom or for private reading. The evidence of the Latin and Old English glosses in L and G certainly suggests that there was in the eleventh century an active group of readers glossing Aldhelm's Riddles in Old English and an active group of scribes transcribing Latin text and Latin glosses.

Who would have read these manuscripts? Certainly not beginners in Latin. A mastery of Donatus' *Ars grammatica* and easier texts in prose and verse would be a minimal prerequisite for reading Aldhelm's Riddles, let alone composing Latin verse.

Everyone in a Benedictine monastery or nunnery needed to know enough Latin to sing the divine office. Once they had fulfilled their religious duties, monks and nuns would use the rest of their time for other work. Alcuin, in a poem about the scriptorium, says:

> Est opus egregium sacros iam scribere libros
>   Nec mercede sua scriptor et ipse caret.
> Fodere quam vites melius est scribere libros
>   Ille suo ventri seruiet, iste animae.[103]

His pious pronouncements on the writing of books (and the copying of sacred books) are the sentiments of a learned man, and one who wrote his own Latin verse; but we must remember that someone was tending the vines, even as the scribes busily pursued their reward (perhaps consisting of wine!). In the Benedictine Rule, we find that the rules for fasting are more lenient for those who work in the fields:

---

[103] "It is exellent work to copy sacred books. / Nor will the writer himself lack his reward. / It is better to write books than to tend vines. / One serves the belly, the other the soul" (Alcuin, *Carmina* 94, MGH: Poet. Lat. 1: 320.

A Pentecoste autem tota aestate, si labores agrorum non habent monachi, aut nimietas aestatis non perturbat, quarta et sexta feria jejunent usque ad nonam: reliquis diebus ad sextam prandeant.[104]

Jean Leclercq also says that not everyone would advance to writing their own Latin:

The schools were then, no doubt, places where an elementary, then later, secondary education was given to young men of all classes; the program of the trivium and quadrivium included different series of lessons, that is classes and courses. But the master was far more than a teacher: he was able to pick out the most talented or the most willing workers in the study-group and train them with particular care. This system of selection and specialization favored the rise of a few men of outstanding personality who, in turn, exercised an enriching influence on the environment from which they had come and on a few select disciples. We know, for instance, that Aimoin had received this kind of formation from Abbo at Fleury. In like manner, in the second half of the eleventh century, Albericus of Monte Cassino dedicated a part of his *Breviarium de dictamine* to two of his disciples, Gunfridus and Guido who, after their elementary studies, wished to brave the difficulties of composition and advance *ad pugnam compositionem*.[105]

One thinks, too, of Leobgyda learning versification from Eadburg.

L is intended for advanced students and this may explain the presence of the long, encyclopedic glosses. They may be intended to give the student guidance in the actual mechanics of versification (as in the long glosses to the Prologue) and material for writing their own verses on the salamander, crab, peacock, etc. These glosses were probably not copied into G because there was insufficient space in the margins; this suggests that the pedagogical intent behind L and G was quite different.

L was intended primarily as a riddle collection; it was planned as a composite volume and has survived with its original gatherings intact. The fact that Aldhelm's Riddles begin in the middle of folio 79v shows that Julian of Toledo's *Prognosticon*, immediately preceding, was also part of the original collection. The manuscript was probably intended for advanced students and may have been read by a teacher and a small group of advanced students learning prosody or by a student learning Latin versification independently.

---

[104] "From Pentecost throughout the summer, unless the monks have work in the fields, let them fast on Wednesdays and Fridays until the ninth hour; on the other days let them dine at the sixth hour" (*The Rule of Saint Benedict*, ed. and trans. Abbot Justin McCann [London, 1952], pp. 98-99).

[105] Jean Leclercq, *The Love of Learning and the Desire for God*, trans. Catharine Misrahi (New York, 1961), pp. 143-144.

Wieland contends that the glosses to Arator and Prudentius in G are evidence of the actual classroom technique of an Anglo-Saxon teacher. This may be true for the early parts of G, but it does not seem to be true for L or the later parts of G. Wieland and Rigg state that G

> consisted initially of a group of three classbooks. They were probably planned to form a complete collection, as the most elaborate initial is the *M* on 1r, which surpasses the simply coloured initials at the beginning of parts *II* and *III*. The three books appear to have been graded according to difficulty and educational value.[106]

The manuscript has been rebound and these sections are now out of order, but Arator and Prudentius occur in the original first part of G, the easiest, while Aldhelm's Riddles occur in the third part, the most difficult. Perhaps the glosses to Arator and Prudentius do represent Anglo-Saxon classroom technique. They are easier texts and more likely to have been taught to a large number of students.

Certainly the evidence of Aldhelm's Riddles in L and G does not suggest that the glosses represent classroom procedure or interaction. One of the main features of Wieland's argument that the glosses on Arator and Prudentius in G represent classroom technique is the appearance of *q:* glosses in the manuscript. The *q:* glosses, Wieland says, are puzzling: "they do not help the reader with the translation; they occur over verbs; and they begin with the letter Q." He says that although they do not "necessarily mean *quare*" they "almost certainly are reminders for the teacher to ask the students a question." [107] He concludes:

> These *q:* glosses offer a singular glimpse into the Anglo-Saxon classroom: we are practically looking over the teacher's shoulder — he stops at a particular word, forgets for the moment about the text, and concentrates on the grammar; possibly he asks a student to parse the form and give the principal parts of the verb under discussion. The *q:* glosses thus confirm what we may reasonably assume to be part of any lesson, i.e., that a questioning of students actually took place in the classroom.
>
> The *q:* glosses suggest that glossator and teacher are one. ... [However,] this is true only to a limited extent. The glosses have their own history, and the glossator of Gg.5.35 is only the last redactor. Nonetheless, he has a great amount of control over the glosses of the exemplar, since he is able to omit some of them or add others, as he sees fit (and probably as his teaching technique demands)." [108]

---

[106] Rigg and Wieland, "A Canterbury Classbook," p. 129.
[107] Wieland, *The Latin Glosses*, p. 194.
[108] Ibid., p. 195.

No *q:* glosses are found in any of the surviving manuscripts of Aldhelm's Riddles, though the abbreviation *q:* for *-que* has been added above the line of text several times, after having been erroneously omitted. A similar gloss is found in L to the Verse Preface:

s. et priusquam fulsissent
quid:
Splendida   formatis fulsisset lumina saeclis (VP:24)

Here is a gloss, complete with the *punctus interrogativus*, which shows that the glossator (teacher? student? independent reader?) is genuinely puzzled. The gloss above *quid:* may be the glossator's eventual answer to this question, though it does not answer either the question why? or what?, but rather explains a difficult reading: *fulsisset* does not take a direct object (*lucifer* in line 23 is the subject of *fulsisset*), so the glossator makes *Splendida ... lumina* the subject of this phrase by changing *fulsisset* to *fulsissent*. This does not really solve the problem, but represents an attempt to deal with a difficult reading (the preferred reading in Ehwald's edition is *fudisset*). Both of these glosses are copied directly into G along with the other interlinear Latin glosses from L. How far we must go back to find the original glossator (who may or may have not been teaching) is impossible to determine. Perhaps the glosses do go back to a teacher who glossed a manuscript for teaching, perhaps they go back to Aldhelm himself. The encyclopedic glosses, copied from many independent sources, may represent research as much as teaching or learning Latin verse. From the evidence of Aldhelm's Riddles, there was more copying of glosses than there was actual glossing.

At some point, the glosses become part of the text, a part of the text worth copying word for word into a new manuscript. But when does this happen? The Latin glosses to L have become part of the text by the time they are copied into G. The Old English glosses in G and L are not part of the Latin text; they are unique to each manuscript and added independently by different glossators. As mentioned above, these glosses may be the real clue to how Latin texts were read by the Anglo-Saxons. Latin glosses have a tendency to become part of the Latin text they gloss and, eventually in their transmission, cease to be the work of reader or teacher and become the work of the scribe. Our mysterious "glossator" is hard to find in the succession of scribes, scholars, teachers and students who have a hand in the transmission of texts and glosses. Perhaps we should think of the "glossator" (who, only for simplicity has been referred to in the singular) not only as all the people who have commented on or copied a text, but also, in some sense, the text itself and its original author. Certainly in the case of Aldhelm and his announced pedagogic purpose, we have someone creating a text that cries out to be explained. In the manuscripts of Aldhelm's Riddles, the same words are glossed over and over again, because they invariably present difficulty to readers. Thus, glossing represents an interaction of author and reader by means of a text, whose real significance is obscured by centuries of manuscript transmission and the ultimate silence of the manuscripts themselves. There is, in spite of all, much to be learned:

Qui cupit instanter sitiens audire docentes.
Tum cito prompta damus rogitanti uerba silenter.   (29:6-7)

Aldhelm's Riddles
in the British Library
MS Royal 12.C.xxiii

Prologue

INCIPIT PROLOGUS ALDHELMI SUPER ENIGMATA.

SIMPHOSIUS VERSIFICUS

1   POETA METRICAE ARTIS PERITIA PREDITUS. OCCULTAS

    enigmatum propositiones exili materia sumptas.
             i. litteris.   *i. uarias*
    ludibundis apicibus legitur cecinisse: et singulas

    quasque propositionum formulas tribus uersi

5   culis terminare: Sed et aristotelis philosophorum
           i. obscura
           difficillima   *i. misteria*
    acerrimus. perplexa nihilominus enigmata
                            i. inuenit
    prosae locutionis facundia fultus ärgumenta
                         i. curiositas
    tur; Quamobrem nostrae exercitationis sollicitu
     s. poetarum   *i. incensa*   *i. machinis*
    do horum exemplis instincta et commentis adin
           s. enigmata
10 uentionum componere nitebatur: et uelut in
                      i. alphabeta
                      uel principia
    quodam gimnasio prima ingenioli rudimenta

    s. nostra sollicitudo
    exercitari cupiens: ut uenire possit deinceps ad

i. ad alias partes perfectiores uel grandiores.   uel post haec
prestantiorem operis materiam: Si tamen poste
     s. enigmata   *s. certis*
rius haec mediocria metricae diffinitionis regu
    i. si non   *i. longam sillabam. et breuis et communis*

15 lis minime caruerint: Tripartitamque sillabarum
s. in longas. et in breues
et communes sillabas. i. iuxta regulam
differentiam iuxta perpendiculam scandendi rite
s. et si   post complendam artem prologum scribit
seruauerint; Denique predicta enigmatum capi
                       i. narranda
tula primitus quaternis uersiculorum lineis di
s. sunt
gesta: sequentia uero iuxta quod se occatio com

20 ponendarum rerum exibuit: quinis iam senis uel etiam
                      i. modulantur
septenis metrorum uersibus et eo amplius canan
   s. uersibus
tur: quibus indesinenter ⟨secundum⟩ poeticae traditio
            i. limes dæl. i. duo pedes et semis.
       * *i. lim. i. per quintam diuisionem.*
      i. duo pedes i. particula uel conclusio
nis disciplinam cola uel commata seu pentimemeren

et ebtimemeren adnectere progressis binis et ternis
         i. ideo
25 pedibus procuraui; alioquin dactilici exametri

regulae legitima aequitatis lance ⟨carentes⟩. lū

bricis sillabarum gressibus uacillarent; Porro

quod etiam muta insensibilium rerum natura.
         i. occulta.
        i. misterium i. occultum eloquium
de qua enigma clancula et latens ⟨propositio⟩ con
s. in commune
30 ponitur. quasi loqui et sermocinari fingitur.

hoc ēt in sacris litterarum apicibus insertum lē
      i. sepe   *i. homo*
gitur: Quia nonnumquam rationabilis creatura
s. creaturarum i. actu
inrationabilium gestu et personis utitur. Et econ

fol 80v1-22

      s. creatura
trario inrationabilis sensu uaria cecitate
  s. hominum

35   intellectualium gestu et uoce fŭngitur. Quem

admodum in libro iudicum diuersa lignorum
                             i. regem uel principem
genera articulata uoce loquentia. monarchum
            i. porrexerunt *i. homines*
quesiuisse rēfertur. Ierunt inquit ligna ungere

super se regem. ubi singulatim sicut supra iam dixi
i. reges   *i. uera* *s. locutus*   *i. malus*
fortes *i. uirginitas* *coniugia*   *est*   *princeps.*

40   ficus et uitis simulque oliua. et ad extremum ramnus
                                   i. homines iustos
igne proprio flammisque uoracibus libani cedros.

⟨consumpturus. iuxta⟩ ritum humanae locutionis
   i. loqui ⁄ *i. testantur*   *dauid*   *i. homines instabiles*
profari perhibentur; Et psalmista omnia ligna
          s. in credendo   *i. doctores*
siluarum exultasse. et flumina plausibus manu

45   um lusisse. camposque gratulabundos extitisse.
                         i. narrauit
Ab inanimali. ad animale. metaforice retulit.
    s. exemplum
Et illud poeticum. mater me genuit eadem mox
           s. legitur s. animalibus. *s. animalibus*
gignitur ex me; Et ⟨quot⟩ de mutis aut brutis ra

tionationis argumenta requiruntur. cum etiam
  i. salomon   *i. ante*
50   sapientissimus cunctorum retro regum et deinceps ⟨nas
           s. libro
citurorum⟩ in ⟨aecclesiaste⟩ frequenter stolidissimorum

personis utitur dicens. Quid habet homo ampli

us iumento. aut sapiens stulto et similia cetera;
  s. exempla
Haec idcirco diximus ne quis forte nouo nos et

55   inusitato dicendi argumento ⟨et⟩ nullis quasi

fol 81r1-22

priorum uestigiis trito. predicta enigmata cecinisse
                        s. syllabarum et uersuum
arbitretur; Et ut euidentius harum rerum ratio cla
              i. xxviii.†
resceret. legitimos septies quaternos metrorum pedes.
ex   *§*
quibus uniuersa non solum principalia octo genera
                        in centimetro sunt.
60   progrediuntur. uerum etiam species quae ex eadem

stirpe pullulantes centuplis metrorum frondibus
                        s. in metro dactilico.
contexuntur subdidimus; Et singulis quibusque

pedibus tantam exemplorum copiam accumulantes
                        regulam
quantum ad presentis opusculi normam prouidentioris
         i. causa
65   iudicii gratia sufficere credimus; Et quod proces

sores celeberrimi uniformi nominis exemplo pro
    i. colligere   *s. celeberrimorum*
palasse noscuntur. nos eorundem uestigia enixius

indagantes uberiorem exemplorum formulam
i. monstrauimus.
enucleamus; Et qualiter uel ex quo pacto longae

70   breues syllabae uel etiam communes utrique com
                        duos temporales. Videlicet quia
    i. conuenientes   *corripi et produci possunt.*
petentes quas greci dicronas dicunt sagaciter dis

criminantur; Ex hac enim triplici sillabarum

diffinitione potius quam de fonte a monte musa

rum de quibus persius flaccus. Nec fonte inquit
         i. ablui
75   labra prolui caballino. nec in bicipiti somniasse

parnaso memini me. omnis metrorum ratio mon

i. qui per omnia   i. qui per quinque
spondeis stant.   loca dactilis stant.

stratur; Et qui uersus monoscemi qui pentascemi

fol 81v1-22

s. iure

uel qui ⟨decascemi⟩ cum .xxiii. temporibus. excepto

si trocheo terminantur. rite dictantur; Hac tri

80   partita discriptionis normula ⟨omnis⟩ heroici ex

ametri uersificatio uel cesurarum scansio principa

liter constat. licet sinalifarum uelut quaedam con

glutinatio et explosa collisionis additamenta

crebro apud poetas liricos et satiricos necessitate
s. additamenta
uel sinalifae   #
85   metri interponantur; Quae maxime ex uocalibus

litteris uel sillabis .M. semiuocali terminandis gig
s. species. sinalifae
et iactalemsi
nuntur; Has utrasque iunius iuuenalis quinto libro

satirarum. unius tenore uersus simul elisit dicens:

Omenta ut uideo nullum discrimen habendum est.

90   Scanditur ita. Omen. spondeus. tut uide. Dactilus per sinalifa onul

spondeus. lumdi. spondeus. scrimina. dactilus. bendest. spondeus per
sinalifa;

Rursus idem dicit liricus libro quarto; Bellorum

excubiae truncis affixa tropheis. Scanditur ita.

Bello. rexcubi. per sinalifa. aetrun. cisad. fixatro. pheis.

95   Sic aennius lucanus cordubiensis poeta uno uer

sinalifa sinalifa
su libro nono bís elisit dicens. Quare agite eoum

comites properemus in urbem; Rursus idem libro .x.
      sinalifa
ait: hinc tergo insultant pedites uia nulla salu
   s. elisit
ti; Unde paulinus questor .M. litteram ita: Tarta

fol 82r1-22

    sinalifa
100 ream in sedem. sequitur noua nupta maritum;

Item prosper ait. Caelestem ad patriam tendens cog

nosce uocantem; Haec eadem sinalipha uersibus
     i. poetae   uel constat
sibillae poetridis continetur: quae ait. Tunc illi

aeterna species pulcherrima regna; Focus quoque

105 gramaticus primo uersu sinalipham explodit:

Ars mea multorum est quos saecula prisca tulerunt;

Virgilius .xi. Oceanum interea surgens aurora reliquit;
      genetiuus
      singularis
Idem libro .vii. eneido⟨s⟩ in uno uersu sinalipham

et iecthilemsin conprehendit ita. Nunc repeto
sinalifa uel
iactalemsi
110 anchises fatorum archana ⟨reliquit;⟩ Scanditur

autem hoc modo. Nunc repe. tanchi. sesfa. torar.

chanare. ⟨liquit;⟩ Sed hos duos metaplasmos.

sepe ambiguitas scandendi conturbat: quos

talis differentia dirimit; Si prior uocalis ex

115 plodatur. erit ⟨sinalipha:⟩ si exterior fuerit

s. libro
explosa. erit iactalemsis꞉ Sicut in nouissimo
　　　　　　　　　　　　　　pro duabus
　　　i. scriptum　　　　　*consonantibus*
regum cautum legitur. Purpurei maior. persarum

in sede tyrannis; Virgilius idem libro quem
　　nomen artis.
pedagogum praetitulauit꞉ Carmina si fuerint

120　te iudice digna fauore. Reddetur titulus pur

pureusque nitor; Si minus estiuas poteris con

fol 82v1-18

uoluere sardas. Aut piper aut caluas hinc ope
　　　　　　　　　　　　　　sinalifa
rire nuces. Sillabam elisit dicens. Durum iter et ui

tae magnus labor; Et arator subdiaconus primo

125　uersu genitiui sillabam elisit dicens. Moenibus
　　　　　　sinalifa
undosis bellorum incendia cernens; Et infra

eleiaco uersu subiungit. Inque humeris ferimur

te reuocante piis; Itaque has duas metaplasmorum

species propetera ex numero .xiiii. explanare

130　nisus sum. quia per omne corpus poeticorum libro

rum satis frequenter insertae sunt꞉ et nisi sagaci

subtilitate precognitae fuerint. diuersa impedi

mentorum ⟨obstacula⟩ scandentibus generare

solent; Idcirco diuersos uersus metrorum

135　ad sinaliphae metaplasmum congruentes cater
　　　　i. colligimus　　　　*s. uersibus*
uatim congessimus꞉ quatinus his perspectis nul

s. duarum
lum deinceps explosae collisionis chaos et latebro

sum confractae sinaliphae barathrum. lucem
s. M
139 scandentis confundant; finit amen.

22 secundum] sicut MS   26 carentes] currentes MS   29 propositio]
propotio MS   42 consumpturus. iuxta] consumptus iuxtum MS
48 quot] quod MS   50 retro *added above the line*   51 nasciturorum]
nascitorum MS   aecclesiaste] aecclesiastico MS   55 et] e MS
78 decascemi] descascemi MS   80 omnis] omnes MS   103 eneidos]
eneido MS   110 reliquit] reliquid MS   112 liquit] liquid MS
115 sinalipha] sinalemsin MS   133 obstacula] obstaculo MS

23 (botmarg80r)

* *Cola. id est maior diuisio uersus in septem*
  i. vii dimidiis pedibus
  semipedibus secundi membri. in tribus pedibus. Commata id est minor
  diuisio prioris membri in tribus pedibus. Aliter comma dicitur.
  ubi post duos pedes nihil remanet. Pentimemeris dicitur cesura.
  uidelicet. quinta sillaba quando ex spondeis constat quae finit
  partem sed non pedem. Eptimemeris dicitur cesura .i. syllaba post
  tres pedes remanens. septima syllaba. tenet semipedem;

Cola ... remanet: Bede *De arte metrica* 12 ("De scansionibus uel caesuris heroici
versus"), pp. 116-118   Pentimemeris ... tenet semipedem: Aldhelm *De
metris* 10, pp. 93, 95

58 (upmarg81r)

† *Septies quaternos pedes id est xxviii. Sunt autem*
  pedes dissyllabi .iiii. Trisyllabi .viii. Tetrasyllabi
  sedecim singuli nominatim distincti. atque ex his
  geminatis adcrescunt sine nomine qui generaliter
  zinzugiae .i. coniunctiones dicuntur; Unde fit omnes
  pedes a disillabis usque ad exasillabas c.xx.iiii
  colligi;

Septies ... colligi: cf. Bede *De arte metrica* 9 ("De pedibus"), p. 107, "Sunt
autem pedes disyllabi IIII, trisyllabi VIII, tetrasyllabi XVI, singuli nominatim
distincti. At qui ex his geminatis adcrescunt sine nomine generaliter 'synzygiae,'
id est, 'coniugationes,' dicuntur. Vnde fit omnes pedes, a disyllabis scilicet usque
ad exasyllabos, CXXIIII colligi, de quibus in Donato plenissime quisque uelit
inueniet."

59 (upmarg81r)

§ *Octo principalia genera metrorum sunt. id est*
Iambicum. Trochaicum. Dactilicum. Anapestum.
Coriambicum. Antispaticum. Ionicum a maiore.
Ionicum a minore;

> Octo ... minore: cf. Malli Theodori *De metris*, Keil 6:588, "Sunt igitur metrorum
> genera haec, dactylicum, iambicum, trochaicum, anapaesticum, choriambicum,
> antispasticum, ionicum a maiore, ionicum a minore." Cf. also Marii Seruii
> Honorati Grammatici *De centum metris*, Keil 4:457, "Metra vel a pedibus
> nomen accipere, vel a rebus quae describuntur, vel ab inventoribus, vel a
> frequentatoribus, vel a numero syllabarum: choriambicum, antipasticum, ioni-
> cum a maiore, ionicum a minore, de quibus carptim tractabimus, eligentes ea
> quae ad palmam lyrae perducit voluptas."

77 (botmarg81r)

Mono enim grece pes latine. Monoscemi unam figuram
qui per .v. loca dactilicis stant. Qui per quinque
loca dactilo uariantur. Aut enim primo et secundo
loco dactilus ponitur. aut primo et tertio ponitur.
aut primo et quarto. aut primo et quinto. aut secundo
et tertio. aut secundo et quarto. aut secundo et
quinto. aut tertio et quarto. aut tertio et quinto
aut quarto et quinto;

85 (botmarg81v)

\# *Fit autem sinalifa duobus modis .i. cum aliqua*
pars orationis in uocalem desinit. incipiente sequente
parte orationis iterum a uocali. Ut arta uia est uere
quae ducit ad atria uitae. Aut in .M. consonantem cum
desinit illa quae sequitur pars orationis. precedentem
uel literam uocalem uel sillabam quae .in .M. desierat
sua uocali absumit. Ut superius diximus. Scanditur
enim ita. Artaui. Dactilus. estue. spondeus intercepta
.A. per sinalifam. Item pars syllabae quae in .M.
desierat sinalifa intercipitur. cum dicit.
Nullus enim est insons sola formidine penae.
Qui sanctum et iustum non amat imperium. Scanditur
enim ita. Nullus e. Dactilus. n est in. spondeus.
absorbta. ⟨im.⟩ per sinalifam. Item. Qui sanc.

spondeus. tet ius. spondeus. absumpte sinalifa
particulam sillabae. um.

.im.] .in. MS

Fit autem sinalifa ... sillabae. um.: Bede *De arte metrica* 13 ("De synalipha"),
pp. 119-120.

PROLOGUE

Symphosius the versifier, a poet, endowed with skill in the poetic art, is said
to have sung obscure riddles on humble subjects in a playful style and he fits
each one of these riddles into three verse lines; Aristotle as well, the most
brilliant of philosophers, who was aided by the eloquence of prose locution,
also wrote perplexing riddles. (8) My natural striving solicitude was inspired
by these poets and in accordance with their creations I began trying to
compose riddles, hoping that the rudiments of my small talent would be
exercised as if in school, so that I might eventually write of more important
subjects. (13) If, when finished, my first mediocre verses do not stray from
the rules of metrical limits and if they preserve the tripartite distinction of
syllables, according to the rule of proper scanning, then, while these early
riddles will be written in verses of four lines, the following ones, as the
opportunity for writing presents itself, will be sung in five, six, or even seven
and more verses. (22) In these verses I have ceaselessly striven according to
the discipline of poetic tradition to join the first and second halves of a line
with a caesura amidst the dactyls and spondees, otherwise dactylic hexa-
meters lacking the proper balance of measured symmetry would stumble
amidst the slippery steps of syllables. (27)

Now, these riddles and puzzling enigmas are written in such a way that
mute and insensible objects speak; we also find this to be true in holy
scriptures, where a rational creature often adopts the persona and posture of
irrational creatures. (33) Likewise, irrational creatures, lacking understand-
ing in their manifold blindness, use the voice and posture of intelligent
beings. (35) For instance, in the Book of Judges, diverse species of trees,
speaking with articulate voice, are said to have sought a king:

"The trees went forth to anoint a king over themselves."

Here, one at a time, the trees are shown to speak, with the power of human
speech (as I explained above): the fig, the vine, the olive, and finally the
bramble, which will consume the cedars of Lebanon in its voracious flames.
(43) In addition, the psalmist told, in metaphors drawn from the inanimate
to the animate, how all the trees of the forest rejoiced, the rivers played to

the clapping of hands and the fields were glad. (47) There is also a poetic example of this:

> "My mother bore me and then she herself is born again from me." (48)

What more argument is required concerning mute and brute creatures when even the wisest of all kings and men ever born, in *Ecclesiastes* frequently takes the part of the dumbest beasts, saying:

> "What more does a man have than a beast or the wise man than the fool?," etc. (53)

I have given these examples lest anyone should think I wrote these riddles using a new and unusual way of speaking that was never used in the writings of our prececessors. (57)

In order that the reason for these things might be made more clear, I have added below the twenty-eight legitimate feet of poetry, out of which are derived not only the eight principal types, but also those kinds which spring from the same root and are woven into the hundredfold branches of meter. (62) I have also collected such a quantity of examples of each and every foot as I believe will suffice for the better understanding of this present little work. (65) Because my predecessors of so famous repute are known to have taught by example, I, following zealously in their footsteps, have given a more full accounting of examples and have shown how short, long and common syllables (which the Greeks call dicrons) can each be distinguished from the others. (72) Persius Flaccus says:

> "I do not recall that I have moistened my lips in the horse's fountain,
> Nor that I have slept on twinpeaked Parnassus"

but it is the triple distinction of syllables and not the fountain or mountain of the Muses that reveals the structure of meter and shows which verses are rightly called monoscemes (containing six spondees), which pentascemes (containing five dactyls) and which decascemes (containing twenty-three syllables, except if it ends with a trochee). (79) Versification of all heroic hexameters and scansion of cesuras consists in this tripartite descriptive rule, although the joining of two syllables into one and the uncounted extra syllable of elision are often found in the lyric and satiric poets, by reason of metrical necessity. (85) These instances arise when a vowel is next to another vowel or to the semi-vocalic letter M at the end of a word. (87) Iunius Iuvenalis, in the Fifth Book of the Satires, has instances of both types of sinalifa in one verse:

> "Omenta ut uideo nulleum discrimen habendum est." (89)

It is scanned thus: Omen, spondee; tut uide, dactyl (by sinalifa); onul, spondee; lumdi, spondee; scrimina, dactyl; bendest, spondee (by sinalifa). (91)

Again, the same lyric poet says in Book Four:

"Bellorum excubiae truncis affixa tropheis." (93)

It is scanned this: Bello; rex cubi (by sinalifa); aetrun; cisad; fixatro; pheis. (94)

Aennus Lucanus, the poet of Cordova, in one verse of Book Nine, also elides twice:

"Quare agite eoum comites properemus in urbem." (97)

Again, the same poet in Book Ten says:

"Hinc tergo insultant pedites uia nulla saluti." (98)

Paulinus Quaestor elides the letter M thus:

"Tartaream in sedem sequitur noua nupta maritum." (100)

In the same way, Prosper says:

"Caelestem ad patriam tendens cognosce uocantem." (101)

This same elision is found in the verses of the poetess Sibyl, who says:

"Tunc illi aeterna species pulcherrima regna." (104)

Also, Focus the Grammarian elides in his first verse:

"Ars mea multorum est quos saecula prisca tulerunt." (106)

Virgil, in Book Eleven of the *Aeneid*, says:

"Oceanum interea surgens aurora reliquit." (107)

The same poet in Book Seven uses both sinalifa and iactalemsis in one verse:

"Nunc repeto anchises fatorum archana reliquit." (109)

It is scanned in this way: Nunc repe: tanchisesfa; torar; chanare; liquit. (110) But ambiguity in scansion often confuses these two metrical irregularities, which are distinguished in this way: if the first vowel is removed, then it is sinalifa; if the last is removed, then it is iactalemsis. (116)

Thus we read in the last book of Kings:

"Purpurei maior persarum in sede tyrannis." (117)

Virgil, in that book which is called *The Pedagogue*, says:

"Carmina si fuerint te iudice digna fauore
Redditur titulus purpureusque nitor,
Si minus estiuas poteris conuoluere sardas
Aut piper aut caluas hinc operire nuces." (123)

He elides a syllable, saying:

"Durum iter et uitae magnus labor." (124)

Arator the Subdeacon also elides a syllable in the genitive case in his first verse, saying:

"Moenibus undosis bellorum incendio cernens." (126)

He adds later, in an elegiac verse:

"Inque humeris ferimur te reuocante piis." (128)

I have tried to explain these two types of metaplasm or metrical irregularity (sinalifa and iactalemsis) through these fourteen (sic) examples, because they are quite frequently found in the entire corpus of poetic works and, unless they are sagaciously understood in advance, can cause many problems for those who are scanning the verse. (134) This is why I have brought together different verses containing the metaplasm of sinalifa, so that when the verses are studied, the chaos of conjoined syllables and the dark abyss of elision may not overshadow the light of the one who is scanning.

It is finished. Amen.

Verse Preface

fol 83r1-20

INCIPIUNT ENIGMATA ALDHELMI POETAE
ANGLI SAXONIS:

1   *s. o censor   i. iudex*
ARBITER. AETHEREO. IUGITER QUI REGMINE SCEPTR A

  s. disponis   s. et
Lucifluumque simul caeli regale tribuna L

  i. eiciens demones et inuitans angelos   s. tribunal
Disponis. moderans aeternis legibus illu D;

                    i. familiam
  s. illum   i. curuasti diaboli †
Horrida nam multans torsisti membra beemot H

         ipse   i. demon
5 Exalta quondam rueret dum luridus arc E;

                      i. dominator
  i. liquida s. mihi   uocatiuus .i. princeps
Limphida dictanti metrorum carmina presu L

    imperatiuus
           neophitus i. ostendere
Munera nunc largire: rudis quo pandere reru M

           i. possim i. obscura.   i. narratione
Versibus enigmata queam clandestina fat U;

  s. ut postulo.   i. reddis uel
    ó   nobis   i. ut posui   tribuis
Sic deus indignis tua gratis dona rependi S;§

  i. a castalido   i. non uoco
    monte   i. deas   quod facio .in   i. huc
10 Castalidas nimphas non clamo cantibus istu C

  i. sicut legimus de sancto ambrosio
  i. ad similitudinem examinis apum.   dulcedine
Examen neque spargebat mihi necta in or E.

  i. nomen montis in dela insula in qua
    natus est appollo pater
Cincti sic numquam perlustro cacumina. sed ne C

  s. monte. Mons in arcadia ubi et appollo adorabitur
    # ||
In parnasso procubui. nec somnia uid I;

Nam mihi uersificum poterit deus addere carme   **N**

i. per spiritum

    sanctum i. stultae   s. meae

15 Inspirans stolidae pia gratis munera ment   **I;**

                        i. reddunt

s. deus   i. sensus s. per poema

Tangit si mentem. mox laudem corda rependun   **T;**

fol 83v1-22

      in deuteronomio

Metrica nam moysen declarant carmina uate   **M**

    i. per auxilium   i. uenire filios israel

    gratiae dei   i. opera per mare rubrum

Iamdudum cecinisse prisci uexilla trophe   **I**

aduerbium s. mundi

Late per populos inlustria. qua nitidus so   **L**

           i. eleuans   i. caput

20 Lustrat ab oceani iam tollens gurgite cepha   **L;**

i. dauid Ut est illud.

    ante luciferum genui te   uel cantica

Et psalmista canens metrorum carmina uoc   **E**

Et illud. permanebit ante solem et lunam i. filium

    in generationes generatum   dei

Natum diuino promit generamine nume   **N**

    illud numen   i. sol

In caelis prius exortum quam lucifer orb   **I.**

s. et priusquam fulsissent

quid: i. pulchris

Splendida formatis fulsisset lumina saecli   **S;**

      s. decursa   cum

25 Verum si fuerint bene haec enigmata uers   **U**

i. deletis

  expulsis   i. maculis s. explosa inprudentia

Explosis penitus neuis et rusticitat   **E**

    i. molimina mentis

    s. et si fuerint s. et si

           hi⟨wung⟩

Ritu dactilico recte decursa: nec erro   **R**

i. pro

seduxerit ablatiuus machina consilia geþoht

Seduxit   uana   specie molimina   menti   **S**

s. canere s. carmina   uel serui

Incipiam potiora: sui deus arida uerb   **I**

contra diabolum

30 Belligero quondam qui uires tradidit io   **B**

:‒ *s. mea*   *s. et*

Viscera perpetui s̈i roris r̈epleat haust   U;

             i. <scopulis> uel

     i. fontium   s. pro   lapidibus   i. flumina

Siccis nam laticum duxisti cautibus amne   S

                   i. mari

Olim c̄um cuneus transgresso marmore rubr   O

    pro penetrauerat

Desertum peñetrat. cecinit quod carmine daui   D;

  in   *s. ó*

35   Arce poli genitor seruas qui saecula cunct   A

           i. culpas

Soluere iam scelerum noxas dignare nefanda   S

INCIPIUNT ENIGMATA AEDITA AB ALDHELMO ARCHIEPISCOPO
THEODORI RETHORIS DISCIPULO DACTILICO CARMINE

fol 84r1-3

QUATERNIS QUOQUE VERSIBUS CONTEXTA QUAE
GRECA LINGUA TETRASTICA DICUNTUR
INCIPIUNT ENIGMATA:

8 possim] possem MS   11 i. sicut legimus de sancto ambrosio *squeezed in*
apum] ap um MS, *with space for an erased* i *between* p *and* u   12 nomen
added above the line   32 scopulis]scopolis MS

12 Cincti: cf. *Scholia Bernensia ad Vergili Bucolica atque Georgica* at *Ecologa*
6.3, "*Cynthius*, Apollo, a Cyntho monte qui in Delo insula est."   13 Par-
nasso: cf. Remigius of Auxerre *Commentum in Martianum Capellam* 1.10.6,
"Elicona pars est Parnasi montis. Duo enim iuga habet ille mons, Eliconem et
Citeronem. Eliconem est Apollonis et Citeron est Liberi."   17 in Deutoro-
nomio: Deuteronomy 32-33   21 i. david: Psalm 109:3   22 Et illud:
Psalm 71:5

T (upmarg83r)

*   *Enigma est obscura sententia. per occultam*
    similitudinem rerum. ut mater me genuit. eadem mox
    gignetur ex me. cum significat aquam in glaciem
    concrescere et ex ea rursum effluere;

    Enigma ... effluere: Donatus *Ars grammatica*, in Keil 4:402

4 (rmarg83r8-10)

Beemoth ex ebrea lingua. in latina animal sonat.
et quadrupes ostenditur. et significat hostem
antiquam .i. diabolum;

> Beemoth ... sonat: Isidore *Etymologiae* 8.11.27

4 (bot marg 83r)

† *Beemoth .i. demon. beemoth hebraica uoce in latinam*
linguam animal ponit. propterquod de excelsis ad
terrena cecidit. et quod tortuosum animal brutum
effectum sit: ipse est et leuiathan serpens de aquis
quia in huius mari uolubili uersatur astutio.
Leuiathan autem interpretatur addimentum eorum. quōrum
scilicet: nisi hominum quibus in paradiso culpam
praeuaricationis intulit. <Et hanc> usque aeternam
mortem cotidie persuadendo adducit uel extendit;

> Et hanc] Ad hanc MS
>
> Bemmoth ... extendit: Isidore *Etymologiae* 8.11.27

11 (lmarg83r15-16)

Nectar .i. quasi nectirassin .i. sine honore.

13 (rmarg 83r13-17)

\# *Parnassus mons thaesaliae iuxta boetiam qui*
gemino uertice est erectus in caelum. hic in duo
finditur iuga cirra et nisa. unde et nuncupatur
eo quod in singulis iugis colebantur appollo et
liber pater;

> Parnassus ... liber: Isidore *Etymologiae* 14.8.11

13 (rmarg83r19-20)

|| *ut faciebant gentiles .i. ostendebant somnia*
poetis. iuxta postulationem musarum postea
faciebant carmina;

17 (lmarg83v2-4)

cantauit canticum domino quando
⟨porrexit⟩ per mare rubrum per
metricam rationem;

> porrexit] prexit MS
>
> Moyses? *damaged:* Exodus 15:1-18

34 (lmarg83v18-19)

Quando dixit. qui diuisit mare rubrum
in diuisiones;

> Quando dixit: Psalm 135:13

VERSE PREFACE

Lord, you who rule forever your kingdom in the heavenly realm
And the royal, light-filled tribunal of the sky,
Governing it by eternal laws;
As punishment, you hurled the horrid limbs of the behemoth,
5   When, long ago, he fell out of the high heaven;
O master, may you now, a mellifluous poem in meter
Grant as a gift to me, that I, though ignorant, may reveal in verse,
The enigmatic nature of things, secret to tell,
For thus you give your gifts freely to unworthy poets.
10   I do not call the Castalian nymphs here in song,
Nor did swarming bees sprinkle nectar in my mouth,
Never do I wander the heights of Cinthius, nor
Have I slept on Parnassus, nor have I seen visions.
God alone could give a versified song to me,
15   Breathing the holy gift into my dull mind,
If god touches my mind, at once my heart gives forth praise.
Metrical poems tell of Moses the prophet, who long ago
Praised that ancient, bannered, triumphant throng
Widely throughout the nations, where the bright sun
20   Shines and lifts its head from the swell of the ocean;
Likewise, the psalmist, singing measured poems with his voice
Foretold the incarnate godhead born of divine generation,
That power created in heaven before Lucifer, the morning star,
Suffused its splendid rays around the newly created world.

25 If these riddles are well put into verse,
    With all stains and rusticity completely removed,
    And the dactyls arranged properly, and if error has not
    Seduced the efforts of my mind with its false semblance,
    I will begin these worthy poems, if the god who
30 Once gave strength to the valiant Job will fill my
    Dry throat with a draught of the eternal dew of the word.
    For you once brought forth rivers of water from dry rocks,
    When the army had passed through the Red Sea
    And come to the desert, as David tells in song.
35 You, o lord, who preserve all the world from on high,
    Deign to destroy the unspeakable blight of sin.

Riddle 1 De terra

DE TERRA

i. nutrix   *s. homines cunctos*   *i. portat*
1 ALTRIX CUNCTORUM QUOS MUNDUS GESTAT IN ORBE
                                        i. tam ualde
   i. cuora   × *i. infantes qui me lacerant.*
Nuncupor et merito quia numquam pignora tantum
                                    i. mamillas
Improba sic lacerant maternas dente papillas;
                    i. quia non gigno fructum
          s. sum   i. in   *in hieme.*   *i. hiemis*
4 Prole uirens aestate. tabescens tempore brumae;

T (upmarg84r)

Terra dicta a superiore parte qua teritur. Humus ab inferiori uel humida. Terra uero sub mari. Tellus autem quia fructus eius tollimus. haec et ops dicta eo quod ⟨fert⟩ opem fructibus eadem et aruus ab⟨arando⟩ et colendo uocatur. Proprie autem terra ad distinctionem ⟨aquae⟩. Arida nuncupatur sicut scriptura ait porro uocauit deus aridam terram;;

> fert] fest MS   arando] querendo MS   aquae] harenae MS

> Terra ... teritur: Isidore *Etymologiae* 14.1.1; Genesis 1:10

2 (rmarg84r4-7)

Pignus pignoris .i. filius uel soboles.
Pignus pigneris .i. uadimonium;
Quomodo me lacerant ⟨filii mei⟩ uel habitatores ⟨mei.⟩
cum alii hoc non faciunt matribus suis;

> me *added above the line*   filii mei] filios meos MS   mei] meos MS

> Pignus: cf. Bede *De orthographia*, p. 42, "Pignera rerum, pignora et affectionum."

4 (rmarg84r9)

Bruma a breui motu dicitur solis;

> Bruma: cf. Isidore *Etymologiae* 5.35.6, "Hiemem ratio hemisphaerii nuncupavit,
> quia tunc breviori sol volvitur circulo, vnde et hoc tempus bruma dicitur."

ON THE EARTH

The nursemaid of all creatures born by the world on its orb
I am called: and rightly so, because never do wicked children
Thus lacerate their mother's breasts with their teeth.
I grow green with fruit in the summer: I decay in the winter.

Riddle 2   De vento

DE VENTO

    i. homines   *i. manibus*
1 Cernere me nulli possunt nec prendere palmis;
        i. sonitum   *i. ostendo* *i. mundum*
  Argutum uocis crepitum cito pando per orbem;
            i. species pro genere pro
     i. possum   *omnibus lignis posuit.*
  Viribus horrisonis ualeo confringere quercus
           i. terras *i. circuo*
4 Nam superos ego pulso polos et rura peragro;

ON THE WIND

No one can see me or catch me in their palms.
I spread the noisy sound of my voice quickly through the world;
I can break to pieces the oak with my loud, crashing strength,
As I beat against the high poles of the sky and traverse the fields.

Riddle 3 De nube

fol 84r15-84v1   Ehwald 3

DE NUBE

s. non teneo locum certum in
caelo uel in terra   *s. relinquo*

1 ⟨Versicolor⟩ fugiens caelum terramque profundam
   i. in terra
Non tellure locus mihi nec in parte polorum est.
                                       uel timet pertimescit
s. meum   *i. sic*   *i. patitur ut me non suscipit*
Exilium nullus modo tam crudele ueretur.   *caelum uel terram;*
   s. quamuis sim exul. tamen per me   *uirescere*
   i. humidis perficitur istud miraculum crescere ablatiuus
4 Sed madidis mundum faciam frondescere guttis.

   1 Versicolor] versiculor MS

3 (botmarg84r)

Quia qui exilium patitur in eo loco uno in quo tunc est manet. et ego totum per mundum discurro;

ON A CLOUD

Multicoloured in hue, I flee the sky and the deep earth;
There is no place for me on the ground nor in any part of the poles
No one fears an exile as cruel as mine,
But I make the world grow green with my rainy tears.

Riddle 4   De natura

DE NATURA. *Natura est ab eo quod nasci aliquid faciat.*

   s. ó lector   *i. disponente*

1   Crede mihi res nulla manet sine me moderante.
                        i. quia substantia eius incorporalis est.
                        i. nullius oculi
   Et frontem faciemque meam lux nulla uidebit;

   Quis nesciat dicione mea conuẹxa rotari
   i. cacumina

      i. caeli .
   A̋lta poli. solisque iubar lunaeque meatus;

       2 nullius oculi *squeezed in*

3 (lmarg84v5-9)

Conuexa autem caeli extrema eius sunt a curuitate dicta ut est illud. conuexam quotiens cludit nox humida. conuexum enim curuum est quasi eius uersum seu inclinatum ad modicum circum flexum;

    Conuexa ... flexum: Isidore *Etymologiae* 13.5.6; Iuuencus *Evageliorum Liber* 3.24

ON NATURE

Believe me, nothing exists without my guidance
And no light will ever see my face and brow.
Who does not know that by my decree are turned
The high vaults of the pole, the radiance of the sun and the course of the
     moon?

Riddle 5   De iri

fol 84v7-11   Ehwald 5

Arcus celestis dictus a similitudine curuati arcus.
                              hiris huic nomen prorpium est. et
DE IRI VEL ARCU CAELESTI.   *dicitur hiris quasi aeris quod per*
                              aera descendit ad terras;

Nomen montis
i. hiris filia taumantis   s. poetarum   i. narratione
1 Taumantis   proles priscorum famine fingor;
                          i. principia
                          uel alphabeta   i. narrabo.
Ast ego prima mei generis rudimenta retexam.
  of
Sole ruber genitus sum partu nubis aquosae;
i. peragro   *s. quia non rutilat sól ab aquilone*
Lustro polos passim. solos non scando per austros;

        1 Nomen montis *squeezed in*

        T Arcus ... terras: Isidore *Etymologiae* 13.10.1

ON THE RAINBOW OR CELESTIAL ARC

I am said to be the child of Taumans in the legends of the ancients,
But I will tell the origins of my kind.
I am brought forth red by the sun, the offspring of a watery cloud;
I wander here and there in the heavens, but I do not appear over southern
        lands.

Riddle 6   De luna

DE LUNA   *De concordia maris et lunae narrat hic*

1   Nunc ego cum pelago fatis communibus insto⸱
       i. iteratis   *i. circulis*
     Tempora reciprocis conuoluens menstrua ciclis;
     i. similiter   *i. minuitur*
     Ut mihi lucifluae decrescit gloria formae⸱
     Swa i. incrementa pro mare
4   Sic augmenta latex cumulato gurgite perdit;

3 (lmarg84v13-16)

Non decifit luna sed obumbratur. non diminutionem sentit corporis sed ⟨obiectu⟩ obumbrantis terre cassum patitur luminis;

   obiectu] obiectio MS

   Non deficit ... luminis: Isidore *De natura rerum* 21.1

ON THE MOON

I share a common fate with the sea,
Spinning the months around in alternate cycles.
When the glory of my light-flowing form wanes
So, too, the sea loses its swollen flood tides.

Riddle 7   De fato

fol 84v17-21   Ehwald 7

DE FATO VEL GENESI.

i. eloquentem   i. uerum est   i. in XII. libris
                                    aeneidae   s. uirgilium
1 Facundum constat quondam cecinisse poetam
i. ubi   i. ad bellum   i. in qua non uincitur
Quo deus et quo dura uocat fortuna sequamur;
i. hoc poetae dicebant   i. aduerbium
Me   ueteres   falso dominum uocitare solebant.
i. regna. poetae hoc dicebant
       s. sum   uel a
4 Sceptra regens mundi dum Christi gratia regnet;

2 Quo ... sequamur: Vergil *Aeneid* 12.677

ON FATE OR GENESIS

It is true that the eloquent poet once sang,
"Where god and harsh fortune call, let us follow!"
The ancients wrongly used to call me lord
When, in truth, the grace of Christ rules the scepters of the world.

Riddle 8   De pliadibus

fol 84v22-85r1-5

Ehwald 8

DE PLIADIBUS.

      nomen montis   *i. genitas*
1   Nos athlante satas stolidi dixere priores;
    i. VII enim filias   *s. pro paruitate una.*
   athlans habuit   *s. nobis*   *i. septena*
Nam septena choors est. sed uix cernitur una; *i. maia*

Arce poli gradimur. nec non sub tartara terrae;
      beoð   *i. in die*
Furius conspicimur tenebris. et luce latemur
     i. uergilia *i. trahentes*
5   Nomina de uerno ducentes tempore prisca;

      4 in *added above the line*

T (botmarg84v)

Pliades dictae a pluralitate quia pluralitatem greci apotopliston appellant. Sunt .VII. stellae ante ianuam tauri ex quibus sex uidentur. nam latet una. has latini uergilias dicunt a temporis significatione quod est uér quando exoriuntur: nam occasu suo ⟨hiemem ortu⟩ aestatem primae nauigationis tempus ostendunt;

    hiemem ortu] hiemem ortum MS The glossator has expunged the last *m* of hiemem, when it is the last *m* of ortum that needs to be expunged.

    Pliades ... appellant: Isidore *Etymologiae* 3.71.13

5 (rmarg85r5)

Quia in uerno tempore meridie surgunt a terra oriundo. et occidunt media nocte. In aestate uero oriuntur matutino et occidunt uespertino. Autumpno media nocte oriuntur et occidunt media nocte. In hieme uero in prima noctis parte oriuntur. et occidunt tempore matutino;

ON THE PLEIADES

The benighted ancients said we were the children of Atlas,
For we are a sevenfold company, but one can hardly be seen.
We climb on the summit of heaven, and sometimes under the infernal depths
  of the earth;
We are seen in the secret shadows and in daylight we are hidden;
We take our ancient names from the springtime.

Riddle 9 De adamante lapide

fol 85r6-10   Ehwald 9

Adamans est genus lapidis durissimi. qui nisi sanguine hyrcino
DE ADAMANTE LAPIDE   *calido molliatur sculpi non potest;*

        i. non timeo   i. duri
1   En ego non uereor rigidi discrimina ferri
            i. ardore.
            i. non timeo
   Flammarum neu torre cremor sed sanguine capri
   i. non domiti
   Virtus indomiti mollescit dura rigoris;
                 i. nominatiuus
   s. capri   *uel quem   singularis*
4   Sic cruor exsuperat quod ferrea massa pauescit;

T (upmarg85r)

Adamans indicus lapis paruus et indecorus. ferrugineum habens colorem. et splen-
dorem ⟨cristalli.⟩ numquam ultra magnitudinem nuclei ⟨Abellano⟩ repertus. Hic nulli
cedit materiae. nec ferro quidem nec igni. nec umquam incalescit;;

   cristalli] cristallini MS   Abellano] Ab ebellano MS

   Adamans indicus ... incalescit: Isidore *Etymologiae* 16.13.2

4 (rmarg85r7-8)

i.Non lacerat ferrum. sed mollescit sanguine
capri. uel hirci;

ON THE DIAMOND

I do not fear the sharp-edged sword,
Nor am I consumed by the flame's heat, but in goat's blood
The hard strength of my unconquerable rigor grows soft.
Thus the blood subdues what intimidated the iron mass.

Riddle 10   De moloso

fol 85r11-15   Ehwald 10

DE MOLOSO

       i. olim   *s. dei*

1 Sic me iamdudum rerum ueneranda potestas
   i. operatus est   s. mei
   Fecerat: ut domini truculentos persequar hostes;
   i. faucibus   i. dentes   s. ego i. portans   i. iram   i. perficio

1 Rictibus   arma   gerens   bellorum proelia patro:
                                        i. pretereo.
     i. de mea familia propria   *uel fugio*

4 Et tamen   infantum   fugiens mox uerbera uito;

ON THE HOUND

The venerable ruler of all things made me thus long ago,
That I should pursue the belligerent enemies of my lord.
Bearing warlike weapons in my jaws I give battle
And yet, fleeing at once, I avoid the blows of children.

Riddle 11   De poaleis

fol 85r16-20

Ehwald 11

DE POALEIS ID EST FOLLIBUS FABRORUM.

1 Flatibus alternis uescor cum fratre gemello;

Non est uita mihi cum sint spiracula uitae;
       i. ornatis   *s. quae ornantur gemmis.*
Ars mea gemmatis dedit ornamenta metallis.
                           i. fabricator
i. merces   *uel faber.*
4 Gratia nulla datur mihi. sed capit alter honorem;

ON THE BELLOWS

I take in alternate breaths with my twin brother;
There is no life in me, though I take the breaths of life.
My art made ornaments out of jewelled metal;
No credit is given to me, but another takes the honour.

Riddle 12   De bombicibus

fol 85r21-85v3   Ehwald 12

i. uermibus sericas uestes digerentibus uel tegentibus
DE BOMBICIBUS ID EST VERMIBUS QUI SERES DICUNTUR.

                    i. ut texem   *i. webb*
1 Annua dum redeunt texendi tempora telas
         i. hirsutis
         ablatiuus   *sint*   *s. mea*
   Lurida setigeris replentur uiscera filis;
              i. miricarum.
   Moxque genestarum frondosa cacumina scando:
     U   :   :
4 Et globulos fabricans tum fati sorte quiescam;

T (botmarg85r)

Bombex .i. uermis ex cuius textura bombilicinium uel bombicinum conficitur.
appellatur hoc nomine ab eo quod euacuetur dum ⟨fila⟩ generat. et aer solus in eo
remaneat. Seres nomen alicuius gentis in oriente. et incertum in quo speciali loco illa
gens habitat. De qua isidorus dixit ex persona alicuius poetae. Ignoti facie noti uellere
seres;

> fila] filam MS

> Bombex ... remaneat: Isidore *Etymologiae* 12.5.8   Seres nomen: cf. Isidore
> *Etymologiae* 9.2.40, "Seres a proprio oppido nomen sortiti sunt, gens ad
> Orientem sita, apud quos de arboribus lana contexitur. De quibus est illud:
> Ignota facie, sed noti vellere seres."

ON THE SILKWORM OR CATERPILLAR

When each year brings back the time for weaving webs,
My yellow entrails are filled with bristly threads,
And soon I climb the leafy heights of the broom plant;
I make little balls of silk, then fate decrees I shall rest.

Riddle 13   De barbito

fol 85v4-8   Ehwald 13

DE BARBITO ID EST ORGANO

i. genus tubae
1   Quamuis aere cauo salpicae classica clangant

Et citharae crepitent strepituque tubae ⟨modulentur⟩

Centenos tamen erŭctant mĕa uiscera cantus;

4   Me presente ⟨stupet⟩ mox musica chorda fibrarum;

2 modulentur] modulantur MS   4 stupet] stupent MS

T (upmarg85v)

Organum est quasi turris quaedam diuersis fistulis fabricata. quibus flatu follium uox copiosissima destinatur. ut eam modulatio ⟨decora⟩ componat. Linguis quibusdam ligneis ab interiore parte construitur. quas disciplina uiliter magistrorum digiti reprimentes grandisonam efficiunt et sauissimam cantilenam;;

eam modulatio decora] eum modulatio decoram (de *added above the line*) MS

Organum ... cantilenam: Cassiodorus *Expositio in Psalterium* 150:4

1 (lmarg85v4-7)

⟨*Classi*⟩*ca cornua* ⟨*qu*⟩*ae uocandi causa erant facta. et a calendo classica dicebantur. de quibus uirgilius ait. classica iamque sonant;*

Classica ... dicebantur: Isidore *Etymologiae* 18.4.5   de quibus ... sonant: Virgil *Aeneid* 7.637

ON THE ORGAN

Though the tones of the trumpet clang in empty bronze,
The citharas murmur and the tubas measure out tunes with a roar,
When my belly pours forth a hundred songs,
My music silences the song of the strings.

Riddle 14   De pavone

fol 85v9-13   Ehwald 14

DE PAVONE

s. sum   s. ego   s. sum
1 Pulcher et excellens specie mirandus in orbe
                                      coadunatus
                              i. pro creatus sum
   Ossibus et neruis ac rubro sanguine cretus;
   i. quamdiu
   Cum mihi uita comes fuerit nihil aùrea fòrma
                              a pululando
   i. nec pulchrior est aurum quam ego.   dicitur pulpa
4 Plus rubet. et moriens mea numquam pulpa putrescit;

4 (lmarg85v9-12)

Pulpa est caro sine pinguedine dicta. eo quod ⟨palpitet.⟩ resilit enim saepe. Hanc plerique et ⟨uiscum uocant⟩ ác propter quod glutinosa sit;

   palpitet] pulpitet MS   viscum uocant] vis convocat MS

   Pulpa ... sit: Isidore *Etymologiae* 11.1.81

ON THE PEACOCK

I am beautiful and wonderful to see, a marvel of the world;
I was created out of bones and nerves and red blood;
As long as life is my companion, no golden form
Shines more brightly than I; when I die, my flesh never decays.

Riddle 15   De salamandra

fol 85v14-18   Ehwald 13

Animal - uiuens in igne.
DE SALAMANDRA QUAE SIMILIS EST LACERTAE.

1   Ignibus in mediis uiuens non sentio flammas.
                        aduerbium
                    s. esse   i. facio
    Sed detrimenta rogi penitus ludibria faxo;
                    i. igni
    Nec crepitante foco nec scintillante fauilla
                                                    s. a me
            i. detrimenta.   i. urenti   i. igni s. meo
4   Ardeo. sed flammae   flagranti   torre tepescunt;

    T (lmarg85v13-18)

*Salamandra uocata quod contra incendia ualeat. cuius inter omnia uenenata uis
maxima est. Viuit enim in mediis flammis ⟨sine⟩ dolore et consummatione. et non
solum quod non uritur. sed extinguit incendium;;*

        sine] super MS

        Salamandra ... incendium: Isidore *Etymologiae* 12.4.36

ON THE SALAMANDER

Living in the midst of fires, I do not feel the flames;
I completely make fun of the ravages of the funeral pyre.
Neither in the crackling hearth or the glowing embers
Do I burn. Instead, in the burning conflagration, the flames grow cool.

Riddle 16   De Iuligine

fol 85v19-86r1   Ehwald 16

DE LULIGINE ID EST PISCE VOLANTE.

i. aliquando   i. scrutanda   s. hominibus
1 Nunc   cernenda   placent nostrae spectacula uitae;
uel qui   finnum
  Cum grege piscoso scrutor maris equora squamis;
                                      accusatiuus
                                      grecus
  Cum uolucrum turma quoque scando per aethera pennis

4 Et tamen aethereo non possum uiuere flatu;

ON THE SQUID OR FLYING FISH

People are pleased when they understand the wonder of my life;
Among a school of fish, I swim the calm field of the sea with my fins;
With a flock of birds, I also climb through the air on wings,
Even though I cannot live by breathing air.

Riddle 17   De perna

fol 86r2-6   Ehwald 17

i. genus cuiusdam piscis qui   CONFICITUR VEST⟨IS⟩

DE PERNA QUAE MULTO MAIOR EST OSTREIS EX CUIUS VELLERIBUS

i. per undas

1   E geminis nascor per ponti cerula conchis
s. ouium

Vellera setigero producens corpore fulua;
i. cibaria

En clamidem pepli. nec non et pabula pulpae
s. in utilitatem   *s. hominibus*

4   Confero.   sic duplex fati persoluo tributum;

T vestis] veste [#] MS

(upmarg86r)

Muricae cocleae sunt maris ab acumine dictae. et asperitate. quae alieno nomine
concilium nominantur propter quod ⟨circumcisae⟩ ferro. lacrimas purpurei coloris
emittant. ex quibus purpura ⟨tingitur;;⟩

circumcisae] circumcisa MS   tingitur] tinguitur MS

Muricae ... tingitur: Isidore *Etymologiae* 12.6.50

ON THE SEA MUSSEL, WHICH IS MUCH GREATER THAN THE OYSTER AND FROM
     WHOSE SHELLS CLOTHING IS MADE

I am born from twin shells under the waves of the sea
And produce golden fleeces from my bristly body.
I give both rich robes and meaty food to people;
Thus I pay the double tribute of fate.

Riddle 18　De formica leone

fol 86r7-12　　　　　　　　　　　　　　　　　Ehwald 18

DE FORMICA LEONE.　　*Formicaleon uocatus quia est formicarum leo. uel*
　　　　　　　　　　　　certe formica pariter et leo. Est enim animal
　　　　　　　　　　　　paruum formicis satis infestum;

1　Dudum compositis ego nomen gesto figuris;
　　　　　i. leo formicis sum. et aliis
i. similiter　bestiis sum formica.　i. greco Leo formica unde nomen compositum;
　Ut leo sic formica uocor sermone pelasgo.
i. species　　　　i. leo peccatores. et formica
uel mistica　　　　　　sanctos significat.
　Tropica nominibus signans praesagia duplis:
　　　　　　　　i. non possum uel resistere frumenta gestantes.
　Cum rostris auium nequeam rescindere rostro
imperatiuus　i. Leo pro fortitudine dicitur.
i. meditetur.　Formica pro sapientia.　　　i. utor
5　Scrutetur sapiens gemino cur nomine fungor;

　　　　2 Isidore *Etymologiae* 12.3.10　　　5 Judges 14:14; Proverbs 6:6

T (botmarg85v and 86r)

Est enim animal paruum. formicis satis infestum. quod se in puluere abscondit et formicas interficit. proinde autem leo et formica appellatur. quia animantibus. aliis ut formica est.· formicis autem ut leo est. Gregorius ait in moralibus quia ‹translatione autem septuaginta› interpretum nequaquam dicitur tigris sed mirmicaleon. Quippe paruum ualde est. Animal formicis aduersum quod se sub puluere abscondit. et formicas frumenta gestantes interficit. et interfectas consumit. Mirmicaleon grece dicitur latine formicarum / leo uel certe expressim formica pariter et leo. Recte autem leo et formica nominatur quia siue uolatilibus seu quibuslibet aliis minutis animalibus formica est. ipsis autem formicis leo: Has enim quasi leo deuorat. sed ab illis animalibus quasi formica deuoratur;;

　　　translatione autem septuaginta] translative aput lxx MS

　　　Est enim ... leo est: Isidore *Etymologiae* 12.3.10　　　translatione ... deuoratur:
　　　Gregory *Moralia in Job* 5.20.40

ON THE ANT-LION

From of old I bear a name compound in form.
For I am called both ant and lion in Greek;
I reveal mystical forebodings with my twofold name.
With my beak I cannot fight off the beaks of birds.
Let the wise consider why I have a double name.

Riddle 19   De sale

DE SALE

i. habundans uel sufficiens
1 Dudum limpha fui squamoso pisce redundans.
i. locum dedit.
i. differentiae   uel sé subdidit.
Sed natura nouo fati discrimine   cessit;

Torrida dum calidos patior tormenta per ignes
s. candido.
s. in duritia   s. mea   s. in albedine   mihi
4 Nam   cineri   facies niuibusque   simillima constat;

4 s. in durita *squeezed in*

ON SALT

Once I was water among the scaly fish,
But by a new decree of fate my nature yielded,
When I suffered burning torments in hot fires;
For my face is as white as ashes or snow.

Riddle 20   De apibus

fol 86r18-86v1   Ehwald 20

De apibus enigmata quinque versibus decurrunt

                                 uel formata
       s. sum   *pro creata. nata*

1   Mirificis formata modis sine semine creta;

Dulcia florigeris onero precordia praedis;
       i. fulua   *obsonia*
Arte mea crocea flauescunt fercula regum;
       i. porto.
Semper acuta gero crudelis spicula belli.

5   Atque carens manibus fabrorum uinco metalla;

(rmarg86r19-20)

⟨*Apes*⟩ *quasi a pedibus dictae sunt. quod sine pedibus nascuntur;*

Apes] Casus apes MS

Apes: cf. Isidore *Etymologiae* 12.8.1, "Apes dictae, vel quod se pedibus invicem alligant, vel pro eo quod sine pedibus nascuntur."

On the bee

Formed in a marvellous way, born without seed,
I load my sweet breast with treasure from flowers;
By my art the golden platters of kings grow yellow;
Always I bear the small, sharp spears of cruel war
And though I lack hands, my spear stings more cruelly than weapons forged
      by smiths.

Riddle 21   De lima

fol 86v2-7   Ehwald 21

DE LIMA QUAE ROSCINA DICITUR.

1   Corpo sulcato nec non ferrugine glauca
                                cinum
    Sum formata: fricans rimis informe metallum;

    Auri materias massasque polire suesco;
                            unsmeþust.
    Plano superficiem constant asperrima rerum;
                                                ic gyrre
5   Garrio uoce carens rauco cum murmure stridens;   *mid haswre*
                                                hroðrunge.

ON THE FILE

Into a furrowed shape of iron grey
I was formed. Rubbing the formless metal with my fissures,
I am used to polish the weighty mass of gold;
I, the harshest of things, smooth the surface.
Though lacking a voice, I chatter and hiss with a grating murmur.

Riddle 22   De achalantida

fol 86v8-13   Ehwald 22

DE ACHALANTIDA QUAE LATINE LUSCINIA DICITUR.

1   Vóx̄ mea diuersis üāriatur pulchra figuris;

Raucisonis numquam modulabor carmina rostris;
s. sum
Spreta colore tamen sed non sum spreta canendo;
s. hiemis
Sic non cesso canens fato terrente futuro;

5   Nam me bruma fugat sed mox aestate redibo;

ON THE NIGHTINGALE

My beautiful voice warbles diverse melodies;
Never shall I sing poems with a raucous-sounding beak.
Though my plumage is spurned, I am not spurned for my singing,
So I do not cease singing, even when the fated future threatens;
Though winter puts me to flight, as soon as summer comes, I will return.

Riddle 23   De draconti gemma

fol 86v14-19   Ehwald 24

genus gemmae
DE DRACONTI GEMMA ID EST SANGUIS DRACONIS.

             i. dicitur   *i. serpentis*
1 Me caput horrentis fertur genuisse draconis;

Augeo purpureis gemmarum lumina fucis
                         s. lucis
Sed mihi non dabitur rigida uirtute potestas
N   *i. moritur*   *i. serpens*
Si prius occumbat squamoso corpore natrix
                                    i
5 Quam summo spolier capitis de uertice rubra;

T (lmarg86v14-20)

Dracontides ex cerebro draconis eruitur. ⟨quae⟩ si uiuenti abscisa fuerit ingemescit.
unde et ⟨eam magi dormientibus draconibus⟩ amputant; Est ut dicunt quiddam genus
serpentum quod uenefici solent incantare ad soporationem. et tunc oculos auellere. et
ex ipsis gemmas pulcherrimas conficere.

quae] quam MS   eam magi dormientibus draconibus] eum magis dormienti
MS

Dracontides ... amputant: Isidore *Etymologiae* 16.14.7

T (botmarg86v)

Draconum inmite genus est serpentium quod naturali obstinatione uerba incantantium
non perhibentur admittere. ne audiat uerba eorum ⟨suas⟩ latebras delinquat. unam
aurem caudae suae inflectione dicitur obdurare. alteram uero in terram deprimere;;

admittere.] admittere MS   suas] suasque MS   delinquet.] delinquat MS

Draconum: cf. *Physiologus* 26

ON THE DRAGON STONE OR DRAGON'S BLOOD

It is said that the head of a horrid dragon engendered me;
I enhance the lights of gems with my purple dye,
But power enduring in strength will not be given to me,
If the serpent with its scaly body falls dead
Before I, red, am plucked from the topmost crown of its head.

Riddle 24   De magnete ferrifero

fol 86v20-87r3   Ehwald 25

genus lapidis
DE MAGNETE FERRIFERO.

    i. fortitudo
                           i. caeli
1 Vis mihi näturae dedit immo creator olimpi
    i. donum naturae
  Id quo cuncta carent ueteris miracula mundi;
                i. ferri
  Frigida nam calibis suspendo metalla per auras.
  i. aliqua uirtute uel
     fortitudine   *i. supero*
  Vi quadam superans sic ferrea fata reuinco;
    adamans genus lapidis in cipro.   *s. mea*
5 Mox adamante cypris presente potentia fraudor;

5 (rmarg87r3-4)

Ciprus insula a ciuit⟨ate⟩ quae in ea est nomen accepit;

    MS damaged; reading supplied from Isidore

    Ciprus ... accepit: Isidore *Etymologiae* 14.6.14

T (botmarg87r)

Magnes lapis indicus ab inuentore uocatus. fuit autem in india primum repertus. clauis crepitarum baculique cuspide herens. cum armenta idem ⟨Magnes⟩ pasceret. Postea et passim inuentus. est in colore ferrugineus. sed cum ferro probatur adiunctus eius fecerit raptum. Nam adeo adprehendit ferrum ut catenam faciat anulorum. Unde et eum uulgus ferrum uiuum appellat;;

    Magnes] magnes MS

    Magnes ... appellat: Isidore *Etymologiae* 16.4.1

ON THE MAGNET

The force of nature, or rather the creatur of Olympus, has given to me
That which all the miracles of the ancient world lack;
I suspend the cold metal of the sword in the air;
Triumphant by a kind of strength, I conquer the ferrous fates,
But my power weakens when adamant of Cyprus is near.

Riddle 25   De gallo

fol 87r4-9   Ehwald 26

DE GALLO

altisonans   *i. uaticinare*
1   Garrulus in tenebris rutilos cecinisse solebam:
Lux enim Christus est. et manens dies. et sol perennis   i. solis
Augustae lucis radios et lumina phoebi;
         i. inuento   *Galli meo nomine*
Penniger experto populorum nomine fungor   *uocantur.*
                    i. facio uel perficio
Arma ferens pedibus belli discrimina faxo.
gecyrnode   *cambas*
5   Serratas capitis gestans in uertice cristas;

ON THE COCK

I used to crow aloud in the shadows to greet the first glimmering
Rays of the splendid light and the radiance of Phoebus;
I am feathered and I bear the well-known name of a people;
Bearing arms on my feet, I can inflict the ravages of war;
I have sawtooth combs on the top of my head.

Riddle 26   De coticulo

DE COTICULO.

s. sum
1   Frigidus ex gelido prolatus uiscere terrae;

Duritiam ferri quadrata fronte polibo.

Atque senectutis uereor discrimina numquam
i. nomen est uulcani
i. flammiger uel mortifer   *i. si non minuit*
Mulcifer annorum numerum ni dempserit ignis;
         i. dura   *i. ignibus   i. nigris*
5   Mox rigida species mollescit torribus   atris;

      4 i. flammiger uel mortifer *squeezed in*

ON THE WHETSTONE

I was brought forth cold from the frozen belly of the earth;
I will polish the hardness of iron with my square brow
And I never fear the effects of old age,
Unless the volcanic fire decreases the number of my years,
Where at once my hard shape grows soft in the black flames.

Riddle 27 De minotauro

fol 87r16-21   Ehwald 28

DE MINOTAURO.

1 Sum mihi dissimilis uultu membrisque biformis
       s. sum   *s. sed*
  Cornibus armatus. horrendum cetera fingunt
                             uel egyptia
                 s. sum   *i. per grecia. i. cretensis*
  Membra uirum. fama clarus per gnosia   rura;
      uel ignobilis
  s. sum   *i. inmundus.*   *s. utrum a tauro án a ioue natus sim*
                   s. in. nomen insulae.
  Spurius incerto creta genitore creatus
    i. minois   *i. tauri*   *i. minotaurus uel semitaurus*
5 Ex hominis pecudisque simul cognomine dicor;

       3 uel egyptia *squeezed in*   4 uel ignobilis, s. in, *and* nomen insulae
       squeezed in   sim *corrected from* sum   5 uel semitaurus *squeezed in*

3 (rmarg87r19-21)

Gnosia et gnosium nomen oppidi est in creta insula; Nothus qui ex nobili matre nutritur. uel progenitus. Spurius uero qui ex ignobili patre;

    Nothus, Spurius: cf. Isidore, *Etymologiae* 9.5.23-24, "Nothus dicitur, qui de patre nobili et de matre ignobili gignitur, sicut ex concubina. Est autem hoc nomen Graecum et in Latinitate deficit. Huic contrarius ʂpurius, qui de matre nobili et patre ignobili nascitur."

5 (lmarg87r21)

Minotaurus i. minois taurus

ON THE MINOTAUR

I am unlike myself: double-formed in face and members,
Armed with horns — my other parts form a horrible
Man. My fame is widespread throughout the Cretan countryside.
I am the shameful creation of an unknown father in Crete;
I am called by the name of both man and beast.

Riddle 28   De aqua

fol 87r22-87v6   Ehwald 29

DE AQUA.

1 Quis non obstupeat nostri spectacula fati
                        i. trabes
   Dum uirtute fero siluarum robora mille;
            i. paruus. uel modicus   i. pondera
   Ast acus   exilis   mox tanta gestamina rumpit;
                    pro natantes   s. maris
   Nam uolucres caeli nantesque per aequora pisces.
            i. in creatione mundi.
5 Olim sumpserunt ex me primordia uitae;
                    i. a me   i. conuenit   ablatiuus
   Tertia pars mundi. mihi   constat   iure tenenda;

1 (lmarg87v1-2)

[...........]*ctus*
[.........]*rsibus*
[.......]*u poeta;*

6 (lmarg87v6-7)

Uniuersitas enim creaturarum ex caelo et terra et mari constat;

ON WATER

Who would not be amazed by my strange lot?
With my strength I bear a thousand forest oaks,
But a slender needle at once pierces me, the bearer of such burdens;
Birds flying in the sky and fish swimming in the sea
Once took their first life from me;
A third of the world is held in my power.

Riddle 29   De elemento

fol 87v7-14   Ehwald 30

i. alfabeto uel abcdario
DE ELEMENTO VEL ABECEDARIO.

    s. sumus
1 Nos denae et septem genitae sine uoce sorores.
      su⟨n⟩derborene   *s. nobiscum*
  Sex alias nothas non dicimus adnumerandas;
               i. stilo uel graphio
  Nascimur ex ferro rursus ferro moribundae.
      i. auis   *i. uolantis*
  Nec non et uolucris penna uolitantis ad aethram;
         i. uaga mente. uel manu scriptoris.
  i. tres digiti scriptoris.   *in carta uel in cera*
5 Terni nos fratres incerta matre crearunt;
                 s. nos.
  uel cum   *i. litteras in scripturis*
  Qui cupit instanter sitiens audire docentes.
        quia non locuntur et tamen docent.
  Tum cito prompta damus rogitanti uerba silenter;

2 (lmarg87v9-11)

Id est. K.Q.H.X.Y.Z. Duae superuacuae .K. et .q:
Duae grece .y. et .Z. X. non fuit ad tempus augusti.
h. autem aspirationis nota est;

> Id est ... nota est: cf. Donatus "De littera" from *Ars grammatica* in Keil 4:334, 368

5 (lmarg87v12-13)

ignoramus utrum cum penna coruina uel anserina siue calamo perscriptae simus;

ON THE ALPHABET

We are seventeen sisters born without a voice;
Six other counterfeits are not counted among us.
We are born from iron and die by iron;
Likewise, with the feather of a high-flying bird,
Three brothers created us from an unknown mother.
To one who thirsts for knowledge and wishes to hear
We quickly and silently give our ready words.

Riddle 30   De ciconia

fol 87v15-22   Ehwald 31

DE CICONIA.

i. alba uel
pulchra   *i. splendens*
1 Candida forma nitens nec non et furua nigrescens

Est mihi. dum uaria conponor imagine pennae
                    i. facio   i. sonos
Voce carens tremula nam faxo crepacula rostro;

Quamuis squamigeros discerpam dira colubros
                                i. serpentium
5 Non mea loetiferis turgescunt membra uenenis;

Sic teneros pullos prolemque nutrire suesco
                i. nigro   i. serpentium
Carne uenenata tetroque cruore draconum;

T (lmarg87v16)

Ciconia auis precipua est quae uenit ab affrica;

ON THE STORK

Resplendent in white and shining dark in black
Am I, since I am cloaked in variegated plumage.
Lacking a voice, I make clacking noises with my beak.
Although I savagely rend the scaly serpents,
My limbs do not swell from their death-bearing venom;
I am accustomed to nourish my tender chicks
With the poisonous flesh and dark blood of dragons.

Riddle 31 De pugillaribus

fol 88r1-9 Ehwald 32

DE PUGILLARIBUS.

　　　　　　　　　　　　　　　　　i. cera
1 Melligeris apibus mea prima processit origo.
　　　　　　　i. tabula
Sed pars exterior crescebat caetera siluis;
þwancgas　　　　　　　　　　*hyda*
Calciamenta mihi tradebant tergora dura;
i. aliquando i. grafium　　　　　　　*i. pulchram.*
Nunc ferri stimulus faciem proscindit amoenam
　　　　　　　s. stimulus ferri
　　　　　　　　i. curuat i. ad similitudinem
5 Flexibus et sulcos obliquat ' ad instar　aratri;
　　　　i. litterae de caelo sunt lapsae
　　　　　　　datiuus　　　　　　*i. sanctum*
Sed semen segeti de caelo ducitur almum
s. semen
Quod largos generat millena fruge maniplos
　　　　s. litterarum.　　　　*i. deletur.*
Heu tam sancta seges diris extinguitur armis;

5 i curuat *squeezed in*　　　6 datiuus *squeezed in*

3 *P⁵ (fol 97v) and S¹ (fol 28) have the following gloss:* sicut uidetur in tabulas scottorum

3 (rmarg88r4)

Tergus. tergoris. i. cutis.
Tergum. tergi. dorsum

Tergus: cf. Bede *De orthographia* p. 54, "Terga hominum sunt tantum, singulariter tergum; tergus quadrupedum, pluraliter facit tergora, id est coria."

On writing tablets

My inner part came from the honey-bearing bees,
But my outer part grew in the woods;
Hard hides supplied my shoes.
Now a goad of iron cuts my pleasant face;
In the likeness of a plough, it bends the furrows with its
     curving motions.
But from heaven comes the nourishing seed for the harvest,
Which brings forth generous sheaves in a thousandfold fruit.
Alas that such a holy crop is destroyed by harsh weapons!

Riddle 32   De lorica

fol 88r10-17   Ehwald 33

DE LORICA.

         i. frigido
1 Roscida me genuit gelido de uiscere tellus;
         i. hyrsuto
  Non sum setigero lanarum uellere facta;
        s. me
  Licia nulla trahunt. nec garrula fila resultant.
    i. fulua i. orientales s. me
  Nec crocea seres taxunt lanugine uermes   *assirisce*
         i. moueor
5 Nec radiis carpor. nec duro pectine pulsor:
           i. populi   *i. uocor*
  Atque tamen uestis uulgi sermone uocabor;
  i. sagittas   i. timeo   i. prolata
  Spicula non uereor longis exempta faretris;

ON THE MAILSHIRT

The dewy earth brought me forth from her cold belly;
I am not made of the woolly skin of sheep;
No loom-leashes pull me, no garrulous threads resound;
No Chinese worms weave with saffron down;
I am not plucked by shuttles, nor am I struck by a comb,
And yet I am called a mere vestment in the vulgar tongue;
I do not fear arrows drawn from a long quiver.

Riddle 33   De locusta

fol 88r18-88v3   Ehwald 34

DE LOCUSTA.

1   Quamuis agricolis non sim laudabilis hospes͗
                              i. terrae
    Fructus agrorum uiridi de cespite ruris
    i. decarpo
                              i. tellure   i. cortices
    Carpo cateruatim. rodens de stipite libros;
                                      i. circumdatum
    Cor mihi sub genibus nam constat corpore septum
                                      ican
5   Pectora poplitibus subduntur more rubetae;
                              dicta a nilo
        s. fui   *flumine.   i. memphitica*
    Nam dudum celebris spolians   nilotica   regna
                                  i. patiebantur.
    Quando decem plagas spurca cum gente luebant;

        3 i. tellure *should gloss* cespite *in line 2.*

T (rmarg88r17-19)

Locusta est animal paruum. de quo iohannes
utebatur in heremo. coquitur namque per
oleum et non fit nisi copiis semper;

        Locusta ...: Matthew 3:4, Mark 1:6

ON THE LOCUST

I am not at all a welcome guest among farmers.
From the green rural land I snatch the fruits of the fields;
In great swarms, I gnaw the tree bark from the trunk.

My heart is enclosed in my body beneath my knees;
My breasts are also under my knees after the fashion of a toad.
Long ago, I despoliated the Egyptian kingdom,
As they, together with the unclean race, suffered the ten plagues.

Riddle 34　De nicticorace

fol 88v4-11　　　　　　　　　　　　　　　　　　Ehwald 35

DE NICTICORACE.

　　　　　　　　　　　i. ex nocte
　　　　i. natura　　*et corace*　　　　*i. iuste*
1　Duplicat　ars　geminis mihi nomen rite figuris:
　　　s. nominis
　Nam partem tenebrae retinent partemque uolucres;
　　　　　　　　　　　　　i. in die　i. clara
　Raro me quisquam cernit sub luce serena.

　Quin magis astriferas ego nocte fouebo latebras
　　　　　　　　　　　　　　　accusatiuus grecus
　Raucisonus media crepitare per　aethra　suescens
　i. latinis uel

　romanis　　　　　　　　　*i. greca*
　Romuleis scribor biblis sed uoce pelasga　　*i. Nycticorax*
　　　s. in
　Nomine nocturnas dum semper seruo tenebras;

T (upmarg88v)

Nicticorax i. noctua. multi bubonem esse contendunt. Sunt etiam qui asserunt esse
orientalem auem quae nocturnus coruus appellatur. Nicticorax grece dicitur noctis
coruus. quam quidam bubonem. quidam noctuam dixerunt. Alii magis coruo
magnitudine et colore consimilem in specie. in asiae partibus inuenire posse testantur;;

> Nicticorax grece ... testantur: Cassiodorus *Expositio in Psalterium* on Psalm
> 101:7

ON THE NIGHT RAVEN

Grammar rightly bestows on me a double name,
For shadows and birds each comprise half of it.

Rarely does anyone see me in the clear light,
Since I prefer the star-filled darkness;
A loud singer, always filling the air with my chattering —
So I am described in Roman books; in the Greek tongue
My name shows that I haunt the nocturnal shadows.

Riddle 35   De scniphe

fol 88v12-19   Ehwald 36

DE SCNIPHE.

i. unguibus
1 Corpore sum gracili stimulis armatus acerbis
      i. turmatim   *i. spatia*
  Scando cateruatim uolitans super ardua pennis
                     i. sanguineo
  Sanguineas sumens predas mucrone cruento.
                  ic þy
  Quadrupedi parcens nulli sed spicula trudo.
  i. hyrsutas
5 Setigeras pecudum stimulans per uulnera pulpas;
          i. de nomine ciuitatis quae dicitur
  s. fui   *memphis quae est metropolis aegypti;*
  Olim famosus uexans   memphitica   rura;
        i. cutes.
  Namque toros terebrans taurorum sanguine uescor;

6 Cf. Isidore *Etymologiae* 15.1.31: "Memphin civitatem Aegypti aedificavit Epaphus Iovis filius, cum in secunda Aegypto regnaret."

ON THE BLACK FLY

I am small of body and armed with sharp goads,
I fly over high places in swarms on the wing,
Seizing bloody plunder with a gory sword;
I spare no quadruped, but thrust forth my spear,
Stabbing and wounding the hairy flesh of cattle.
Once I was famous for annoying the country of Egypt
For biting the skin of bulls and drinking their blood.

Riddle 36 De cancro

fol 88v20-89r4   Ehwald 37

DE CANCRO QUAE NEPA VOCATUR.

i. nec petens
1 Nepa mihi nomen ueteres dixere latini;
                    i. ambulo
    Humida spumiferi spatior per litora ponti
                    hindergenga
    Passibus oceanum retrograda transeo uersis

    Et tamen aethereus per me decoratur olimphus
                    s. cum
                    i. XII. sidera
5 Dum ruber in caelo bis seno sidere scando.
                    s. in.
    Ostrea quem metuit duris perterrita saxis;

    5 s. cum *squeezed in*

T (botmarg88v and 89r)

Animal quod sit in mari duo capita habens et quattuor manus. quando autem pergit tú putas ad té uenire. et ⟨quando⟩ ad té uenit. síc a té uadit. quippe illud efficitur. eo quod geminas facies habet. prima ad té deducitur. altera post sé.

⟨Cancri uocantur⟩ conchae sed crura habentes inimica ostreis. Animalia autem haec cornibus uiuunt miro ingenio. Nam quia ualidam testam eius aperire non potest. explorat quando ostrea claustra testarum aperiat. tunc / cancer latenter lapillum inicit. Atque inpedita ⟨conclusione⟩ testae ostream erodit. Ostrea dicta a testa quibus mollities interior carnis minuitur. Greci autem testam ostream uocant. Ostrea autem neutrum. carnes uero eius feminino dicunt;;;

> quando] quondo MS   Cancri uocantur] Cancro uocant MS   conclu-
> sione] conclusionem MS

> Cancri ... erodit: Isidore *Etymologiae* 12.6.51   Ostrea ... dicunt: Isidore
> *Etymologiae* 12.6.52

On the crab

The ancient Romans called me by the name "nepa".
I amble across the wet planes of the foamy sea;
I cross the ocean backwards with reversed steps,
But even ethereal Olympus is decorated by me,
For I climb in the sky among the twelve constellations,
I, who terrify the oyster in its hard shell.

Riddle 37   De tippula

fol 89r5-12   Ehwald 38

DE TIPPULA ID EST VERMIS QUI NON NANDO SED
   GRADIENDO AQUAS TRANSIT;

1   Pergo super latices plantis suffulta quaternis

    Nec tamen in limphas uereor quod mergar aquosas

    Sed pariter terras et flumina calco pedester;
                 s. me
    Nec natura sinit celeres ⟨natare⟩ per amnes
             s. nec sinit
5   Pontibus aut ratibus fluuios transire feroces.

    Quin potius pedibus gradior super aequora siccis;

    4 natare] nataṛae MS

ON THE WATER STRIDER, AN INSECT THAT CROSSES THE WATER
   BY WALKING INSTEAD OF SWIMMING

I cross over the water supported by four feet,
But I do not fear drowning in the watery streams,
Since I walk as well on rivers as I do on land.
Nature does not allow me to swim through fast-running brooks
Or to cross fierce torrents by bridge or raft,
Rather I walk on the wet surface with dry feet.

Riddle 38   De leone

DE LEONE.

1   Setiger in siluis armatos dentibus apros
    :-

    Cornigerosque simul ceruos licet ora rudentes
                                        i. brachia
    Contero. nec parcens ursorum quasso lacertos
      :-

    Ora cruenta ferens. morsus rictusque luporum
        s. ego   i. non timeo   i. dignitate
5   Horridus haud uereor regali culmine fretus;
                                            i. oculis
    Dormio nam patulis non claudens lumina gemmis;

> 5 haud] *corrected from* haut

T (rmarg89r13-17)

Tres sunt naturae leonis. quarum una dum uenatores eum insecuntur. Cauda sua
uestigia operit propria. sic et Christus humanitate operuit diuinitatem. ne diabolus eum
agnosceret. Alia autem quia oculis semper dormit apertis. ita et Christus in cruce
positus. potentia diuinitatis ubique uigilauit. Tertia cum leena suos genuerit catulos
scotomaticos. i. apertis oculis nil uidentes producit patre uero in facie illorum flante
illuminantur. Ita et Christus in sepulchro dormiens. potentia est patris resuscitatus;

> Tres ... resuscitatus: cf. *Physiologus Latinus* 1, s.v. "Leo"

ON THE LION

I have bristly skin and I destroy the fierce-tusked boars of the forests
And the horned deer; although they roar
I do not spare them, but strike even the shoulders of bears.
I am bloody-mouthed and fear not the snapping jaws of wolves;
I am savage, relying on my royal dignity;
I sleep without closing my luminous, gem-bright eyes.

Riddle 39   De pipero

fol 89r20-89v4   Ehwald 40

DE PIPERO

Serpentes custodiunt siluas in quibus nascitur.
sed incolae regionis illius cum maturi fuerint
incendunt. et serpentes fugantur. et ex flamma
nigrum efficitur. Nam natura piperis alba est;

geryflodre

1   Sum niger exterius rugoso cortice tectus.

Sed tamen interius candentem gesto medullam;

Dilicias epulas regum luxusque ciborum.   ⊦
                                  i. aspergo   coquinae
                i. carnes   *a celando*
Ius simul et pulpas battutas   condo   culinae;
         proficientem uel
         suffultum
5   Sed me   subnixum   nulla uirtute uidebis
         s. mea
Viscera ni fuerint nitidis quassata medullis;

T Serpentes ... alba est: Isidore *Etymologiae* 17.8.8

ON PEPPER

I am black outside, covered with a wrinkled shell,
But inside I have a white marrow.
I season the dainty meals and luxurious feasts of kings,
As well as the soup and pounded meats of a common kitchen.
You will never know my strength,
Unless you crush the inner part of my shining marrow.

Riddle 40   De puluillo

fol 89v5-11   Ehwald 41

DE PULUILLO ID EST MINIMUM CERVICAL

                    unsoðe
      s. ut   *i. uana uel falsa* *s. homines*

1 Nolo fidem frangas licet   irrita   dicta putentur:

Credula sed nostris pande precordia uerbis;
comparatiuus
Celsior ad superas possum turgescere nubes
  s. hominis   *a*   *i. diminuto*
Si   caput   aufertur mihi toto corpore dempto;

5 At uero capitis si pressus mole grauabor

Ima petens iugiter minorari parte uidebor;

4 (lmarg89v9)

i. Non caput tantum sed corpus totum.

ON THE PILLOW OR SMALL BOLSTER

Do not disbelieve me, though my assertions seem false,
But open your credulous heart to my words.
I can fluff up higher toward the lofty clouds,
If a head is taken away from me and my body thus diminished.
If pressed by the weight of a head I will sink
And seem smaller by half as I shrink down.

Riddle 41   De strutione

fol 89v12-18   Ehwald 42

DE STRUTIONE.

               feðriað
1 Grandia membra mihi plumescunt corpore denso;
   s. est   s. mihi
  Par   color   accipitri. sed dispar causa uolandi;
                       i. uolito
  Nam summa exiguis non trano per aethera pennis
             i. pergo   *i. sordida*
  Sed potius pedibus spatior per squalida rura⁚
   s. meorum
5 Ouorum teretes prebens ad pocula testas;
         i. affricorum
  Affrica poenorum fertur me gignere tellus;

     3 exiguis] exsiguis MS

T (lmarg89v12-22)

Strutio nomen auis est ferox. penna nigra. cuius uox similis uoci tonitrui et eiusdem generis sunt licet non eiusdem magnitudinis. Strutio et erodion similes cum grecis. Strutio pennas habet sed non uolat a terra. et confouere oua sua neglegit. sed cineres ea confouere solent; Strutio auis est magna quae fit in heremo affricae. in dextera parte. et natura est illius oua in heremis dimittere sua. et postea estu solis fouentur;

    Strutio ... fouentur: cf. Isidore *Etymologiae* 12.7.20, "Struthio Graeco nomine dicitur, quod animal in similitudine avis pinnas habere videtur; tamen de terra altius non elevatur. Ova sua fovere neglegit; sed proiecta tantummodo fotu pulveris animantur. Ardea vocata quasi ardua, id est propter altos volatus."

ON THE OSTRICH

My large limbs plume forth from my densely feathered body;
I am like the hawk in color, but unlike it, I cannot fly.
I do not mount into the high heavens on my tiny wings,
But rather I cross the dirty fields on foot.
I lay round eggs, whose shells become goblets for men.
Africa, the land of the Carthaginians is said to be my native land.

Riddle 42   De sanguisuga

fol 89v19-90r3   Ehwald 43

DE SANGUISUGA.

             i. pergo
1 Lurida per latices cenosas lustro paludis;
    ;   *;i. fortunatis rebus*
  Nam mihi conposuit nomen   fortuna   cruentum
                                 i. oris
  Rubro dum bibulis uescor de sanguine buccis;
                       i. careo
  Ossibus et pedibus geminisque carebo lacertis
                      per dolorem
5 Corpora uulneribus sed mordeo   dira   trisulcis
       ablatiuus   *i. sanitatem uel medicinam*   *s. meis*
  Atque salutiferis sic   curam   presto   labellis;

ON THE LEECH

I wander, pale and ghostly, through the foul waters of the swamp;
Fortune gave me a gory name,
For I feed on red blood with my sucking mouth.
I have no bones nor feet nor matching arms,
Yet I inflict three-cornered wounds on unlucky people
And offer a cure with my health-bringing lips.

Riddle 43   De igne

fol 90r4-12

Ehwald 44

DE IGNE.

i. ferrum   i. silex   i. uirtute
1   Me pater et mater gelido genuere rigore
i. principia
Fomitibus siccis dum mox rudimenta uigebant;
s. patrum   i. frigorem eorum
Quorum ui propria   fortunam   uincere possum
i. aquae   i. meam naturam
Cum nil ni latices mea possit uincere   fata;

5   Sed saltus. scopulos. stagni ferrique metalla

Comminuens penitus naturae iura resoluam
i. quando magnus sum   i. similitudo
Cum   me   uita   fouet sum clari sideris instar;
i. extinctus   i. sum
Post haec et fato   uictus   pice nigrior exsto;

ON FIRE

My mother and father created me in cold hardness;
I flourished at first in dry kindling.
With my own strength I can overcome my parent's lot,
Since nothing but water can change my fate.
Meadows, rocks, iron and tin
I destroy utterly, when I dissolve the laws of nature.
When life nourishes me I am as bright as a star,
But afterwards, extinguished by fate, I am blacker than pitch.

Riddle 44   De fuso

fol 90r13-20   Ehwald 45

DE FUSO QUO FILA TORQUENTUR.

non sum nunc
    ramosus   *geþiⱡſ⟩*
1 In saltu nascor   ramoso   fronde uirescens

Sed natura meum mutauerat ordine fatum
        i. porto   i. circa   *tyrninge*
Dum   ueho   per collum teretem uertigine molam;
                                        i. dominus
Tam longa nullus zona precingitur heros.

                                        i. iii. deae dictae
        pro   s. homines   *sunt parcae eoquod*
        uirorum   gentiles   uel decernere   minime parcant;
5 Per me fata   uirum   dicunt   decerpere   parcas
i. ex me   *i. uestimenta*
Ex quo conficitur regalis stragula pepli;
        i. perimunt   s. frigoribus illis;
Frigora dura uiros sternunt ni forte resistem;

6 iii deae ... parcant: Isidore *Etymologiae* 8.11.93

6 (rmarg90r19)

Stragula est proprie uestis picta qua utuntur saeculi potentes.

Stragula: cf. Isidore *Etymologiae* 19.26.1, "Stragulam vestis est discolor quod
manu artificis diversa varietate distinguitur: dictum autem quod et in stratu et in
amictu aptus sit. De quo Salomon (Prov. 31,22): 'Stragulum vestem sibi fecit.'"

ON THE SPINDLE WHICH TWISTS THREAD

I was born in a woody meadow and grew green with leaf,
But nature altered the order of my fate

And now I bear a smoothed spool turning about my neck.
No hero is clad in such a long girdle as I am;
Through me the Fates allot the lives of men.
Out of me the cloth of a regal gown is made;
The harsh, cold winter would kill men if I did not intervene.

Riddle 45   De urtica

fol 90r21-90v4   Ehwald 46

DE URTICA.

        i. tangentes   *s. mea*

1 Torqueo torquentes sed nullum torqueo sponte

Ledere nec quemquam uolo ni prius ipse reatum
    i. tangit   *s. ante*
Contrahat. et uiridem studeat decerpere caulem;

Feruida mox hominis turgescunt membra nocentis;

5 Vindico sic noxam stimulisque ulciscor acutis;

T (rmarg90r21-22)

Urtica ex eo uocatur quod tactus eius corpus adurat. Est autem igneae omnino naturae et ⟨tactu⟩ perurat et pruriginem facit;;

    tactu] tactus MS

    Urtica ... facit: Isidore *Etymologiae* 17.9.44

ON THE NETTLE

I torment tormenters, but I torment none willingly;
Nor do I wish to harm anyone unless he first commits
A crime and tries to pluck my green stalk.
The limbs of the harmful man grow hot and swell;
Thus I repay his harm and take vengeance with stinging pains.

Riddle 46   De hirundine

fol 90v5-14   Ehwald 47

DE HIRUNDINE.
In estate enim uenit et in kalendis
october recedit.

1   Absque cibo plures degebam marcida menses
       ideo sustinui quia in somno fui.   abs i. tenuerunt
Sed sopor et   somnus   ieiunia longa tulerunt   ⌜*a;*
           i. crescunt   i. semine
          i   uel germine
Pallida purpureo dum glescunt gramine rura

Garrula mox crepitat rubicundum carmina guttur;
       i. pullos   cnosle cynnes
5   Post teneros foetus et prolem gentis adultam

Sponte mea fugiens umbrosas quaero latebras;
               i. oculos
Si uero quisquam pullorum lumina ledat
   inuentum   i. medicina clyþan
Affero conpertum medicans cataplasma salutis
         s. floris   i. celedonia
Quaerens campestrem proprio de nomine florem;

9 (lmarg90v12-16)

Caeledonia dicitur eoquod pullis hirundinum necessaria sit. uel quod aduentu hirundi-
num uidetur erumpere. si oculi auferantur matres eorum illis ex hac herba mederi
dicuntur;

     Caeledonia ... dicuntur: Isidore *Etymologiae* 17.9.36

ON THE SWALLOW

Wasted with lack of food, I passed many months,
But sleep and dreams sustained the long fast.

When the pale fields burst forth in purple flower,
My red throat soon warbles garrulous songs;
Later, I flee my tender chicks and the company of my full-fledged kin
And willingly seek the shadowy hiding places.
If anyone should harm the eyes of my chicks,
I cure them with a healthful poultice which I have found;
I seek and bring a field-growing flower whose name is my own.

Riddle 47 De vertigine poli

fol 90v15-91r2

Ehwald 48

DE VERTIGINE POLI. *Firmamentum per uiginti quattuor horas terram circuit.*

    s. ut sum   *i. uniuscuiusque naturae*

1 Sic me formauit naturae conditor almus;

        i. rotundus   *s. per*   *i. circulis*

  Lustro   teres   tota spatiosis saecula ciclis

Latas in gremio portans cum pondere terras;

                      s. a similitudine

                      coloris caerae

Sic maris undantes cumulos et   cerula   claudo

                      uel uelox

                  i. quasi celerior

5 Nam nihil in rerum natura tam   celer   esset

                    s. per

                i. accussatiuus *i. uolitet*

Quod pedibus pergat quod pennis   aethera   tranet

i. piscis   *i. tranans*

Accola neu ponti uolitans per cerula squamis;

           i. circuitum   *i. conpellit*

Nec rota per   girum   quam trudit machina limphae

                    i. tardent

                trico i. soluo

Currere sic posset ni septem sidera tricent;

      5 uel uelox *squeezed in*   9 i. tardent *squeezed in*

9 (rmarg91r2-3)

Septem sider⟨a⟩
sol. luna. mar⟨s⟩
Ioppiter. Ven⟨us⟩
Saturnus;

    Septem: cf. Germanici Caesaris Aratea cum Scholiis p. 226, "Involutio Sphaerae ... per cuius circuli obliquitatem septem errantes stellae feruntur id est Saturnus Iouis Mars sol Venus Mercurius luna."

ON THE TURNING OF THE HEAVENLY AXIS

The nourishing creator of nature made me thus —
Smooth and round, I wander the wide world in huge circles;
Bearing the broad lands and their weight on my lap,
I enclose the blue and wave-crested depths of the sea.
Nothing in all of nature could be so swift,
Nothing that walks on feet or flies through the air on wings,
Neither a scaly fish swimming through the azure sea,
Nor a millwheel spinning in its water-driven circle
Could run as fast as I, if the seven stars did not impede me.

Riddle 48 De caccabo

fol 91r3-8   Ehwald 49

DE CACCABO SIVE LEBETE.

i. niger sum

1 Horrida curua capax patulis fabricata metallis

Pendeo. nec caelum tangens terramue profundam.
                    s. sum
Ignibus ardescens nec non et gurgite feruens;
                    s. inter ignem et aquam   i. proelia
Sic geminas uario   patior   discrimine pugnas

5 Dum latices limphae tolero flammasque feroces;

T (upmarg91r)

Caccabus et coquina a sono feruoris cognominantur. haec in grecis et latinis communia habentur. Sed utrum latini a grecis. an greci a latinis haec uocabula mutuassent incertum;

Caccabus ... incertum: Isidore *Etymolgoiae* 20.8.3

ON THE CAULDRON

Black, curved, capacious and of beaten metal made,
I hang, touching neither the sky nor the deep earth.
Growing hot from fires and sometimes bubbling like a whirlpool,
I suffer the twinned onslaught of a variable threat,
As I endure the surging of water and the ferocious flames.

Riddle 49　De mirifolio

fol 91r9-14　　　　　　　　　　　　　　　Ehwald 50

<gearwe>
DE MIRIFOLIO GRECE QUOD EST MILLEFOLIUM LATINE.

　　　　i. grecorum
1　Prorsus achiuorum lingua pariterque latina

　Mille uocor uiridi folium de cespite natum;
　　　　　　　　　　　　　　　i. habeo
　Idcirco decies centenum nomen habebo
　　　　　　　　　　　　　s. ut ego　i. germinat
　Cauliculis florens quoniam sic nulla　frutescit
　　　　　　　　　　　i. termine
5　Herba. per innumeros telluris limite sulcos;

　　　T gearwe] wearwe MS

ON THE MILLIFOIL OR YARROW

In the language of the Greeks and the Latin
I, born from the green sod, am called the thousand-leaved.
I bear the name of ten hundreds,
Since no other herb blooms thus on its stalks
In all the countless fields of the earth.

Riddle 50   De trutina

fol 91r15-21

Ehwald 23

wegan
DE TRUTINA QUAE MOMENTANA DICITUR EO QUOD
AD MOMENTUM INCLINATA VERGIT.

1   Nos geminas olīm genuit natura sorores.
                                    i. iudicium
    Quas iugiter rectae legis censura gubernat;
    i. spernere   *i. rectitudinem*
    Tempnere personas et   ius   seruare solemus;
                                    i. hominibus
    Felix in terra fieret mortalibus aeuum:
            i. regulam   pro seruarent
5   Iustitiae   normam   si seruent more sororum;

ON SCALES

Sometime ago nature bore us, twin sisters,
Governed eternally by the law of true judgment;
We spurn the claims of people and preserve justice.
A blessed age would come for mortals on earth
If they would preserve the will of justice as we sisters do.

Riddle 51   De eliotropo

fol 91r22-91v4

Ehwald 51

goldwyrt
DE ELIOTROPO GRECE QUOD EST SOLSEQUIUM LATINE.

i. crescens

1   Sponte mea nascor foecundo cespite uernans;
i. fuluo
Fulgida de croceo flauescunt culmina flore;
i. uesperi
Occiduo claudor sic orto sole patesco
s. mihi   i. elitropium
4   Unde prudentes posuerunt nomina greci;

T (botmarg 91r)

Eliotropi in grece. a latinis solissequa nominatur. nam et sole oriente flores suos aperit;

Eliotropi ... aperit: Isidore *Etymologiae* 17.9.37

ON THE HELIOTROPE OR SUN-SEEKER

I am born and I flourish freely in the fertile field;
My shining crown culminates in a golden flower.
I close at sunset and open at dawn;
For this, the wise Greeks named me.

Riddle 52   De candela

fol 91v5-13   Ehwald 52

DE CANDELA.

1 Materia duplici palmis plasmabar apertis;

Interiora mihi candescunt uiscera lino
                    s. uiscera
Seu certe gracili iunco spoliata nitescunt;
    i. aliquando   *ablatiuus*
Sed   nunc   exterius flauescunt corpora   flore
s. corpora   *i. faces pro calore*
5 Quae   flammasque focosque   laremque uomentia fundunt
                        i.   humidae
Et crebro lacrimae stillant de frontibus   udae;

Sic tamen horrendas noctis extinguo latebras;
                    i. exusta
Relliquias cinerum mox uiscera tosta relinquunt;

ON THE CANDLE

Open-palmed hands formed me out of two substances.
My inner core glows white, made of flax,
Or else shines bright, plundered from a slender rush,
But when my outward body bursts into yellow flower,
It pours forth, spewing flames, heat and fire
As moist tears drop in profusion from my brows.
Yet, in this way, I destroy the horrid shadows of night
And soon my burned heart leaves behind only ashes.

Riddle 53　De arcturo

fol 91v14-92r1　　　　　　　　　　　　　　　　　Ehwald 53

nomen sideris
DE ARCTURO.

　　　　　　　　　uel bis　　　　　　　*i. caeli*
1　Sidereis stipor turmis in uertice mundi;
　　　　　　　　　　　　　　i. septentrio de septem bobus iouis.
　　　　　　i. plaustrum　i. porto　triones autem antiqui boues dicebant;
　Famosum　nomen　gesto　cognomine　uulgi.
　i. in circuitu circa cardinem caeli　　　　*i. infra terram*
　In　giro　uoluens　iugiter non uergo deorsum
　　　　　　i. quasi　　　　　　　*i. sidera*　　*i. mari*
　Caetera　ceu　properant caelorum lumina　ponto;
　　　　　　　　　　　　　　　　i. polo
5　Hoc dono ditor. quoniam sum proximus axi
　　　　　　　　　　i. praepositus
　　　　　　　　　uel eleuatus　　　　　　　*hwearft*
　Qui ripheis scithiae　praelatus　montibus errat
　i
　Vergilias numeris aequans in arce polorum
　　　　　　　　　　　　　　　　　inferens hominibus.
　i. axi　　　　　　　　　*lacus*　　*Nomen paludis inferni somium*
　uel cui　i. mihi　　　　*inferni　i. mortifera*
　Pars　cuius　inferior　stigia　letheaque palude
　dicitur　　　　　　　　*asigan*
　Fertur. et inferni fundo succumbere nigro;

> 2 septentrio ... dicebant: cf. Isidore *Etymologiae* 3.71.6, "Signorum primus
> Arcton, qui in axe fixus septem stellis in se revolutis rotatur. Nomen est
> Graecum, quod Latine dicitur ursa; quae quia in modum plaustri vertitur, nostri
> eam Septentrionem dixerunt. Triones enim proprie sunt boves aratorii, dicti eo
> quod terram terant, quasi teriones."

2 (lmarg91v14-15)

Plaustrum penes uulgus nominor.
Arcturus uero apud perfectos;

8 (lmarg91v20-21)

Lethus nomen fluminis in inferno.
et obliuiosus interpretatur;

8 (botmarg91v)

Tria sunt flumina inferni. Acheros. quod sine gaudio interpretatur. ex quo nascitur
secundum stix. i. tristitia quia ubi gaudium non est. consequens est. ut tristitia sit.
Rursus ex isto oritur cocitus i. luctus. quia nimirum ubi tristitia est sequitur ut simul
sit luctus;

> Tria sunt ... luctus: cf. *Commentaire anonyme sur Prudence* on *Psychomachia*
> 520, "Stix ABDIT palus Inferni quae tristitia interpretatur"; and on *Hamartigenia*
> 502, "IPSE CHARON ipse portitor inferni: dicitur autem Charon quasi acharon id
> est sine gaudio."

ON THE BIG DIPPER

Surrounded by starry throngs, I am set at the high point of the world;
I bear a vulgar name in the common tongue.
Revolving ever in my circular course, I do not turn downward,
Like other stars of the heavens that hasten into the sea;
I am enriched with this gift, since I am close to the pole,
Which wanders above the Riphean mountain of Scythia.
I am equal in number to the Pleiades, set in the sky,
Whose lower part is said to extend to the Stygian marsh of Lethe
And to lie under the black depth of Hell.

Riddle 54　De cacuma dupplici

fol 92r2-9　　　　　　　　　　　　　　　　　　Ehwald 54

DE CACUMA DUPPLICI.　*Quam pyrate in nauibus solent habere*
　　　　　　　　　　　　uel tantis uel rerum uel causis
1　Credere quis poterit tantarum foedera rerum.
　　s. quis. nisi ego　ablatiuus　uel rerum
　Temperet　et　fatis.　morum contraria fata;
　　　　ignem i. aquam　　　　　　　　　　　　*wambe*
　Ecce larem laticem quoque gesto in uiscere uentris

　Nec tamen undantes uincunt incendia limphae
　　　　　　　　s. nec
5　Ignibus haud atris siccantur flumina fontis

　Foedera sed pacis sunt flammas inter et undas;
　　　　　　s. tempore　　　　　　　　*haec incus. dis*
　Malleus in primo memet formabat et incus;

ON THE DOUBLE BOILER

Who could believe the union of such things?
Who can reconcile such contrary fates to a common fate?
Behold, I bear both fire and water in the depth of my belly,
And the boiling liquid cannot vanquish the flames,
Nor can the black fires boil away the welling waters;
Thus there is a pact of peace between flame and wave.
A hammer and anvil shaped me originally.

Riddle 55　De chrismale

DE CHRISMALE.

        i. corpore Christi uel benedictione
1　Alma domus ueneror　diuino　munere　plena
       aperit　　　　*undeð*
　Valuas sed nullus reserat nec limina pandit
      pro angulis
　Culmina ni fuerint　aulis　sublata quaternis;
     uel redolent
　Et licet exterius　rutilent　de corpore gemmae
⋮
         uel gemma uel bula
5　Aurea dum fuluis flauescit　bulla　metallis.
        ⋮　　　*s. corpore salutis*
　Sẽd tamen uberius ditantur uiscera　crassa
    i. ubi i. corpus Christi r　l
　Intus　qua　species　flagrat pulcherrima Christi;

　Candida sanctarum sic floret gloria rerum
            uel na templi
　Nec trabes in templo surgunt nec culmine tecta;

ON THE CHRISMAL

I am revered as a beautiful house full of the divine gift,
But no one can open my doors or throw wide my portals
Unless my roof has been lifted from its four corners.
Although jewels gleam on the outside of my body
And a golden gem glows yellow against my shining surface,
Nevertheless, my full belly is enriched more fully
Within, where the beauteous body of Christ burns bright.
Thus the radiant glory of holy things shines forth
Where no timbers hold the roof at the top of the temple.

Riddle 56   De castore

fol 92r20-92v7   Ehwald 56

DE CASTORE QUI LATINE FIBER DICITUR.

        i. fractis   *staðum.*

1   Hospes preruptis habitans in margine ripis

                       kene

   Non sum torpescens. oris sed belliger armis

   Quin potius duro uitam sustento labore;

                     i. obliquis dentibus

   Grossaque prosternens mox ligna securibus uncis.

5   Humidus in fundo tranat quo piscis aquoso

   Sepe caput proprium tingens in gurgite mergo;

   Vulnera fibrarum nec non et lurida tabo

                   de testiculo eius

          ge wole   *medicamenta faciunt*

   Membra medens. pestemque luemque resoluo   necantem;

                  i. utor

   Libris conrosis et cortica uescor amaro;

T (botmarg92r)

Castores a castrando dicti sunt. Nam testiculi

               uel medicinae

eorum apti sunt medicinalibus. propter quod cum persenserint uenatorem ipsi se castrant et morsibus uirilia sua amputant;

    Castores ... amputant: Isidore *Etymologiae* 12.2.21

ON THE BEAVER

I am a dweller on the edge of steep stream banks,
And not at all lazy. But warlike, with the weapons of my mouth,

I sustain my life with hard labour,
Laying low huge trees with my hooked axes.
I dive into the water, where the fish swim,
And immerse my own head, wetting it in the watery surge.
The wounds of sinews and limbs foul with gore
I can cure. I destroy pestilence and the deadly plague.
I eat the bitter and well-gnawed bark of trees.

Riddle 57   De aquila

fol 92v8-16   Ehwald 57

DE AQUILA   *Non sum illa aquila troiana quae ganimidem in caelum*
             fertur rapuisse

                                        i. filius troi regis
1   Armiger infausti iouis et raptor ganimedis
     ⸫   *pro fallaces*
     Quamquam pellaces cantarent carmine uates

                                        i. de genere dardanii
              s. non fueram   *Dardanus rex troianorum*
                     ⟨*s. propterea*⟩ *s. ad caelum* *erat inde troiani.*
     Nön fueram. prĕpes   quo   fertur   dardana proles.

     Sed magis in summis cignos agitabo fugaces
     arsis. i. eleuatio
     i. uociferantes
5   Arsantesque grues perturbo sub aetheris axe;
                   ablatiuus
     Corpora dum   senio   corrumpit fessa senectus
                        s. mea
     Fontibus in liquidis mergentis membra madescunt;

     Post haec restauror preclaro lumine phoebi;

          3 propterea] propea MS   5 i. uociferantes *squeezed in*

1 (lmarg92v9-12)

Pulcherrimus puer erat ipse qui aquilam in celum rapuisse dicitur. ut pincerna iouis
fuisset. De quo dicit uirgilius. qui et eius concubitor fuit

     Pulcherrimus ... fuisset: Vergil *Aeneid* 1.28

ON THE EAGLE

The shield-bearer of unlucky Jove and the abductor of Ganymede
So the false prophets named me in their poems,

But I was not the bird who stole away that son of Troy;
Rather I put the swans to flight, high in the air
And scatter the honking geese beneath the vault of heaven.
When age has tired my worn body with feebleness,
I wash my limbs, immersing them in clear streams.
Afterwards, I am renewed in the clear light of Phoebus.

Riddle 58 De vespero sidere

fol 92v17-93r2   Ehwald 58

DE VESPERO SIDERE.

　　　　　　　　　　　　　　　i. uesper
1　Tempore de primo noctis. mihi nomen adhesit;
　　　　　　　　　　　ablatiuus
　　　　i. caeli　　　　　*termino*
　Occiduas mundi conplector cardine partes
　　　　i. sol
　Oceano titan dum corpus tinxerit almum;
　　　s. dum
　Et polus in glaucis descendens uoluitur undis
　　　　　　　　　　i. recondens i. sidera
5　Tum sequor in uitreis abscondens lumina campis;
　　　　　　i. ditatus
　s. essem　uel felix
　Et　　fortunatus subito ni tollar ab aethre
　　　　　s. meum
　Ut furuas lumen noctis depelleret umbras;

　　　6 aethre] aethr_e MS

2 (lmarg92v19)

Oriens. occasus. auster. Septentrio;

> Oriens: cf. Isidore *Etymologiae* 13.1.3, "Quattuor autem esse climata mundi, id est plagas: Orientem et Occidentem, Septentrionem et Meridiem."

ON THE EVENING STAR

From the early hours of night I take my name;
I wander the western parts of the world.
When Titan bathes its life-giving body in the ocean,

And the axle of heaven rolls down beneath the gray-gleaming waves,
I follow, hiding my light under the glassy field of the sea.
I would be happy to dispel dark night,
If I were not suddenly removed from the air.

Riddle 59   De penna scriptoris

fol 93r3-11

Ehwald 59

DE PENNA SCRIPTORIS.

i. nomen auis
1 Me dudum genuit candens onocratulus albam
        s. onocratulus
   Gutture   qui   patulo sorbet de gurgite limphas.

   Pergo per albentes directo tramite campos
                    i. nigra
   Candentique uiae uestigia cerula linquo
                i. obliquis
5 Lucida nigratis fuscans anfractibus arua.
                        i. pergere
   Nec satis est unam per campos pandere callem

   Semita quin potius milleno tramite tendit
            i. iustos uel
   s. semita   fideles
   Quae   non errantes ad caeli culmina uexit;

ON THE WRITER'S QUILL

I am shining white, born long ago of the gleaming pelican,
Who takes the waters of the sea into his open mouth.
Now I travel a narrow path over white-glowing fields;
I leave cerulean footprints along the shining way,
Obscuring the bright fields with my blackened windings.
It is not enough for me to open one pathway through the fields;
Rather, the road runs its course in a thousand byways
And leads those who stray not to the heights of heaven.

Riddle 60   De monocerote

fol 93r12-93v1   Ehwald 60

DE MONOCEROTE GRECE. UNICORNU LATINE.

i. belli
1 Collibus in celsis saeui discrimina martis

Quamuis uenator frustra latrante moloso
i. uociferet uel arcifer.
                  i. arcum ferens   i. iactans   i. sagittas
Garriat   arcister   contorquens spicula ferri

Nil uereor. magnis sed fretus uiribus altos
                              s. per   uel a
5 Belliger inpugnans elefantes uulnere sterno;

Heu fortuna ferox quae me sic arte fefellit
          uel trudo   s. elefantes
Dum trudico grandes. et uirgine uincor inermi
                                                    s. me
Nam gremium pandens mox pulchra puerpera prendit.
          i. particeps   s. me
Et uoti   compos   celsam deducit ad urbem;
i. inseruit monoceron.   i. unicornus.   i. greca
10 Indidit   ex cornu   nomen   mihi lingua pelasga;
          i. iterum s. nomina.   i. unicornis
Sic itidem   propria   dixerunt uoce latini;

ON THE UNICORN

I fear not the battles of fierce Mars, in the high hills,
Though the hunter calls and his dog barks in vain,
And the archer hurls his arrows of iron.
A warrior armed with great strength,
I fight the tall elephants and fell them with a blow.

But, alas, ferocious fortune tricked me in this way —
Although I can slay the mighty, I am conquered by an unarmed virgin;
A beautiful maiden who bares her breast may seize me
And, mistress of her will, lead me to the turreted city.
I am named for my single horn in the Greek tongue
And I am called by this same name in Latin.

Riddle 61   De pugione

fol 93v2-9   Ehwald 61

DE PUGIONE VEL SPATA.

1   De terrae gremiis formabar primitus arte.

Materia trucibus processit caetera tauris.
                    i. foetidis   ipsa   *.i. capris*
Aut potius putidis constat fabricata capellis;

Per me multorum clauduntur lumina loeto

5   Qui domini nudus nitor defendere uitam;
                                                    i. raso
Nam domus est mihi constructa de tergore secto

Nec non et tabulis quas findunt stipite rasis;

T (lmarg93v2-3)

[.........] *pugnando*
[.....] *est enim gla*
[.....] *aruus et bis*
[....] *s lateri adhe*
[...] *us*

> The source is Isidore *Etymologiae* 18.6.6; the full text reads: "Pugio a pungendo
> et transfigendo uocatus. Est enim gladius paruus et bis acutus lateri adhaerens."

ON THE DAGGER OR SHORT SWORD

One part of me was shaped with skill from the bosom of the earth,
The other half either came from a savage bull
Or was made from a fetid-smelling goat.

Many eyes are closed in death by me
When, naked, I try to defend the life of my lord.
My home is made from a well-scraped hide
And smooth wood split from trees.

Riddle 62   De famfalica

fol 93v10-17

Ehwald 62

DE FAMFALICA GRECE. BULLA AQUATICA LATINE.

                      pro aere
1 De madido nascor rorantibus aethere guttis.
                                 fylle
   Turgida concrescens liquido de flumine lapsu;

   Sed me nulla ualet manus udo gurgite nantem

   Tangere. ni statim rumpantur uiscera tactu
  ni
5 Et fragilis tenues flatus discedat in auras;
                        pro duxi
   Ante cateruatim per limphas duco cohortes
                   i. socientur
   Dum plures ortu comites potiuntur eodem;

ON THE BUBBLE

I come in dewy drops from the wet sky,
And grow fat in my fall through the rainy shower,
But no hand can touch me, as I swim in the limpid water,
For my delicate interior bursts at once from the touch
And my fragile breath departs into thin air.
Once, through the watery ways, in a great crowd, I led the companions
And many fellows who share my same birth.

Riddle 63   De corvo

fol 93v18-94r6   Ehwald 63

DE CORVO.

1 Dum genus humanum truculenta fluenta necarent
             i. punirent
  dum   *ipsa*
  Et noua mortales multarent aequore cunctos
          i. paucis
  Exceptis raris gignunt qui semina saeclis.

  Primus uiuentum perdebam foedera iuris
          i. noe
5 Imperio patris contempnens subdere colla;
                       i. sedulium
  Unde puto dudum uersu dixisse poetam

  Abluit in terris quicquid deliquit in undis;
        Quos deus per quindecim ieiunos seruat dies. Unde dicitur
        qui dat iumentis escam. et pullis coruorum et reliqua
  Nam sobolem   numquam   dapibus   saturabo   ciborum

  Ni prius in pulpis plumas nigrescere cernam;
  i.c. quia antiqui u. pro b. ponebant dicentes oruus pro orbus.
  s. prima   s. si
10 Littera   tollatur   post   haec   sine   prole manebo;

2 ipsa *squeezed in*

7 Abluit ... undis: Sedulius *Carmen Paschale* 1.175   8 Unde dicitur:
Psalms 146:9   10 quia antiqui: cf. Priscian *Institutionem grammaticarum*
libri xviii 1.23

10 (rmarg94r6)

i. orbus dicitur qui filios numquam genuit.
  orbatus qui filios genuit et amisit;

ON THE RAVEN

When fierce floods destroyed the human race
And drowned all mortal creatures in the ocean,
Except those few who preserved the new seeds for the world,
I was the first of the survivors to break the pact of the law,
By refusing to bend my neck to the will of the father.
Concerning this, I think the poet once sang in verse,
"He pays on land for the sin he committed at sea."
I will never feed my young with nourishing food
Until I first see the plumes grow black on their bodies.
If you remove a letter from my name, I will be childless.

Riddle 64   De columba

fol 94r7-13   Ehwald 64

DE COLUMBA

i. puniret
1   Cum deus infandas iam plecteret aequore noxas

Ablueretque simul scelerum contagia limphis.
i. precipientis
Prima precepti conpleui iussa parentis
i. demonstrans   · ⁻
uel significans
Portendens fructu terris uenisse salutem;

5   Mitia qua propter semper precordia gesto
i. ales
Et felix prepes nigro sine felle manebo;

2 -que *added above the line*

ON THE DOVE

When god destroyed unspeakable offenses in the flood
And washed away the stain of sin in the water,
I was the first to fulfill the laws of my commanding parent,
Showing by the fruit I brought that salvation had come to the earth.
Because of this, I have a gentle heart forever
And am a happy bird, devoid of dark and bitter gall.

Riddle 65   De catto

fol 94r14-94v1   Ehwald 65

DE CATTO VEL MURICIPE VEL PILACE.

s. sum
1   Fida satis custos conseruans peruigil aedes.

Noctibus in furuis caecas lüstrabo latebras
                                i. uisum
Atris haut perdens oculorum lumen in antris;
            i. execrabilibus   *i. similae   mugan cumulos*
Furibus   inuisis   uastant qui   farris   aceruos

5   Insidiis tacite dispono scandala mortis;
         wo⟨h⟩   *denn uel fereldu*
Et uage uenatrix rimabor   lustra   ferarum
                            i. surices
Nec uolo cum canibus turmas agitare fugaces
s. canes   *i. mouent*
Qui mihi latrantes crudelia bella ciebunt;
        s. suricum
Gens exosa mihi tradebat nomen habendum;

ON THE CAT, THE MOUSE-CATCHER

I am a faithful vigilant guardian, always watching the house;
In the deep night, I walk through the unseeing shadows,
For I do not lose the sight of my eyes, even in black caverns.
Against the hateful thieves who ravage the stores of grain,
I ambush, I silently set a snare of death.
A roaming huntress, I invade the lairs of wild beasts,
But I do not wish to chase fleeing herds alongside dogs
Who bark and bring cruel war against me.
A race I despise has given me my name.

Riddle 66   De mola

DE MOLA.

1   Nos sumus equales communi sorte sorores.

   Quae damus ex nostro cunctis alimenta labore
   s. est   *s. sed*
   Par labor ambarum dispar fortuna duarum;
              i. uergit
   Altera nam cursat quod numquam altera gessit

5   Nec tamen inuidiae stimulis agitamur acerbis;
          i. comedit   *ceuwð*
   Utraque quod mandit quod ruminat ore patenti

   Comminuens reddit. famulans sine fraude maligna;

> 7 *the first a in* maligna *is added below the line.*

ON THE MILLSTONE

We are two sisters, equal in our common lot,
Who give food to all by our labor.
While our labor is the same, our fortunes are quite different;
One of us turns in a circle, which the other never has done,
Yet we are not made jealous by envy's bitter sting;
Each of us, grinding what she eats, through her open mouth
Returns what she chews; thus we serve, with no evil intent.

Riddle 67　De crebello

fol 94v10-19　　　　　　　　　　　　　　　　　Ehwald 67

i. cribro uel capisterium quo furfures a farina sequestrantur.
DE CREBELLO QUO FURFURAE A FARINA SEQUESTRANTUR.

1　Sicca pruinosa in crebris effundo fenestris　　*syfeda*

Candentemque niuem iactans de uiscere furuo;
　　　　　s. homo　s. eam niuem
Et tamen　omnis　amat　quamuis sit frigida nimbo
　　　　s. quamuis
Densior et nebulis late spargatur in aula;
　　　　　i. inpugnantur
s. niue　　　　　　*suffocantur*
5　Qua sina mortales grassantur funere loeti;

Sic animae pariter pereunt dum uita fatescit.
　s. niue　　　　　　　　　*i. mortis*
Et qua ditati contempnunt limina ditis;

Liquitur in prunis numquam torrentibus haec nix;
　　　　　　　s. in
Sed mirum dictuque magis durescit ad ignem;

　　　9　-que *added above the line*

ON THE SIEVE IN WHICH THE CHAFF IS SEPARATED FROM THE GRAIN

I, dry and hoary, pour out through my many windows
White snow, throwing it from my dark belly;
All men love this snow, though it is cold,
Denser than a rain cloud and wide-flung in clouds throughout the room.
Without it, mortals wander in a mad procession of death
And their spirits perish as their life grows weak.
Wealthy ones who possess it scorn the portals of death,
For this snow is never destroyed by burning coals
But, amazing to say, grows harder in the fire.

Riddle 68   De salpice

DE SALPICE.

1   Sum caua bellantum crepituque corda ciebo
           i. instigans
    Vocibus horrendis stimulans in bella cohortes

    Idcirco reboans tanto clamore resulto.
       eo
    Quod nulla interius obtundunt uiscera uocem

5   Spiritus in toto sed regnant corpore flabra;

    Garrula me poterit numquam superare cicada
                          i. frutectibus
    Aut arguta simul cantans luscinia ruscis
                  i. nominant.
    Quam lingua propria dicunt achalantida greci;

        6 numquam *added above the line*

ON THE TRUMPET

I am hollow and I excite the hearts of warriors with my call;
Urging armies to war with my horrid clamor,
And resounding, I ring with a great noise,
Because no inner parts weaken my voice,
And breath and winds rule my entire body.
The garrulous cricket can never outsing me,
Nor can the high-pitched nighintgale that sings in the broom plant
And is called "achalantida" in the Greek tongue.

Riddle 69   De taxo

DE TAXO.

1   Semper habens uirides frondenti in corpore crines

Tempore iam nullo uiduabor tegmine spisso:
              uel flu
Circius et boreas quamuis et flamina chauri

Viribus horrendis studeant deglobere frondem.
     s. illum taxum.
5   Sed me pestiferam fecerunt fata reorum;

Cumque uenenatus glescit de corpore stipes
i. raptores   *i. cupidi*
Lurcones   rabidi quem carpunt rictibus oris

Occido mandentum mox plura cadauera loeto;

ON THE YEW

I always wear green curls on my leafy body,
For at no time am I deprived of my dense cloak,
Although the northwesterly winds Boreas, Circius, and Caurus
Try to strip my foliage with their fearsome strength.
The fates made me the destroyer of the guilty.
Poisoned branches grow from my body,
And when rapacious thieves seize them with their open jaws,
I send to death their gluttonous corpses.

Riddle 70 De tortella

DE TORTELLA.

                                      i. scutum

1   De terris orior candenti corpore pelta
               deus ignium   *uel rigescens*
   Et niue foecunda   ulcani   torre nigrescens;
     s. sum
   Carior et multo quam caetera scuta duelli

   Nec tamen in medio clipei stat ferreus umbo;
                      i. scutum uel pelta

5   Me sine quid prodest dirorum   parma   uirorum
  i. statim   *uel rent*
   Vix   artus animaeque carebunt tramite mortis
             i. contradicam. resistam   *i. loeti*
   Ni forsan ualidis   refrager   uiribus   orco;

ON THE HEARTH CAKE

I am a small white buckler born from the earth;
Made of snowy grain, I grow dark in the fire of Vulcan.
I am far more precious than other shields of war,
Though no iron boss adorns my center.
Without me, of what use are grim warrior's shields?
Body and soul will travel the path to the underworld,
Unless I firmly oppose death with all my might.

Riddle 71   De pisce

fol 95v2-8   Ehwald 71

DE PISCE.

1   Me pedibus manibusque simul fraudauerat almus

Arbiter. inmensum primum dum pangeret orbem;

Fulcior haut uolitans ueloci prepetis ala;
　　　　　i. confortat
Spiritus alterno uegetat nec corpora flatu;

5   Quamuis in caelis conuexa cacumina cernam

Non tamen undosi contempno marmora ponti;

ON THE FISH

The bouteous lord deprived me of both feet and hands,
When he first created the boundless earth.
Flying, I am not supported by the fast wing of a bird,
Nor does the spirit quicken my body with regular breaths.
Although I see the curved heights of the sky,
I do not spurn the bright expanse of the wave-filled sea.

Riddle 72   De coloso

fol 95v9-17   Ehwald 72

DE COLOSO VEL TORACICLO.

                              i. pictor

1   Omnia membra mihi plasmauit corporis auctor;
          s. auctore   *uel munia*
   Nec tamen ex isdem membrorum munera sumpsi;

   Pergere nec plantis oculis nec cernere possum

   Quamquam nunc patulae constent sub fronte fenestrae;
        i. spiranti
5   Nullus anhelanti procedit uiscere flatus.

   Spicula nec geminis nitor torquere lacertis;
         i. pictor
   Heu frustra factor confinxit corpus inorme

   Totis membrorum dum fraudor sensibus intus;

       2 isdem] hisdem MS

ON THE COLOSSUS

My maker gave me all the parts of a body,
But I have not received any benefit from my limbs;
I cannot walk with my feet or see with my eyes,
Though my lids are open wide like windows beneath my brow.
No breath of life comes forth from my panting chest;
Nor can I throw spears with my two arms.
Alas! my creator made my huge body in vain,
Since I am deprived of all the inner bodily senses.

Riddle 73   De fonte

fol 95v18-96r3   Ehwald 73

DE FONTE

1   Per caua telluris clam serpo celerrimus antra

Flexos uenarum gyrans anfractibus orbes;

Cum caream sensu uita quoque funditus expers:

Quis numerus capiat uel quis laterculus equet
s. in   s. in aquis
5   Vita uiuentum generem quot milia partu;

His neque per caelum rutilantis sidera sperae

Fluctiuagi ponti nec conpensantur harenae;

ON THE WELLSPRING

I slither quickly and secretly through the dark caves of the earth,
Rolling my bubbling surface along the windings of waterways.
Though I lack sensation and am entirely devoid of life,
What number can tell or abacus count
The thousands of creatures I bring to life?
The stars in the shining sphere of the sky cannot equal them
Nor the sands of the restless, wave-worn sea.

Riddle 74   De fundibalo

fol 96r4-13   Ehwald 74

DE FUNDIBALO.

1 *i. planitudine*
Glauca seges lini uernans ex equore campi
Et tergus mihi tradebant primordia fati;   *uel uitae*

Bina mihi constant torto retinacula filo
Ex quibus inmensum trucidabam mole tyrannum   *i. goliam*

5 Cum cuperent olim ingentes seuire phalanges;

Plus amo cum tereti bellum decernere saxo

Quam duris pugnans ferrato cuspide contis;

Tres digiti totum uersant super ardua corpus;

Erro caput circa tenues extendor in auras;   *s. et*

ON THE SLING

The bright fruit of flax growing green in the broad field
And a leather back provided my start in life.
Two straps bind me with a twisted thread;
With these and a massive stone I killed the enormous tyrant,
When the pagan armies were longing to fight.
I would rather wage war with a round stone,
Than fight with the iron point of sharp spears.
Three fingers whirl my entire body up high;
I circle round the head and fly out into thin air.

Riddle 75   De crabrone

fol 96r14-96v4   Ehwald 75

DE CRABRONE.

1   Aera per sudum nunc binis remigo pennis

Horridus et grossae depromo murmura uocis;
i. ego maneo
Namque cauo densis conuersor stipite turmis

Dulcia conficiens propriis alimenta cateruis:

5   Et tamen humanis horrent haec pabula buccis;

Sed quicumque cupit disrumpens foedera pacis
:-
Dirus commaculare domum sub culmine querno.
i. cito
Extimplo socios in bellum clamo cohortes;

Dumque cateruatim stridunt et spicula trudunt

10   Agmina diffugiunt iaculis exterrita diris;

Insontes hosti sic torquent tela nocenti
i. mixta
Plurima. quae constant tetris infecta uenenis;

ON THE HORNET

I fly through the bright air on doubled wings;
A horrid creature, I send forth the murmur of my heavy voice.
I live in a hollow tree in huge swarms,
Making sweet food for my young ones,
Though these meals seem sour to human mouths.

If anyone cruelly wishes to destroy my peace and tries
To defile my home beneath the oaken tree top,
At once I call my comrades in arms to war,
And when, together, they buzz in rage and thrust out spears,
The invaders flee, terrified by their sharp stings;
Guiltless, they thrust into the harmful enemy many spears,
Which are dipped in black poisons.

Riddle 76   De melario

DE MELARIO VEL MALO.

1 Fausta fuit prima mundi nascentis origo
              s. mundus
  Donec prostratus succumberet arte maligni;

  Ex me tunc priscae processit causa ruinae
                     i. ade et eue
  Dulcia quae rudibus tradebam mala colonis;
      s. ex me
5 En iterum mundo testor remeasse salutem

  Stipite de patulo dum penderet arbiter orbis
    s. dum   *i. passus est.*
  Et poenas   lueret soboles ueneranda tonantis;

ON THE APPLE TREE

The nascent world was blessed in its birth
Until it fell, laid low by the deceit of the evil one.
From me came the cause of that ancient ruin −
I, who gave sweet apples to those innocent garden dwellers.
But, lo! I swear that salvation came again to the world
When the lord of the universe hung on my spreading trunk
And the holy son of the thunderer paid the penalty of death.

Riddle 77   De ficulnea

fol 96v13-20   Ehwald 77

DE FICULNEA.

1   Quis prior in mundo depromsit tegmina uestis
                                 i. adam
   Aut quis clementer miserum protexit egenum;

   Irrita non referam uerbis nec friuola fingam;

   Primitus in terra proprio de corpore peplum
     ablatiuus
5   Ut fama fertur produxi frondibus altis;
        quas
   Carica me curuat dum massis pabula prestat

   Sedulus agricola brumae quas tempore mandit;

ON THE FIG TREE

Who before me in the world gave leaves as vestments
Or so gently shielded a wretched, needy man?
I do not repeat vain words or speak frivolously;
First of all on earth, raiment from my own body,
I produced (as the story goes), from my tall green fronds.
The dry fig bows me down when it ripens in heavy clusters,
Which the diligent farmer eats in the winter.

Riddle 78　De cuppa vinaria

fol 96v21-97r9

Ehwald 78

DE CUPPA VINARIA

i. uini uel falerni

1 En plures debrians inpendo pocula bachi
i. maturis
Vinitor expressit quae flauescentibus uuis;
s. quae　　　　　　　s. cum
Pampinus et uiridi genuit de palmite botris
cum　i. pincerni
Nectare cauponis conplens ex uite tabernam;

5 Sic mea turgescunt ad plenum uiscera musto;

Et tamen inflatum non uexat crapula corpus
ða swe⟨tnysse⟩　　s. corpus
Quamuis hoc nectar centenis hauserit urnis;

Proles sum terrae gliscens in saltibus altis;

Materiam cuneis findit sed cultor agrestis

10 Pinos euertens altos et robora ferro;

ON THE WINE CASK

Lo, I intoxicate many when I pour forth the drink of Bacchus,
Which the wine maker pressed from the ripe grapes,
And the vine engendered with grapes from its green shoot.
I fill the innkeeper's tavern with nectar from the vine.
Thus my belly grows full with new wine,
Yet drunkenness does not disturb my filled body,
Even if I drink the nectar from one hundred urns.
I am a child of the earth, born in the mountain valleys,
Where the rustic farmer splits wood with his wedge,
Felling the high pines and oaks with his axe.

Riddle 79   De sole et luna

fol 97r10-21   Ehwald 79

DE SOLE ET LUNA.

1   Non nos saturni genuit spurcissima proles

Ioppiter. inmensum fingunt quem carmina uatum;
     i. nomen insulae
Nec fuit in   delo   mater. latona creatrix;

Cinthia non dicor. nec frater apollo uocatur
     s. nos
5   Sed potius summi genuit regnator olimpi

Qui nunc in caelis excelsae presidet arci;

Diuidimus mundum communi lege quadratum;

Nocturnos regimus cursus et frena dierum;
     ablatiuus
Ni soror et frater uaga saecula iure gubernent

10   Heu chaos inmensum fuscaret cuncta latebris.

Atraque nunc erebi regnarent tartara nigri;

    5 olimpi] olimphi MS

3 (rmarg97r11-12)

Latona mater apollinis quae matrem mercurii. magiam nomine genuit;

> Latona: cf. *Scholia Bernensia* at *Georgica* 3.6, "Latona quo tempore a Pythonte premebatur, quem draconem Iuno inmisit, Delon confugit, ubi Apollinem Dianamque procreauit." Cf. also *Commentum in Martianum Capellam* 3.82.10, "LATOIDES id est Apollo, Latonae filius"; and ibid. 7.364.1, "ATHLANTIADES patronomicum, id est Mercurius, filius Maiae, filiae Athlantis." Latona is traditionally the mother of Apollo and Diana, not of Maia.

4 (rmarg97r13-16)

Cinthia nomen deae i. diana. et sic nec diana. i. cinthia dicor. nec frater apollo. sicut
pagani pro sole appollinem. et pro ⟨luna⟩ cinthiam dicunt;

> luna] lunam MS

> Cinthia: cf. Augustine *De ciuitate Dei* 7.16, "Apollinem quamuis diuinatorem et
> medicum uelint, tamen ut in aliqua parte mundi statuerent, ipsum etiam solem
> esse dixerunt, Dianamque germanam eius similiter lunam."

4 (botmarg97r)

Isidorus dicit. Fuere apud gentiles ⟨duae⟩ sorores apud aliquem uirum qui uocabatur
apollo. et ⟨duae⟩ sorores. i. ops et deana. Postquam mortui sunt isti. translata sunt
nomina eorum super elementa. Apollo super solem. ops super terram. Deana super
lunam. et putauerunt gentiles lunam et terram facere zelum circa solem. ut terra zelum
contra lunam ut efficiat eclipsis;

> duae] duas MS   duae²] duas MS

ON THE SUN AND MOON

The villainous son of Saturn did not create us,
That Jupiter, who the songs of the poets say was enormous;
Nor was our mother Latona, of the isle of Delus;
I am not called Cinthia, nor is my brother named Apollo,
But rather the ruler of high Olympus created us,
Who now presides over the high citadel in the heavens.
We have divided the four-cornered world according to a mutual law;
We rule the courses of the night and hold the reins of the day.
If we, brother and sister, were not to govern the wandering world by our law
Alas! Immeasurable chaos would bury everything in the shadows
And the infernal regions of black Erebus would reign supreme.

Riddle 80   De calice vitreo

fol 97r22-97v9   Ehwald 80

DE CALICE VITREO.

1   De rimis lapidum profluxi flumine lento

Dum frangunt flammae. saxorum uiscera dura

Et laxis ardor fornacis regnat habenis;

Nunc mihi forma capax glacieque simillima lucet;
                                                        s. manu
5   Nempe uolunt plures collum constringere dextra

Et pulchre digitis lubricum conprendere corpus

Sed mentes muto dum labris oscula trado
            toaset
Dulcia conpressis inpendens bassia buccis

Atque pedum gressus titubantes sterno ruina;

> 5 Nempe] Nemphe MS

ON THE GLASS CHALICE

I poured forth in a slow river from rocky fissures
When flames broke the hard cores of stones,
And the heat of the furnace was given free rein.
Now my capacious form glimmers like ice.
Many wish to squeeze my neck in their right hand
And seize my beautifully smooth body with their fingers,
But I befuddle their minds when I put my mouth to their lips.
Giving sweet kisses to their tight-pressed lips,
I cause their staggering footsteps to fall.

Riddle 81   De lucifero

fol 97v10-20   Ehwald 81

DE LUCIFERO.

            meo
1 Semper ego clarum precedo lumine lumen.

Signifer et phoebi lustrat qui limpidus orbem
     i. pergens
Per caelum gradiens obliquo tramite flector
proprium
Eoas partes amo dum iubar inde meabit
         s. solis
5 Finibus indorum. cernunt qui lumina primi
    s. fui
O felix olim seruata lege tonantis

Heu post haec cecidi proterua mente superbus;

Ultio qua propter funestum perculit hostem;

Sex igitur comites mecum super aethera scandunt
  i. prudens
10 Gnarus quos poterit per biblos pandere lector;

> 4 prorium (*short for* proprium nominum): *The gloss* proprium *occurs over* amodum *in the* MS. *It makes better sense to read it over* Eoas, *although evidence from two other manuscripts shows that* amodum *was read as one word, perhaps mistakenly for* amodo. *P⁵ (fol. 103v) and S¹ (fol 43) both read:* amodum: i. magnopere.

9 (lmarg97v18-20)

Sex sidera errantia. i. sol. luna. mars. mercurius. ioppiter. ueneris. saturnus;

> *This gloss is repeated from Riddle 47 and is also found in the "Germanici Caesaris Aratea cum scholiis" p. 226.*

ON LUCIFER

I, with my light, always precede the bright sun;
I am the luminous standard-bearer of Phoebus, who wanders the world;
Climbing across the sky, I am bent on an oblique path.
I love the regions of Dawn, when the brilliant sun travels
To the land of the Indians, who first see the light.
Oh, I was happy once, when I obeyed the law of the Thunderer
But, alas! I fell, proud in my shameless soul,
When vengeance destroyed me, the fatal enemy.
Six companions now climb the heavens with me,
The learned reader can best explain who they are in books.

Riddle 82   De mustela

DE MUSTELA.

              s. ego
1 Discolor in curuas deflecto membra cauernas

   Pugnas exercens dira cum gente draconum;

   Non ego dilecta turgesco prole mariti
           ablatiuus
   Nec fecunda uiro sobolem sic edidit aluus

5 Residuae matres ut sumunt semina partus;
   pro sed
   Quin magis ex aure pregnantur uiscera foetu;

   Si uero proles patitur discrimina mortis

   Dicor habere rudem conponens arte medelam;

T (botmarg97v)

Duo genera mustellarum sunt. alterum siluestrae distans magnitudine. alterum in domibus oberrans. falso autem opinantur qui dicunt mustelam ore concipere aure effundere partum;

     Duo genera ... partum: Isidore *Etymologiae* 12.3.3

7 (rmarg98r5-7)

Si mortua fuerit eius proles potest suscitare uel uiuificare sua arte;

ON THE WEASEL

A many-hued creature, I bend my limbs in curved caverns,
Waging war against the savage race of snakes.

I do not grow big with the beloved child of my mate,
Nor does my womb, made fecund by a male, bring forth a child,
As other mothers do who receive the seed of birth,
But rather my belly is made pregnant through my ear;
And if my offspring suffer death
I am said to make a natural remedy with my skill.

Riddle 83   De iuvenco

DE IUVENCO.

1 Arida spumosis dissoluens faucibus ora

   Bis binis bibulus potum de fontibus hausi;

   Viuens nam terrae glebas cum stirpibus imis
                                    i. fructuosas
   Nisu uirtutis ualidae disrumpo feraces;

5 At uero linquit dum spiritus algida membra

   Nexibus horrendis homines constringere possum;

ON THE BULLOCK

Quenching my dry throat with foamy mouthfuls,
I have freely drunk the draughts of four fountains.
While alive, clods of fruitful earth, full of deep roots,
I break to pieces with the effort of great strength,
But when the spirit leaves my limbs cold,
I can bind men with fearful bonds.

Riddle 84   De scropha pregnante

fol 98r15-98v2   Ehwald 84

DE SCROPHA PREGNANTE

.*XII.*

1 Nunc mihi sunt oculi bisseni in corpore solo
s. caput uel nant
Bis ternumque caput sed caetera membra gubernat;

Nam gradior pedibus suffulta bis duodenis   *XXIIII. pedes*
XCVI. et VI.
Sed nouem decies sunt et sex corporis ungues;
i. coniunctos
uel congregatos
5 Sinzugias numero pariter similabo pedestres;
pluralis
Populus et taxus uiridi quoque fronde salicta

Sunt inuisa mihi; sed fagos glandibus uncas
et
Fructiferas itidem florenti uertice quercus

Diligo; sic nemorosa simul non spernitur ilex;

ON THE PREGNANT SOW

I have twelve eyes in one body
And six heads, but the one head governs these other members.
I walk supported by twenty-four feet,
Yet there are ninety-six claws in my body.
I appear in number like so many conjoined pedestrians.
The poplar, the yew and the willow with its green foliage
I despise, but the crooked beech with its nuts
And the fruit-bearing oaks with flowering tops
I love; nor do I scorn the bushy scarlet oak.

Riddle 85   De caeco nato

fol 98v3-9   Ehwald 85

DE CAECO NATO.

1   Iam referam uerbis tibi quod uix credere possis
      hit wunað
   Cum constet uerum. fallant nec friuola mentem.

   Nam dudum dederam soboli munuscula grata
      s. munuscula
   Tradere quae numquam poterat mihi quislibet alter
   i. postquam   *s. me*
5   Dum deus ex alto fraudaret munere claro.

   Inquo cunctorum gaudent precordia dono;

ON THE MAN BORN BLIND

My words will tell you something you can scarcely believe,
Although it is true and no tricks deceive your mind.
For I once gave a precious gift to my child,
Which no one else had been able to give to me,
Since god on high deprived me of a shining gift
In which the hearts of all rejoice.

Riddle 86   De ariete

DE ARIETE.

1   Sum namque armatus rugosis cornibus horrens.

Herbas aruorum buccis decerpo uirentes;
et tamen
Nec non astrifero procedens agmine stipor
         s. agmina   *s. cum*
Culmina caelorum quae scandunt celsa cateruis;

5   Turritas urbes capitis certamine quasso
                i. ciuitatibus
Oppida murorum prosternens arcibus altis;

Induo mortales contorto stamine pepli;

Littera quindecima prestat quod pars domus adsto;

     In other words, add p *to* aries *to obtain* paries *("wall").*

ON THE RAM

I am a fearful beast, armed with wrinkled horns;
I crop the green herbs of the fields with my mouth;
Yet also, I travel surrounded by a starry troop,
Which climbs the highest heights of heaven in bands.
I shake turreted cities with the ramming force of my head,
Laying low walled cities with their high citadels.
I clothe mortals in garments made of twisted thread;
The alphabet's fifteenth letter placed before my name makes me part of a
       house.

Riddle 87   De clipeo

fol 98v19-99r3   Ehwald 87

DE CLIPEO.

1   De salicis trunco pecoris quoque tergore raso
    i. pangor
    Conponor. patiens discrimina cruda duelli;
                        s. me
    Semper ego proprio gestantis corpore corpus
                            i. mors
    Conseruabo. uiri uitam ni dempserit orcus;
                    s. suscipit
5   Quis tantos casus aut quis tam plurima loeti

    Suscipit in bello. crudelis uulnera miles.

ON THE SHIELD

From the trunk of a willow and the scraped hide of a cow
I am made. Suffering the fierce savagery of war
I, with my own body, always save my bearer's body,
Unless death takes the man's life.
What fierce soldier endures such a fate
Or receives so many deadly wounds in war?

Riddle 88 De aspide

fol 99r4-11   Ehwald 88

DE ASPIDE VEL BASILISCO.

s. sum.

1 Callidior cunctis aura uescentibus aethrae;
            ex persona diaboli dicit. s. adae
   Late per mundum   dispersi   semina   mortis
            s. uirorum   i. malis.
   Unde horrenda seges diris succreuit   aristis
            i. maculator s. diaboli
   Quam metit ad scelera scortator falce maligna;
            pro ualde
   Cornigeri multum uereor certamina cerui;

   Namque senescenti spoliabor pelle uetustus

   Atque noua rursus fretus remanebo iuuenta;

3 (rmarg99r7)

Arista ab ariditate dicta;

> Arista ... dicta: Isidore *Etymologiae* 16.3.11 and 17.3.16, "Arena ab ariditate
> dicta"; "Arista appellata quod prius ipsa arescat."

ON THE SERPENT

I am more cunning than all other creatures who breathe the bright air;
I have scattered the seeds of death widely throughout the world,
And from the evil seed has grown a horrible grain,
Which the evil one with his wicked scythe reaps as sin.
I fear greatly the enmity of the antlered stag.
When old, I will be stripped of my withering skin
And clothed afresh, I will live with new youth.

Riddle 89 De arca libraria

fol 99r12-17   Ehwald 89

DE ARCA LIBRARIA.

1 Nunc mea diuinis complentur uiscera uerbis

   Totaque sacratos gestant precordia biblos;

   At tamen ex isdem nequeo cognoscere quicquam;
           ablatiuus
   Infelix fato fraudabor munere tali
           i. demunt.   *munera uel acumina*
5 Dum tollunt dirae librorum lumina parcae;

5 (rmarg99r16)

Dicunt gentiles quod parce habent potestatem fati;

> parcae: cf. Isidore *Etymologiae* 8.9.93, "Parcas ... appellatas, quod minime parcant. Quas tres esse voluerunt: unam, quae vitam hominis ordiatur; alteram, quae contexat; tertiam, quae rumpat."

ON THE BOOKCHEST

My inside is filled with divine words,
And my entire heart carries sacred books,
But I understand nothing of them
For I, cursed by destiny, am denied such a gift,
When the cruel Fates darken for me the light of books.

Riddle 90   De puerpera geminos enixa

DE PUERPERA GEMINOS ENIXA.

                                                     i. audiui
1 Sunt mihi sex oculi totidem simul auribus hausi;
         i. lx.
   Sed digitos decies senos in corpore gesto;
                     .x.
   Ex quibus ecce quater denis de carne reuulsis
                                     s. digitos
   .xx.   *uel tantum*   *i. iiii*
4 Quinquies at tamen uideo remanere quaternos;

ON THE WOMAN BEARING TWINS

I have six eyes and I hear with as many ears;
I bear sixty fingers and toes in my body.
Lo! when forty of these are torn from my flesh
I will have left only twenty.

Riddle 91   De palma

fol 99v1-12   Ehwald 91

DE PALMA

1   Omnipotens auctor nutu qui cuncta creauit

    Cui dedit. in mundo tam uictrix nomen habendum;

    Nomine nempe meo florescit gloria regum.
    s. gloria   s. florescit
    Martyribus nec non dum uincunt prelia mundi.
            upli⟨can⟩   s. dum
5   Aedita caelestis prensant et premia uitae;
                                he⟨k⟩mum⟩
    Frondigeris tegitur bellantum turma coronis
    s. densescit   in
    Et uiridi ramo uictor certamine miles.
                    s. et
    In summo capitis densescit uertice uellus
    s. uellere
    Ex quo multiplicis torquentur tegmina pepli;
                            s. homines i. pinguibus
10 Sic quoque mellifluis aescarum pasco   saginis
    ablatiuus
    Nectare per populos tribuens alimenta ciborum

        nempe] nemphe MS

ON THE PALM

To whom did almighty god, who created all things by his command,
Give such a name? To me in this world he gave the name 'Victorious'.
For in my name the glory of kings flourishes,
And martyrs, when they have won the struggles of the world,
Gain the outstanding prize of heavenly life.

The crowd of warriors is covered by my leafy crowns
And the soldier, the victor in battle, by my green branch.
A fleecy wool grows thick on the top of my head
From which are twisted many-folded robes.
I also nourish humans with honey-sweet food
And give rich feasts of nectar to the people.

Riddle 92 De pharo

fol 99v13-100r1

Ehwald 92

DE PHARO EDITISSIMO IN RUPIBUS PELAGI POSITO.

　　　　　　　　　　　　　　　　　　　　i. nœssas
1　Rupibus in celsis qua tundunt cerula cautes.
　　　i. maris　　　　　*s. qua*
　Et salis undantes turgescunt equore fluctus.
　　　　　　　i. magnis　　　　*i. ponderibus*
　Machina me summis construxit molibus amplam
　　　　　　　　i. uias
　Nauigeros calles ut pandam classibus index;

5　Non maris aequoreos lustrabam remige campos

　Nec ratibus pontum sulcabam tramite flexo;

　Et tamen inmensis errantes fluctibus actos
　　　　　　　　　　i. indicans
　Arcibus excelsis signans. ad litora duco;
　s. sum　　　　　　*i. ignes*　　*cautibus*
　Flammiger inponens torres in turribus altis
　　　　　　　　　i. abscondunt
10　Ignea brumales dum condunt sidera nymbi

ON A TALL LIGHTHOUSE STANDING ON THE ROCKS OF THE SEA

Among the high rocks, where the sea rushes into the headlands
And the flowing waves swell out of the salt sea,
Mechanic art built me on the highest ridge,
A signal to show a safe channel to ships.
I do not wander by oar over the watery field of the ocean,
Nor do I plow a rudder's crooked furrow in the sea,
But those wanderers driven by mountainous waves
I lead to shore, when I signal from the heights.
I am a flame-bearer burning bright in my high tower,
When wintry storm clouds hide the fiery stars.

Riddle 93   De scintilla

fol 100r2-13   Ehwald 93

DE SCINTILLA.

1   Quae rés in terris armatur robore tanto
    s. quae res   i. uti
    Aut paribus fungi nitatur uiribus audax;
                                    i. initia
    Parua mihi primo constant exordia uitae

    Sed gracilis grandes soleo prosternere loeto
        i. mortem   *s. mei uel silicis.*
5   Quod loetum proprii gestant penetralia uentris;

    Nam saltus nemorum densos pariterque frutecta

    Pinniferosque simul montes cum collibus altis.

    Truxque rapaxque capaxque feroxque sub aethere spargo;
        s. fui
    Et minor existens gracili quam corpore scnifes
            i. silex   s. me   i. silicis
10 Frigida dum genetrix dura generaret ab aluo.
                            i. scintillas.
    Primitus ex utero producens pignora gentis;

ON THE SPARK

What creature in this world is armed with such strength
Or is brave enough to use such powers?
At the beginning of my life I was small;
Though tiny, I can send great creatures to their death.
Both the shady depths of the forest and the open field,
Both the pine-covered mountains and the barren hills
I scatter, warlike, rapacious, all-embracing and fierce, beneath the sky.
And yet, with my tiny body, I was smaller than a flea,
When my cold mother first gave birth to me from her stony belly,
Bringing forth the heir of her race from her womb.

Riddle 94   De ebulo

fol 100r14-100v1   Ehwald 94

DE EBULO.   *wælwyrt*

                                  on   *hit*
1 Sambucus in silua. botris dum fronde rubescit
                   uel Nam   *truncus*   *on.*
  Est mihi par foliis: dum glesco surculus aruis

  Nigros baccarum portans in fronde corimbos;
  me   *i. per campos*
  Quem medici multum ruris per terga uirentem

5 Cum scabies morbi pulpas inrepserit aegras.
                                i. perhibentur.
  Lustrantes orbem crebro. quaesisse feruntur;
                         ablatiuus
  Clades horrendae dum uexant uiscera tabo.
                   i. adiuuare
  Ne uirus serpat possum succurrere leprae.

  Sic olidas hominum restaurans germine fibras;

ON THE DWARF ELDER

The elder tree, when it grows red with fruit in the forest,
Has leaves like mine, when I spring up in the fields,
Bearing black clusters of berries on my boughs.
I am the green plant that doctors are said to have sought in the country fields,
When scabies and sickness crept into ailing flesh;
They searched over all the world for me.
When the horrid leprosy torments people's viscera with its gore,
I can hinder the creeping virus
And restore evil-smelling bowels with my seed.

Riddle 95   De Scilla

fol 100v2-15   Ehwald 95

DE SCILLA. ID EST MARIS NIMPHA.

1   Ecce molosorum nomen mihi fata dederunt;
   i. grece
Argolicae gentis sic promit lingua loquelis
s. tempore   *i. filia apollinis*
Ex quo me dirae fallebant carmina circae

Quae fontis liquidi maculabat flumina uerbis.
cruraque   uel cruribus   s. et   *ge*
5   Femora cum coxis surras cum polite bino
       ipsa
Abstulit inmiscens crudelis uerba uirago;
               i. sonantia
Pignora nunc pauidi referunt ululantia nautae
i. remis   *i. naues*   *i. undas*
Tonsis dum trudunt classes. et cerula findunt
       nauigantes. uel
       trahentes
Vastos uerrentes fluctus grassante procella.
      ibi   *i. adiuuit   i. aperta*
10   Palmula qua remis succurrit panda per undas.
i. audiere

Auscultare procul quae latrant inguina circum
      i. fefellit.
      fraudauerat.
Sic me pellexit dudum titania proles

Ut merito uiuam salsis in fluctibus exul;

T (upmarg100v)

[Scilla filia] porci et cretidis nimphae pulcherrimae a glauco deo maris adamata est.
[et Circe] filia solis quae glaucum amauerat cum uiderit scillam frequentare ad alium
    fontem

[*ad lauan*]*dum iecit ueneficia in fontem. et in beluam marinam transfigurata est. et*
   fretum ⟨*siculum*⟩
obsedit. ibique pretereuntes naufragio afficiebat. eam neptunus percussit tridenti. et in
   scopulum
mutauit. et sonos undarum ⟨*populi*⟩ *putant. Unde uirgilius. canes in inguine scillae;;*

titania] ti_tania MS   siculum] silicum MS   populi] scopuli MS. *The
phrase* sonos undarum scopuli putant *makes little sense. The glossator seems to
be saying that people hear the sound of the waves on the rocks and think that these
are the dogs barking around Scilla's waist. This section of the gloss does not
appear in the "Scholia Bernensia."*

Scilla: cf. *Scholia Bernensia ad Vergili Bucolica atque Georgica* at *Ecloga*
6.74-77

T (lmarg100v1-2)

[... *rg. liæ . i.*] *filia*
[.... *is que*] *armi*
[.... *subm*]*ersit clas*
[......]*icis;*

T (lmarg100v3-6)

[.... *circ*]*e forsceop*
[*ða wif*] *þet hi of þem*
[*æfp*]*rigum gewiton*
[*in*] *sæ* ⏋ *wurdon to hun*
[*d*]*um.* ⌠ *gecweden;*
Scilla ðet is sǽhund

ON THE SEA NYMPH SCILLA

Lo! the fates gave me the name of a dog,
For so I am called in the Greek tongue,
From the time when the songs of savage Circe deceived me,
That Circe who stained the waters of the clear fountain with her words.
My legs, my knees, my calves and my thighs
The fierce witch stole way, chanting her spells.
Now frightened sailors say that they hear my wailing children,
When they row their ship with oars and split the sea,
Sailing the vast deeps before a pursuing storm;
As their flat oars help them through the waves,
From afar, they hear the creatures barking around my waist,
Thus the child of Titan deceived me long ago
And now I live, justly exiled, amid the salty waters.

Riddle 96   De elefanto

fol 100v16-101r10

Ehwald 96

DE ELEFANTO.

     s. et
1 Ferratas acies et denso milite turmas
       uel a   *uel quas*
    Bellandi miseros stimulat quos uana cupido.
          s. homines
    Dum maculare student armis pia foedera regni
    i. tuba bellandi s. dum
    Salpix et   sorbet uentosis flatibus auras
       i. sonanti   *uel resultant* . _   *genus tubae*
5 Raucaque clangenti rebohant dum classica sistro. *tuba*
                     i. tumultus   *i. belli*
    Cernere non pauidus didici trux murmura martis;

    Quamquam me turpem nascendi fecerat auctor

    Editus ex aluo dum sumpsi munera uitae.
               i. succedit   *uel formae*
    Ecce tamen morti successit gloria famae

10 Loetifer in fibras dum finis serpit apertas;
    i. lamina
    Brattea non auri fuluis pretiosa metallis.

    Quamuis gemmarum constent ornata lucernis
    s. me s. et   *s. ornamentorum*
    Vincere non quibunt falerarum floribus umquam;
              contra lignum iacet quando dormit;
    Me flecti genibus fessum natura   negauit
          i. oculis
15 Poplite seu curuo palpebris tradere somnos;

    Quin potius uitam conpellor degere stando;

ON THE ELEPHANT

Those dense crowds of soldiers and armed battalions,
Who are urged forward by the vain desire for war,
Who stain the noble peace of the kingdom with their arms,
When the trumpet fills its windy, hollow tubes with air
And the loud bugle resounds with a clanging rattle —
All this tumult of war I have learned to hear, fierce and unafraid.
Although god created me base of birth
When I came forth from the womb and received the gift of life,
Lo! the glory of my fame overtakes death,
When the final deathbringer creeps into my sinews and veins.
No gold leaf, most precious of tawny metals,
Though it be ornamented with lamplike gems
Can ever surpass me with its flowery trappings.
Nature forbade me, when tired, to fold my legs,
Or to give my eyes rest on bended knee,
Instead I am compelled to spend my life standing.

Riddle 97   De nocte

fol 101r11-21   Ehwald 97

Tres filiae ⟨plutonis⟩
DE NOCTE.   *regis inferni et noctis.*
                                   Megena. Allecto. et Tisiphone;

1 Florida me genuit nigrantem corpore tellus

   Et nil fecundum sterili de uiscere promo;
                    ipsi s. hoc   suo
   Quamuis eumenidum narrantes carmine uates
   i. infernalem   s. me
   Tartarem partu testentur gignere prolem.

5 Nulla mihi constat certi substantia partus;

   Sed modo quadratum complector cerula mundum;
        s. lux
   Est inimica mihi quae cunctis constat amica
        i. quamdiu   i. sol
   Saecula dum lustrat lampas titania phoebi;

   Diri latrones me semper amare solebant

10 Quos gremio tectos nitor defendere fusco;

   T plutonis] platonis MS

   T Tres filiae: cf. *Saeculi Noni auctoris in Boetii Consolationem Philosophiae
   commentarius* p. 219, "Utrices Deae dicuntur filiae Noctis, quae sunt tres quae
   puniunt sontes: Tisiphone, Megaera, Alcto."

   ON NIGHT

   The blooming earth bore me, black of hue,
   And I send forth no seed from my sterile womb,

Though the ancient prophets of the Eumenides tell in their poetry,
How I gave birth to the children of the underworld.
There is no substance to any part of me,
Yet even so, I embrace the sea and the four cornered earth.
My enemy, though it is a friend to all,
Is Phoebus' lamp, which traverses and illumines the earth.
Fierce thieves always love me, thieves
Whom I wrap in my dark bosom and try to defend.

Riddle 98   De fama

fol 101r22-101v6   Ehwald 97.11-16

DE FAMA.

      uel constat   *i. famam filiam terrae*

1 Virgilium fateor caram cecinisse sororem

    i. pergit   *i. terra*

Ingrediturque solo et caput inter nubila condit

                      s. sunt

Monstrum horrendum ingens cui quot sunt corpore plumae

Tot uigiles oculi subter mirabile dictu.

     s. et   *et* *s. monstrum*

5 Tot linguae totidem ora sonant tot subrigit aures;

Nocte uolat caeli medio terraeque per umbras;

    2-6 Virgil *Aeneid* 4.177, 181-184

ON FAME

I tell you that Virgil once described my dear sister thus:
'She walks on the earth and hides her head in the clouds,
A huge, horrible monster who has countless feathers on her body,
And under each, amazing to say, as many eyes, unblinking;
As many tongues and mouths call out; as many ears listen
She flies at night through the shadows, midway between earth and sky.'

Riddle 99   De elleboro

DE ELLEBORO.   *tunsinwyrt*

brunba⟨su⟩   i. crescebam   i. hirsutis
1   Ostriger en aruo uernabam frondibus hirtis
weolcscille.
Conquilio similis sic. cocci murice rubro.
                    uel de palmite   cum
Purpureus stillat sanguis de uertice   guttis;
                s. me i. gustanti
Exuuias uitae mandenti   tollere nolo;
i. lenia   s. homines   in
5   Mitia nec penitus spoliabunt mente uenena

Sed tamen insanum uexat dementia cordis
        s. homo
Dum rotat in gyro uechors uertigine membra;

    1 en] in MS

T (lmarg101v6-12)

Elleborum memorant greci circa eleborum fluuium ⟨quendam⟩ plurimum gigni atque
grecis appellatur. Hunc romani alio nomine uenatrum dicunt pro eo quod ⟨sumptum
motam⟩ mentem in sanitatem reducit. Duo autem sunt genera eius. album et nigrum;;

    quendam] quodda [*sic*] MS   sumptum motam] sumpta mutatim MS

    Elleborum ... nigrum: Isidore *Etymologiae* 17.9.24

ON THE HELLEBORE

I am purple and I grow on hairy stalks;
I am like a whelk, with a red shell of a berry;

A purple dye drips down from my crown like blood.
I do not wish to take the life of one who eats of me,
Nor will my mild venom fully destroy his reason,
Yet madness of the heart will make him a madman
And he will turn his limbs in circles, addle-brained.

Riddle 100   De camelo

fol 101v15-22   Ehwald 99

DE CAMELO.   *Camelus humiliatus interpretatur.*

Quia aliquis consul in roma sic nominatus erat. s. et
1   Consul eram quondam romanus miles equester

Arbiter imperio dum regni sceptra regebat;
                                    i. reportant
Nunc onus horrendum conuectant corpora gibbi
                        aduerbium
Et premit inmensum truculente sarcina molis;

5   Terreo cornipedum nunc uelox agmen equorum
                        uel u   i. cursu
Qui trepidi fugiunt mox quadripedante meatu
                s. illi equi
Dum trucis aspectant inmensos corporis artus;

> T Camelus humiliatus: cf. Isidore *Etymologiae* 12.1.35, "Camelis causa nomen dedit, sive quod quando onerantur, ut breviores et humiles fiant, accubant." Cf. also Gregory *Moralia in Job* 1.28.39, "Camelos quippe possidemus, si quod altum sapimus, humiliter deponamus."

T (lmarg 101v13-16)

Camelus animal est quod minime capitur a uenatoribus et cuicumque animali adheret.
sui coloris similitudinem retinet;

> The glossator has obviously confused the *camel* with the *chameleon*. Cf. Isidore *Etymologiae* 12.2.18, "Chamaeleon non habet unum colorem, sed diversa est varietate consparsus, ut pardus. Dictus autem ita ... Huius chamaeleontis corpusculum ad colores quos videt facillima conversione variatur, quod aliorum animalium non est ita ad conversionem facilis corpulentia."

ON THE CAMEL

I was once a Roman consul and knight
When the emperor carried the scepters of the reign.
Now an onerous burden lies on my humped body
And the weight of the pack cruelly crushes me, big though I am.
I terrify the swift herd of hoofed horses,
Who thunder away in swift, four-footed flight
When they glimpse the enormous limbs of my fierce body.

Riddle 101   De creatura

fol 102r1-22

Ehwald 100

DE CREATURA.

1 Conditor aeternis fulcit qui saecla columnis

Rector regnorum frenans et fulmina lege
i. quamdiu
Pendula dum patuli uertuntur culmina caeli:
i. mundus dicit

Me uariam fecit primo dum conderet orbem;
iuuabit
5 Peruigil excubiis numquam dormire ualebo

Sed tamen extimplo clauduntur lumina somno:
Ex natura elementorum dicit hanc sententiam;
Nam deus ut propria mundum dicione gubernat

Sic ego conplector sub caeli cardine cuncta;

*
Segnior est nullus quoniam me larbula terret;
s. sum
10 Setigero rursus constans audacior apro;

Nullus me superat cupiens uexilla triumphi

Ni deus aethrali summus qui regnat in arce;
s. sum   *reocende*
Prorsus odorato ture fraglantior halans
i. dulcedinis. proprium nomen holeris.
i. fetorem   *s. et*   *i. terrae.*
Olfactum ambrosiae nec non crescentia glebae

15 Lilia purpureus possum conexa rosetis

Vincere: spirantis nardi dulcedine plena;

Nunc olido ceni squalentis sorde putresco;

Omnia quaeque polo sunt subter et axe reguntur

i. postquam uel quamdiu   *i. natura quam deus condidit in me;*

Dum pater arcitenens concessit.   iure gúberno;

i. scrutor.
20   Grossas et graciles rerum conprenso figuras;

Altior en caelo rimor secreta tonantis

fol 102v1-22

Et tamen inferior terris tetra tartara cerno;

Nam senior mundo precessi tempora prisca.
                    i. annali
Ecce tamen matris orno generabar ab aluo;
            s. sum
25   Pulchrior auratis dum fulget fibula bullis
            s. sum
Horridior ramnis et spretis uilior algis;

Latior én patulis terrarum finibus exsto

Et tamen in media concludor parte pugilli;
        s. sum   *s. et   fulgente*
Frigidior brumis nec non candente pruina

30   Cum sim ulcani flammis torrentibus ardens;
            sum   *i. habundantis*
Dulcior in palato quam lenti nectaris haustus;
    i. amarior s. sum
Dirior   et   rursus quam glauca absinthia campi;
                    i. auidorum   ciclops. i. circulus.
Mando dapes mordax lurconum more cyclopum

Cum possim iugiter sine uictu uiuere felix;
        s. sum   suðernes   et
35   Plus pernix aquilis. zephiri uelocior alis
            s. sum
Nec non accipitre properantior. et tamen horrens   *hor‹sc›*
                    i. boïraca
Lumbricus et limax et tarda testudo palustris.

Atque fimi soboles sordentis cantarus ater.

on   *genetiuus*
Me dicto citius uincunt certamine cursus;

i. inclino
40 Sic grauior plumbo scopulorum pondera uergo

Sum leuior pluma cedit cui tippula limphae;
s. sum

Nam silici densas fundit quae uiscere flammas
s. sum durior   *s. sum*
Durior. aut ferro tostis sed mollior exstis;

fol 103r1-22

Cincinnos capitis nam gesto cacumine nullos
s. cincinni

45 Ornent qui frontem pompis et timpora setis;

Cum mihi cesaries uolitent de uertice crispae
gewalcudum

†   *of wolcspinle*
Plus calamistratis se comunt quae calamistro;

i. uerno.
Pinguior en multo scrofarum auxungia glesco

§
Glandiferis iterum referunt dum corpora fagis.
s. dum

50 Atque saginata laetantur carne subulci;

i. pauperum
Sed me dira fames macie torquebit egenum

Pallida dum iugiter dapibus spoliabor opimis;

i. circulo
Limpida sum fateor titanis clarior orbe;
s. sum

Candidior niuibus dum ningit uellera nimbus;
s. sum

55 Carceris et multo tenebris obscurior atris
s. sum obscurior
Atque latebrosis ambit quas tartarus umbris;

Ut globus astrorum plasmor teres atque rotunda.
sineweaʒlt> s. plasmor   *nominatiuus*
Sperula   seu pilae. nec non et forma cristalli;
swa seolcen ðræd
Et uersa uice protendor ceu serica pensa

i. uestem

60 In gracilem porrecta pannum ceu stamina pepli;
altus
Senis ecce plagis latus qua panditur orbis

Ulterior multo tendor mirabile fatu;
  #
Infra me supraue nihil per saecula constat

Ni rerum genitor mundum sermone coercens;
  s. sum ||
65 Grandior in glaucis ballena fluctibus atra

fol 103v1-19

s. sum
Et minor exiguo sulcat qui corpora uerme
mote
Aut modico phebi radiis qui uibrat atomo;
i. campos
Centenis pedibus gradior per gramina ruris

Et penitus numquam per terram pergo pedester;

70 Sic mea prudentes superat sapientia sophos

Nec tamen in biblis docuit me littera diues
i. scire
Aut numquam quiui quid constet sillaba nosse;
s. sum.
Siccior estiuo torrentis caumate solis
ablatiuus   s. sum
Rore   madens iterum plus udo flumine fontis;
  s. sum
75 Salsior et multo tumidi quam marmora ponti
i. maneo.
Et gelidis terrae limphis insulsior erro;
s. sum
Multiplici specie cunctorum compta colorum

Ex quibus ornatur presentis machina mundi

Lurida cum toto nunc sim fraudata colore;
uel mihi   s. ó i. fideles   i. dicta
80 Auscultate mei   credentes   famina uerbi

     ða   *ex*
Pandere quae poterit gnarus uix ore magister
     i. negans.
     contradicens i. arbitratur s. esse   ista
Et tamen inficiens non retur fribula lector;
s. ego creatura i. superbos
Sciscitor inflatos fungor quo nomine sophos;

EXPLICIUNT ENIGMATA ALDHELMI:

    9 me *added above the line*

T (upmarg102r)

Diuersitas creaturarum diuersitatem locutionis
in ista sententia ostendit de personis omnibus. et
naturis uniuscuiusque creaturae inter mortales et
uiuentes uisibilia et inuisibilia;

9 (rmarg102r9-12)

* *Larbas ex hominibus demones factos aiunt.*
qui meriti mali ⟨fuerint.⟩ quarum esse dicuntur
terrere paruulos et in angulis garrire tenebrosis;

      fuerint] fuerit MS

      Larbas: cf. Augustine *De civitate Dei* 9.11, "Laruas quippe dicit esse noxios
      daemones ex hominibus factos."

? (lmarg102v1-3)

[.........]*reuis*
[.......]*bus nas*
[......]*rporibus*
[..]*rastinus. hor*
[..]*notinus. diu*
[..]*atenus;*

47 (rmarg103r4-7)

† *Calamistrum ⟨acus est⟩ quae calefacta*
et ⟨adhibita⟩ calefacit et intorquet

⟨*capillos.*⟩ ⟨*Unde*⟩ *calamistrati appellantur*
qui comam torquent;

> acus est] acute MS   adhibita] adlibita MS   capillos] capillo MS
> Unde] Ante MS
>
> Calamistrum ... torquent: Isidore *Etymologiae* 20.13.5

49 (rmarg103r8-12)

§   *Fagus et esculus arbores glandiferae ideo*
uocatae creduntur. quia earum fructibus olim
homines uixerunt cibumque sumpserunt et escam
habuerunt. Esculus esca dicta;;

> Fagus ... dicta: Isidore *Etymologiae* 17.7.28

63 (rmarg103r19)

\#   *Dextram. et sinistram. sursum. et deorsum.*
supra. et infra;

65 (rmarg103r20-22)

‖   *Ballenae bestiae inmensae magnitudinis.*
uocatae ab emittendo. et fundendo aquas.
ceteris autem maris animalibus altius iaciunt
undas; Bal enim grece. mittere dicitur;

> Ballenae ... dicitur: Isidore *Etymologiae* 12.6.7

82 (lmarg103v16-17)

Negator. i. inficiator quia non fatetur. sed
contra ueritatem mendacium nititur;

> Negatur ... nititur: Isidore *Etymologiae* 10.49

ON CREATION

The creator who supports the world on eternal pillars,
The ruler of kingdoms, who reins in the lightning bolt,
As the pendulant dome of wide heaven turns,
Gave me many forms when he created the world.

5   Ever wakeful, I keep watch by night,
    Yet my eyes close at once in sleep;
    As god rules the world by his own governance,
    So I embrace all things beneath the bounds of the sky.
    No one is more of a coward than I, who am terrified by a ghost,
10 Yet I am also braver than a bristly boar;
    No one desiring the banners of victory can triumph over me,
    Except highest god who rules over the heavenly sphere.
    In truth, I am more fragrant than spicy incense
    Wafting forth its ambrosial smell; I surpass
15 The lilies of the field, entwined among the red roses,
    With the full sweetness of redolent balsam;
    Yet now I rot, in filthy, nasty, stinking foulness.
    I govern all things beneath the guiding vault of heaven
    As long as god the father, the ruler of heaven allows;
20 I encompass all things, large or small,
    Higher than the sky, I contemplate the secrets of the thunderer,
    And lower than the earth, I watch over black Tartarus.
    I was created in the beginning, older than the earth,
    Yet I emerged from my mother's womb just this year;
25 I am more beautiful than golden knobs on a shining clasp,
    More prickly than the buckthorn, cheaper than scorned seaweed;
    I am wider than the broad expanses of the earth,
    Yet I can be shut up in a tight-closed fist;
    I am colder than winter and the hoary frost,
30 Though I burn like the fierce flames of Vulcan;
    I am sweeter to taste than a draught of thick nectar,
    More bitter than the field's gray wormwood;
    A glutton, I eat my food like a greedy cyclops,
    Yet I could be happy with nary a meal;
35 I am faster than eagles, more fleet than Zephyrus' wings,
    Swifter than a hawk; and yet a timid
    Worm or snail or lumbering marsh turtle
    Or black worm, that springs from filthy dung,
    Can beat me in a race, faster than one could tell it;
40 Heavier than lead, I outweigh huge masses of rocks,
    Yet I am lighter than down, to which even the water strider yields;
    I am harder than flint, scattering sparks from my core,
    Harder than iron, yet softer than cooked liver;
    I wear no locks of hair to crown my head,
45 Adorning my brow and temples with showy curls;

Yet ringlets in masses fall around my face,
More crimped than if curled by an iron;
I am fatter by far than the larded sows
Who refresh their bodies from the nut-bearing beech trees,

50   Whose fatted flesh delights the swineherds,
Yet cruel hunger makes my body lean
As I, deprived of rich meals, grow pale;
I am more brilliant than the bright orb of Titan,
Whiter than snows falling like fleece from the clouds;

55   I am far darker than the black shades of prison
And darker than the shadows that Tartarus encloses;
I am shaped like the smooth, round globe of the stars,
Or the sphere of a ball or contour of crystal;
Contrarily, I am stretched out thin as Chinese silk,

60   Spread out like fine gauze or the threads of a robe;
I stretch beyond the six regions that measure the world,
And farther yet I extend, incredible but true;
Nothing in the world is higher or lower than I am,
Except the creator of all things, who constrains the world with a word.

65   I am larger than the black whale in the shining waves,
And smaller than the minute worm who feeds on corpses,
Or the tiny mote that dances in the rays of the sun.
I walk through the country fields on a hundred feet
Yet I have never been a pedestrian on this earth;

70   My wisdom surpasses that of the wisest scholars,
Yet no one learned in letters has taught me to read books
And I have never even known what constitutes a syllable;
I am drier than the summer heat of the burning sun,
Yet, moister than dew, I give more water than a gushing well;

75   I am more salty than the waves of the swelling sea,
Yet I flow sweeter than the cold, clear waters of the land;
I am rich-hued, adorned with every colour
Of the spectrum, that glorifies this present world,
Yet I am also pale and wan, deprived of all colour.

80   Take heed, oh believers, and listen to my words,
Which can scarce be explained by a work-skilled master;
Even a scornful infidel will not find them frivolous.
I ask all proud philosophers what name I bear!

Appendix A

Latin-Latin Lexical Glosses (Lemmata)

abscondens: i. recondens (58:5)
aceruos: cumulos (65:4)
achiuorum: i. grecorum (49:1)
aethere: pro aere (62:1)
alioquin: i. ideo (Prol:25)
almum: i. sanctum (31:6)
altrix: i. nutrix (1:1)
alta: i. cacumina (4:4)
ambrosiae: i. dulcedinis (101:14)
amnes: i. flumina (VP:32)
amoenam: i. pulchram (31:4)
anfractibus: i. obliquis (59:5)
anhelanti: i. spiranti (72:5)
apicibus: i. litteris (Prol:3)
arbiter: s. o censor i. iudex (VP:1)
arcibus: i. ciuitatibus (86:6)
arcister: uel arcifer i. arcum ferens
 (60:3)
argolicae: i. grece (95:2)
ars: i. natura (34:1)
arsantes: i. uociferantes (57:5)
atris: i. nigris (26:5)
auctor: i. pictor (72:1)
augmenta: i. incrementa (6:4)
aulis: pro angulis (55:3)
axi: i. polo (53:5)

bachi: i. uini uel falerni (78:1)
brattea: i. lamina (96:11)
brumae: i. hiemis (1:4)
buccis: i. oris (42:3)
bulla: uel gemma uel bula (55:5)

calibis: i. ferri (24:3)
calles: i. uias (92:4)

canantur: i. modulantur (Prol:21)
candente: fulgente (101:29)
candida: i. alba uel pulchra (30:1)
capellis: i. capris (61:3)
cardine: termino (58:2)
carmina: uel cantica (VP:21)
carpo: i. decarpo (33:3)
carpor: i. moueor (32:5)
cataplasma: i. medicina (46:8)
cateruatim: i. turmatim (35:2)
cauponis: i. pincerni (78:4)
cautibus: i. ⟨scopulis⟩ uel lapidibis
 (VP:32)
cautum: i. scriptum (Prol:117)
cecinisse: i. uaticinare (25:1)
celer: uel uelox (47:5)
censura: i. iudicium (50:2)
cephal: i. caput (VP:20)
cernenda: i. scrutanda (16:1)
(per) cerula: i. per undas (17:1)
cerula: i. nigra (59:4)
cerula: i. undas (95:8)
* cespite: i. tellure (33:2,3) (ms. stipite: i.
 tellure)
cessit: i. locum dedit uel se subdidit
 (19:2)
ceu: i. quasi (53:4)
ciclis: i. circulis (6:2, 47:2)
ciebunt: i. mouent (65:8)
(non) clamo: non uoco (VP:10)
clancula: i. occula i. misterium (Prol:29)
clandestina: i. obscura (VP:8)
clangenti: i. sonanti (96:5)
classes: i. naues (95:8)
cola: i. duo pedes (Prol: 23)

commata: i. particula uel conclusio (Prol:23)

commentis: i. machinis (Prol:9)

competentes: i. conuenientes(Prol:71)

compos: i. particeps (60:9)

condo: i. aspergo (39:4)

condunt: i. abscondunt (92:10)

congessimus: i. colligimus (Prol:136)

conpertum: inuentum (46:8)

conponor: i. pangor (87:2)

constat: i. uerum est (7:1)

constat: i. conuenit (28:6)

continetur: uel constat (Prol:103)

contorquens: i. iactans (60:3)

conuectant: i. reportant (100:3)

conuersor: ego maneo (75:3)

corda: i. sensus (VP:16)

coxis: uel cruribus (95:5)

crebello: i. cribro uel capisterium (67:T)

credentes: i. fideles (101:80)

crepacula: i. sonos (30:3)

crepitum: i. sonitum (2:2)

creta: pro creata nata uel formata (20:1)

cretus: i. pro creatus sum (14:2)

cretus: coadunatus (14:2)

crocea: i. fulua (20:3, 32:4)

croceo: i. fuluo (51:2)

cruento: i. sanguineo (35:3)

culinae: coquinae (39:4)

culmine: i. dignitate (38:5)

cum: i. quamdiu (14:3)

curam: i. sanitatem uel medicinam (42:6)

cursat: i. uergit (66:4)

decrescit: i. minuitur (6:3)

(ni) dempserit: i. si non minuit (26:4)

demto: i. diminuto (40:4)

deorsum: i. infra terram (53:3)

dicronas: duos temporales (Prol: 71)

dicunt: i. nominant (68:8)

digesta: i. narranda (Prol: 18)

dirior: i. amarior (101:32)

discrimine: i. differentiae (19:2) (sic)

ditis: i. mortis (67:7)

draconis: i. serpentis (23:1)

draconum: i. serpentium (30:7)

ducentes: i. trahentes (8:5)

dum: i. postquam uel quamdiu (101:19)

dum: i. postquam (85:5)

dum: i. quamdiu (97:8, 101:3)

durescit: s. in⟨durescit⟩ (67:9)

duxisti: s. pro⟨duxisti⟩ (VP:32)

egenum: i. pauperum (sic) (101:51)

elemento: i. alfabeto uel abdcario (29:T)

enigmata: i. misteria (Prol:6)

enucleamus: i. monstrauimus (Prol:69)

equore: i. planitudine (74:1)

erro: i. maneo (101:76) (sic) (read meo?)

exempta: i. prolata (32:7)

exilis: i. paruus uel modicus (28:3)

exordia: i. initia (93:3)

experto: i. inuento (25:3)

explosis: i. deletis. expulsis (VP:26)

exsto: i. sum (43:8)

extimplo: i. cito (75:8)

extinguitur: i. deletur (31:8)

factor: i. pictor (72:7)

facundum: i. eloquentem (7:1)

falerarum: s. ornamentorum (96:13)

famina: i. dicta (101:80)

famine: i. narratione (5:1)

farris: i. similae (65:4)

fata: i. naturam (43:4)

fati: uel uitae (74:2)

fatu: i. narratione (VP:8)

faxo: i. facio uel perficio (25:4)

fecerat: i. operatus est (10:2)

femora (cum): cruraque (95:5)

feraces: i. fructuosas (83:4)

fercula: obsonia (20:3)

ferro: i. stilo uel graphio (29:3)

fertur: dicitur (53:9). *See also* tulerunt

fertur: i. dicitur (23:1)

feruntur: i. perhibentur (94:6)

flagranti: i. urenti (15:4)
flammae: i. detrimenta (15:4)
flauescentibus: i. maturis (78:2)
foco: i. igni (15:3)
focos: faces (52:5)
foetus: i. pullos (46:5)
formatis: i. pulchris (VP:24)
fortunatus: i. ditatus uel felix (58:6)
frondescere: uirescere crescere (3:4)
frutescit: i. germinat (49:4)
fungi: i. uti (93:2)
fungor: i. utor (18:5)

garriat: i. uociferet (60:3)
garrulus: altisonans (25:1)
gelido: i. frigido (32:1)
gemmatis: i. ornatis (11:3)
genestarum: i. miricarum (12:3)
gerens: i. portans (10:3)
gero: i. porto (20:4)
gestamina: i. pondera (28:3)
gestat: i. portat (1:1)
gesto: porto (53:2)
gestu: i. actu (Prol:33)
girum: i. circuitum (47:8)
glebae: i. terrae (101:14)
glesco: i. uerno (101:48)
glescunt: i. crescunt (46:3)
gnarus: i. prudens (81:10)
gradiens: i. pergens (81:3)
gramina: i. campos (101:68)
gramine: i. semine uel germine (46:3)
grassantur: i. inpugnantur suffocantur (67:5)
gratia: i. causa (Prol:65)
gratia: i. merces (11:4)

heros: i. dominus (44:4)
hirtis: i. hirsutis (99:1)
horrida: i. niger (sum) (48:1)

iamdudum: i. olim (10:1)
ierunt: i. porrexerunt (Prol:38)
indidit: i. inseruit (60:10)

indomiti: i. non domiti (9:3)
infecta: i. mixta (75:12)
inficiens: i. negans. contradicens (101:82)
inflatos: i. superbos (101:83)
ingreditur: i. pergit (98:2)
instar: i. similitudo (43:7)
(ad) instar: i. ad similitudinem (31:5)
instincta: i. incensa (Prol:9)
inuisis: i. execrabilibus (65:4)
irrita: i. uana uel falsa (40:1)
istuc: i. huc (VP:10)
itidem: i. iterum (60:11)
ius: i. rectitudinem (50:3)

lacertos: i. brachia (38:3)
larem: ignem (54:3)
latens propositio: i. occultum eloquium (Prol:29)
latex: pro mare (6:4)
laticem: i. aquam (54:3)
latices: i. aquae (43:4)
laticum: i. fontium (VP:32)
latus: altus (101:61)
lethae: i. mortifera (53:8)
libros: i. cortices (33:3)
limite: i. termine (sic) (49:5)
limphida: i. liquida (VP:6)
loetum: i. mortem (93:5)
luce: i. in die (8:4)
(sub) luce: i. in die (34:3)
lucifer: i. sol (VP:23)
luebant: i. patiebantur (33:7)
lueret: i. passus est (76:7)
lumen: i. uisum (65:3)
lumina: i. oculos (46:7)
lumina: i. sidera (53:4, 58:5)
lurcones: i. raptores (69:7)
lurconum: i. auidorum (101:33)
lustro: i. peragro (5:4)
lustro: i. pergo (42:1)

madidis: i. humidis (3:4)
mandenti: i. gustanti (99:4)

mandit: i. comedit (66:6)
marmore: i. mari (VP:33)
martis: i. belli (60:1, 96:6)
meatu: i. cursu (100:6)
mihi: i. a me (28:6)
(si) minime: i. si non (Prol:15)
mitia: i. lenia (99:5)
moderante: i. disponente (4:1)
molibus: i. ponderibus (92:3)
molimina: machina consilia (VP:28)
monarchum: i. regem uel principem (Prol:37)
mortalibus: i. hominibus (50:4)
mulcifer: i. flammiger uel mortifer (26:4)
multarent: i. punirent (63:2)
multum: pro ualde (88:5)
mundi: i. caeli (53:1, 58:2)
munera: uel munia (72:2)
murmura: i. tumultus (96:6)

nantes: pro natantes (28:4)
natrix: i. serpens (23:4)
nec: s. etsi (VP:27)
nec non: et tamen (86:3)
nec non: s. et (101:14,29)
nequeam: i. non possum (18:4)
neuis: i. maculis (VP:26)
ni: see dempserit
nilotica: i. memphitica (33:6)
nimphas: i. deas (VP:10)
nitens: i. splendens (30:1)
nonnumquam: i. sepe (Prol:32)
normam: regulam (Prol:64)
normam: i. regulam (50:5)
nosse: i. scire (101:72)
noxas: i. culpas (VP:36)
nunc: i. aliquando (16:1, 31:4, 52:4)
nuncupor: i. uocor (1:2)

obliquat: i. curuat (31:5)
occiduo: i. uesperi (51:3)
occumbat: i. moritur (23:4)
olfactum: i. fetorem (101:14)

olimpi: i. caeli (24:1)
orbe: i. circulo (101:53)
orbem: i. mundum (2:2)
orco: i. loeti (70:7)
orcus: i. mors (87:4)
ornamenta: s. quae ornantur gemmis (11:3)
orno: i. annali (101:24)

pabula: i. cibaria (17:3)
palmis: i. manibus (2:1)
palpebris: i. oculis (96:15)
panda: i. aperta (95:10)
pandere: i. ostendere (VP:7)
pandere: i. pergere (59:6)
pando: i. ostendo (2:2)
pannum: i. uestem (101:60)
papillas: i. mamillas (1:3)
parma: i. scutum uel pelta (70:5)
patro: i. perficio (10:3)
pecudis: i. tauri (27:5)
pelasga: i. greca (34:6, 60:10)
pelasgo: i. greco (18:2)
pellaces: pro fallaces (57:2)
pellexit: i. fefellit. fraudauerat (95:12)
pelta: i. scutum (70:1)
pentimemeren: i. per quintem diuisionem (Prol:23)
per: i. circa (44:3)
peragro: i. circuo (2:4)
perhibentur: i. testantur (Prol:43)
(iuxta) perpendiculam: i. iuxta regulam (Prol:16)
perplexa: i. obscura dificillima (Prol:6)
phoebi: i. solis (25:2)
pignora: i. infantes (1:2)
plecteret: i. puniret (64:1)
poenorum: i. affricorum (41:6)
poetridis: i. poetae (Prol:103)
poli: i. caeli (4:4)
ponto: i. mari (53:4)
portendens: i. demonstrans uel significans (64:4)
posterius: uel post haec (Prol:13)

potiuntur: i. socientur (62:7)

praelatus: i. praepositus uel eleuatus (53:6)

prepes: i. ales (64:6)

preruptis: i. fractis (56:1)

presul: i. princeps i. dominator (VP:6)

profari: i. loqui (Prol:43)

prolui: i. ablui (Prol:75)

propalasse: i. colligere (Prol:67)

propositio: *see* latens

pugnas: i. proelia (48:4)

pulpas: i. carnes (39:4)

putidis: i. foetidis (61:3)

qua: ibi (95:10)

qua: i. ubi (55:7)

quadam: *see* ui

queam: i. possim (VP:8)

quin: pro sed 82:6)

quo: i. ubi (7:2)

rabidi: i. cupidi (69:7)

raris: i. paucis (63:3)

rationabilis creatura: i. homo (Prol:32)

rebohant: uel resultant (96:5)

reciprocis: i. iteratis (6:2)

redundans: i. habundans uel sufficiens (19:1)

refrager: i. contradicam. resistam (70:7)

rependis: i. reddis uel tribuis (VP:9)

rependunt: i. reddunt (VP:16)

rescindere: uel resistere (18:4)

reserat: aperit (55:2)

retexam: i. narrabo (5:2)

retro: i. ante (Prol:50)

retulit: i. narrauit (Prol:46)

retur: i. arbitratur (101:82)

reuinco: i. supero (24:4)

rictibus: i. faucibus (10:3)

rigida: i. dura (26:5)

rigidi: i. duri (9:1)

rigore: i. uirtute (43:1)

rimor: i. scrutor (101:21)

rite: i. iuste (34:1)

robora: i. trabes (28:2)

romuleis: i. latinis uel romanis (34:6)

rudimenta: i. alphabeta uel principia (Prol:11)

rudimenta: i. principia uel alphabeta (5:2)

rudimenta: i. principia (43:2)

rudis: neophitus (VP:7)

rura: i. terras (2:4)

ruris: i. terrae (33:2)

ruscis: i. frutectibus (68:7)

rusticitate: inprudentia (VP:26)

saginis: i. pinguibus (91:10)

salis: i. maris (92:2)

salpix: i. tuba bellandi (96:4)

satas: i. genitas (8:1)

sceptra: i. regna (7:4)

scortator: i. maculator (88:4)

scrutetur: i. meditetur (18:5)

secto: i. raso (61:6)

septum: i. circumdatum (33:4)

serena: i. clara (34:3)

seres: i. orientales (32:4)

setigeras: i. hyrsutas (35:5)

setigeris: i. hirsutis (12:2)

setigero: i. hyrsuto (32:2)

signans: i. indicans (92:8)

singulas: i. uarias (Prol:3)

sinzugias: i. coniunctos uel congregatos (84:5)

sistro: tuba (96:5)

sollicitudo: i. curiositas (Prol:8)

solo: i. terra (98:2)

spatior: i. pergo (41:4)

spatior: i. ambulo (36:2)

spicula: i. sagittas (32:7, 60:3)

spurius: i. inmundus uel ignobilis (27:4)

squalida: i. sordida (41:4)

sternunt: i. perimunt (44:7)

stimulans: i. instigans (68:2)

stimulis: i. unguibus (35:1)

stipite: *see* cespite

stolidae: i. stultae (VP:15)

stragula: uestimenta (44:6)

sub: *see* luce

subnixum: proficientem uel suffultum (39:5)

succurrere: i. adiuuare (94:8)

succurrit: i. adiuuit (95:10)

summis: i. magnis (92:3)

surculus: truncus (94:2)

tam: i. sic (3:3)

tantum: i. tam ualde (1:2)

tartaream: i. infernalem (97:4)

tellure: i. in terra (3:2)

tempnere: i. spernere (50:3)

teres: i. rotundus (47:2)

tetro: i. nigro (30:7)

titan: i. sol (58:3)

tollens: i. eleuans (VP:20)

tollunt: i. demunt (89:5)

tonsis: i. remis (95:8)

toros: i. cutes (35:7)

torre: i. igni (15:4)

torre: i. ardore (9:2)

torres: i. ignes (92:9)

torribus: i. ignibus (26:5)

torsisti: i. curuasti (VP:4)

tosta: i. exusta (52:8)

(aethera) tranet: i. uolitet (47:6)

trano per aethera: i. uolito (41:3)

tricent: i. tardent (47:9)

tropica: uel mistica (18:3)

trucido: uel trudo (60:7)

trudit: i. conpellit (47:8)

tulerunt: i. tenuerunt (46:2). *See also* fertur

tulerunt: abs⟨tulerunt⟩ (46:2)

ualeo: i. possum (2:3)

udae: i. humidae (52:6)

uegetat: i. confortat (71:4)

ueho: i. porto (44:3)

(haud) uereor: i. non timeo (38:5)

uereor: i. timeo (32:7)

(non) uereor: i. non timeo (9:1)

ueretur: uel timet pertimescit (3:3)

uergo: i. inclino (101:40)

uernabam: i. crescebam (99:1)

uernans: i. crescens (51:1)

uerrentes: nauigantes uel trahentes (95:9)

uescor: i. utor (56:9)

uexilla: i. opera (VP:18)

ui quadam: i. aliqua uirtute uel fortitudine (24:4)

uictus: i. extinctus (43:8)

uis: i. fortitudo (24:1)

uito: i. pretereo uel fugio (10:4)

uix: i. statim (70:6)

ululantia: i. sonantia (95:7)

uolitans: i. tranans (47:7)

uolitantis: i. uolantis (29:4)

uolucris: i. auis (29:4)

ut: i. similiter (6:3, 18:2)

uulgi: i. populi (32:6)

Appendix B

Latin-Latin Lexical Glosses (Glosses)

a: (28:6). *See* me
abcdario: elemento (29:T)
ablui: prolui (Prol:75)
abscondunt: condunt (92:10)
abs⟨tulerunt⟩: tulerunt (46:2)
actu: gestu (Prol:33)
ad: (31:5). *See* similitudinem
adiuuare: succurrere (94:8)
adiuuit: succurrit (95:10)
aere: aethere (62:1)
affricorum: poenorum (41:6)
alba: candida (30:1)
ales: prepes (64:6)
alfabeto: elemento (29:T)
aliqua uirtute: ui quadam (24:4)
aliquando: nunc (16:1, 31:4, 52:4)
alphabeta: rudimenta (Prol:11, 5:2)
altisonans: garrulus (25:1)
altus: latus (101:61)
amarior: dirior (101:32)
ambulo: spatior (36:2)
angulis: aulis (55:3)
annali: orno (101:24)
ante: retro (Prol: 50)
aperit: reserat (55:2)
aperta: panda (95:10)
aquae: latices (43:4)
aquam: laticem (54:3)
arbitratur: retur (101:82)
arcifer: arcister (60:3)
arcum ferens: arcister (60:3)
ardore: torre (9:2)
aspergo: condo (39:4)
auidorum: lurconum (101:33)

auis: uolucris (29:4)

bellandi: (96:4). *See* tuba
belli: martis (60:1)
brachia: lacertos (38:3)
bula: bulla (55:5)

cacumina: alta (4:4)
caeli: mundi (53:1, 58:2)
caeli: olimpi (24:1)
caeli: poli (4:4)
campos: gramina (101:68)
cantica: carmina (VP:21)
capisterium: crebello (67:T)
capris: capellis (61:3)
caput: cephal (VP:20)
carnes: pulpas (39:4)
causa: gratia (Prol:65)
censor: arbiter (VP:1)
cibaria: pabula (17:3)
circa: per (44:3)
circuitum: girum (47:8)
circulis: ciclis (6:2, 47:2)
circulo: orbe (101:53)
circumdatum: septum (33:4)
circuo: peragro (2:4)
cito: extimplo (75:8)
ciuitatibus: arcibus (86:6)
clara: serena (34:3)
coadunatus: cretus (14:2)
colligere: propalasse (Prol:67)
colligimus: congessimus (Prol:136)
comedit: mandit (66:6)
conclusio: commata (Prol:23)

confortat: uegetat (71:4)

congregatos: sinzugias (84:5)

coniunctos: sinzugias (84:5)

conpellit: trudit (47:8)

consilia: (VP:28). *See* machina

constat: continetur (Prol:103)

contradicam: refrager (70:7)

contradicens: inficiens (101:82)

conuenientes: competentes (Prol:71)

conuenit: constat (28:6)

coquinae: culinae (39:4)

cortices: libros (33:3)

creata: creta (20:1)

creatus sum: cretus (14:2)

crescebam: uernabam (99:1)

crescens: uernans (51:1)

crescere: frondescere (3:4)

crescunt: glescunt (46:3)

cribro: crebello (67:T)

cruraque: femora (cum) (95:5)

cruribus: coxis (95:5)

culpas: noxas (VP:36)

cumulos: aceruos (65:4)

cupidi: rabidi (69:7)

curiositas: sollicitudo (Prol:8)

cursu: meatu (100:6)

curuasti: torsisti (VP:4)

curuat: obliquat (31:5)

cutes: toros (35:7)

deas: nimphas (VP:10)

decarpo: carpo (33:3)

dedit: (19:2). *See* locum

deletis: explosis (VP:26)

deletur: extinguitur (31:8)

demonstrans: portendens (64:4)

demunt: tollunt (89:5)

detrimenta: flammae (15:4)

dicitur: fertur (53:9)

dicta: famina (101:80)

(in) die: luce (8:4)

(in) die: (sub) luce (34:3)

differentiae: discrimine (19:2)

dificillima: (Prol:6). *See* obscura

dignitate: culmine (38:5)

diminuto: dempto (40:4)

disponente: moderante (4:1)

ditatus: fortunatus (58:6)

diuisionem: (Prol:23). *See* quintem

dominator: presul (VP:6)

dominus: heros (44:4)

domiti: (9:3). *See* non

dulcedinis: ambrosiae (101:14)

duo pedes: cola (Prol:23)

duos temporales: dicronas (Prol:71)

dura: rigida (26:5)

duri: rigidi (9:1)

ego: (75:3). *See* maneo

eleuans: tollens (VP:20)

eleuatus: praelatus (53:6)

eloquentem: facundum (7:1)

eloquium: (Prol:29). *See* occultum

est: (10:2). *See* operatus

est: (76:7). *See* passus

est: (7:1). *See* uerum

et: (86:3). *See* tamen

et: nec non (101:14, 101:29)

etsi: nec (VP:27)

execrabilibus: inuisis (65:4)

expulsis: explosis (VP:26)

extinctus: uictus (43:8)

exusta: tosta (52:8)

faces: focos (52:5)

falerni: bachi (78:1)

fallaces: pellaces (57:2)

falsa: irrita (40:1)

faucibus: rictibus (10:3)

fefellit: pellexit (95:12)

felix: fortunatus (58:6)

ferens: (60:3). *See* arcum

ferri: calibis (24:3)

fetorem: olfactum (101:14)

fideles: credentes (101:80)

flammiger: mulcifer (26:4)

flumina: amnes (VP:32)

foetidis: putidis (61:3)

fontium: laticum (VP:32)
formata: creta (20:1)
fortitudine: ui quadam (24:4)
fortitudo: uis (24:1)
fractis: preruptis (56:1)
fraudauerat: pellexit (95:12)
frigido: gelido (32:1)
fructuosas: feraces (83:4)
frutectibus: ruscis (68:7)
fugio: uito (10:4)
fulgente: candente (101:29)
fulua: crocea (20:3, 32:4)
fuluo: croceo (51:2)

gemma: bulla (55:5)
gemmis: (11:3). See quae
genitas: satas (8:1)
germinat: frutescit (49:4)
germine: gramine (46:3)
graphio: ferro (29:3)
greca: pelasga (34:6, 60:10)
grece: argolicae (95:2)
greco: pelasgo (18:2)
grecorum: achiuorum (49:1)
gustanti: mandenti (99:4)

habundans: redundans (19:1)
haec: (Prol:13). See post
hiemis: brumae (1:4)
hirsutis: hirtis (99:1)
hirsutis: setigeris (12:2). See hyrsutas,
    hyrsuto
hominibus: mortalibus (50:4)
homo: rationabilis creatura (Prol:32)
huc: istuc (VP:10)
humidae: udae (52:6)
humidis: madidis (3:4)
hyrsutas: setigeras (35:5). See hirsutis
hyrsuto: setigero (32:2)

iactans: contorquens (60:3)
ibi: qua (95:10)
ideo: alioquin (Prol:25)
ignem: larem (54:3)

ignes: torres (92:9)
igni: foco (15:3)
igni: torre (15:4)
ignibus: torribus (26:5)
ignobilis: spurius (27:4)
in: (8:4, 34:3). See die
in: (3:2). See terra
incensa: instincta (Prol:9)
inclino: uergo (101:40)
incrementa: augmenta (6:4)
indicans: signans (92:8)
in<durescit>: durescit (67:9)
infantes: pignora (1:2)
infernalem: tartaream (97:4)
infra terram: deorsum (53:3)
initia: exordia (93:3)
inmundus: spurius (27:4)
inprudentia: rusticitate (VP:26)
inpugnantur: grassantur (67:5)
inseruit: indidit (60:10)
instigans: stimulans (68:2)
inuento: experto (25:3)
inuentum: conpertum (46:8)
iteratis: reciprocis (6:2)
iterum: itidem (60:11)
iudex: arbiter (VP:1)
iudicium: censura (50:2)
iuste: rite (34:1)
iuxta: (Prol:16). See regulam

lamina: brattea (96:11)
lapidibus: cautibus (VP:32)
latinis: romuleis (34:6)
lenia: mitia (99:5)
liquida: limphida (VP:6)
litteris: apicibus (Prol:3)
locum dedit: cessit (19:2)
loeti: orco (70:7)
loqui: profari (Prol:43)

machina consilia: molimina (VP:28)
machinis: commentis (Prol:9)
maculator: scortator (88:4)
maculis: neuis (VP:26)

magnis: summis (92:3)
mamillas: papillas (1:3)
maneo: erro [sic; ?meo] (101:76)
(ego) maneo: conuersor (75:3)
manibus: palmis (2:1)
mare: latex (6:4)
mari: ponto (53:4)
mari: marmore (VP:33)
maris: salis (92:2)
maturis: flauescentibus (78:2)
(a) me: mihi (28:6)
medicina: cataplasma (46:8)
medicinam: curam (42:6)
meditetur: scrutetur (18:5)
memphitica: nilotica (33:6)
merces: gratia (11:4)
(non) minuit: (ni) dempserit (26:4)
minuitur: decrescit (6:3)
miricarum: genestarum (12:3)
misteria: enigmata (Prol:6)
misterium: clancula (Prol:29)
mistica: tropica (18:3)
mixta: infecta (75:12)
modicus: exilis (28:3)
modulantur: canantur (Prol:21)
monstrauimus: enucleamus (Prol:69)
moritur: occumbat (23:4)
mors: orcus (87:4)
mortem: loetum (93:5)
mortifer: mulcifer (26:4)
mortifera: lethae (53:8)
mortis: ditis (67:7)
mouent: ciebunt (65:8)
moueor: carpor (32:5)
mundum: orbem (2:2)
munia: munera (72:2)

narrabo: retexam (5:2)
narranda: digesta (Prol:18)
narratione: famine (5:1)
narratione: fatu (VP:8)
narrauit: retulit (Prol:46)
nata: creta (20:1)
natantes: nantes (28:4)

natura: ars (34:1)
naturam: fata (43:4)
naues: classes (95:8)
nauigantes: uerrentes (95:9)
negans: inficiens (101:82)
neophitus: rudis (VP:7)
niger: horrida (48:1)
nigra: cerula (59:4)
nigris: atris (26:5)
nigro: tetro (30:7)
nominant: dicunt (68:8)
(si) non: (si) minime (Prol:15)
non: (26:4). See minuit
non: (9:1, 38:5). See timeo
non domiti: indomiti (9:3)
non possum: nequeam (18:4)
nutrix: altrix (1:1)

obliquis: anfractibus (59:5)
obscura: clandestina (VP:8)
obscura dificillima: perplexa (Prol:6)
obsonia: fercula (20:3)
occulta: clancula (Prol:29)
occultum eloquium: latens propositio
  (Prol:29)
oculis: palpebris (96:15)
oculos: lumina (46:7)
olim: iamdudum (10:1)
opera: uexilla (VP:18)
operatus est: fecerat (10:2)
orientales: seres (32:4)
oris: buccis (42:3)
ornamentorum: falerarum (96:13)
ornantur: (11:3). See quae
ornatis: gemmatis (11:3)
ostendo: pando (2:2)
ostendere: pandere (VP:7)

pangor: conponor (87:2)
particeps: compos (60:9)
particula: commata (Prol:23)
paruus: exilis (28:3)
passus est: lueret (76:7)
patiebantur: luebant (33:7)

paucis: raris (63:3)

pauperum: egenum (101:51)

pedes: (Prol:23). *See* duo

pelta: parma (70:5)

peragro: lustro (5:4)

perficio: faxo (25:4)

perficio: patro (10:3)

pergens: gradiens (81:3)

pergere: pandere (59:6)

pergit: ingreditur (98:2)

pergo: lustro (42:1)

pergo: spatior (41:4)

perhibentur: feruntur (94:6)

perimunt: sternunt (44:7)

pertereo: uito (10:4)

pertimescit: ueretur (3:3)

pictor: auctor (72:1)

pictor: factor (72:7)

pincerni: cauponis (78:4)

pinguibus: saginis (91:10)

planitudine: equore (74:1)

poetae: poetridis (Prol:103)

polo: axi (53:5)

pondera: gestamina (28:3)

ponderibus: molibus (92:3)

populi: uulgi (32:6)

porrexerunt: ierunt (Prol:38)

portans: gerens (10:3)

portat: gestat (1:1)

porto: gero (20:4)

porto: gesto (53:2)

porto: ueho (44:3)

post haec: posterius (Prol:13)

postquam: dum (85:5)

possim: queam (VP:8)

possum: ualeo (2:3)

possum: (18:4). *See* non

postquam: dum (85:5)

praepositus: praelatus (53:6)

princeps: presul (VP:6)

principem: monarchum (Prol:37)

principia: rudimenta (Prol:11, 5:2, 43:2)

pro⟨duxisti⟩: duxisti (VP:32)

proelia: pugnas (48:4)

proficientem: subnixum (39:5)

prolata: exempta (32:7)

prudens: gnarus (81:10)

pulchra: candida (30:1)

pulchram: amoenam (31:4)

pulchris: formatis (VP:24)

pullos: foetus (46:5)

punirent: multarent (63:2)

puniret: plecteret (64:1)

quae ornantur gemmis: ornamenta (11:3)

quamdiu: dum (97:8, 101:3)

quamdiu: cum (14:3)

quasi: ceu (53:4)

(per) quintem diuisionem: pentimemeren (Prol:23)

raptores: lurcones (69:7)

raso: secto (61:6)

recondens: abscondens (58:5)

rectitudinem: ius (50:3)

reddis: rependis (VP:9)

reddunt: rependunt (VP:16)

regem: monarchum (Prol:37)

regna: sceptra (7:4)

(iuxta) regulam: (iuxta) perpendiculam (Prol:16)

regulam: normam (50:5)

remis: tonsis (95:8)

reportant: conuectant (100:3)

resistam: refrager (70:7)

resistere: rescindere (18:4)

resultant: rebohant (96:5)

romanis: romuleis (34:6)

rotundus: teres (47:2)

sagittas: spicula (60:3)

sanctum: almum (31:6)

sanguineo: cruento (35:3)

sanitatem: curam (42:6)

scire: nosse (101:72)

scopulis: cautibus (VP:32)

scriptum: cautum (Prol:117)

scrutanda: cernenda (16:1)
scrutor: rimor (101:21)
scutum: parma (70:5)
scutum: pelta (70:1)
se subdidit: cessit (19:2)
sed: quin (82:6)
semine: gramine (46:3)
sensus: corda (VP:16)
sepe: nonnumquam (Prol:32)
serpens: natrix (23:4)
serpentis: draconis (23:1)
serpentium: draconum (30:7)
sic: tam (3:3)
sidera: lumina (53:4, 58:5)
significans: portendens (64:4)
similae: farris (65:4)
similiter: ut (6:3, 18:2)
(ad) similitudinem: (ad) instar (31:5)
similitudo: instar (43:7)
socientur: potuntur (62:7)
sol: lucifer (VP:23)
sol: titan (58:3)
solis: phoebi (25:2)
sonanti: clangenti (96:5)
sonantia: ululantia (95:7)
sonitum: crepitum (2:2)
sonos: crepacula (30:3)
sordida: squalida (41:4)
spernere: tempnere (50:3)
spiranti: anhelanti (72:5)
splendens: nitens (30:1)
statim: uix (70:6)
stilo: ferro (29:3)
stipite: (33:2,3). See tellure
stultae: stolidae (VP:15)
sub luce: (34:3). See (in) die
subdidit: (19:2). See se
sufficiens: redundans (19:1)
suffocantur: grassantur (67:5)
suffultum: subnixum (39:5)
sum: (14:2). See creatus
sum: exsto (43:8)
superbos: inflatos (101:83)
supero: reuinco (24:4)

tam ualde: tantum (1:2)
(et) tamen: nec non (86:3)
tardent: tricent (47:9)
tauri: pecudis (27:5)
tellure: cespite [MS stipite] (33:2,3)
temporales: (Prol:71). See duos
tenuerunt: tulerunt (46:2)
termine [sic]: limite (49:5)
termino: cardine (58:2)
(in) terra: tellure (3:2)
terra: solo (98:2)
terrae: glebae (101:14)
terrae: ruris (33:2)
terras: rura (2:4)
testantur: perhibentur (Prol:43)
timeo: uereor (32:7)
(non) timeo: (non) uereor (9:1)
(non) timeo: (haud) uereor (38:5)
timet: ueretur (3:3)
trabes: robora (28:2)
trahentes: ducentes (8:5)
trahentes: uerrentes (95:9)
tranans: uolitans (47:7)
tribuis: rependis (VP:9)
trudo: trucido (60:7)
truncus: surculus (94:2)
tuba: sistro (96:5)
tuba bellandi: salpix (96:4)
tulerunt: (46:2). See abs⟨tulerunt⟩
tumultus: murmura (96:6)
turmatim: cateruatim (35:2)

ualde: multum (88:5)
ualde: (1:2). See tam
uana: irrita (40:1)
uarias: singulas (Prol:3)
uaticinare: cecinisse (25:1)
ubi: qua (55:7)
ubi: quo (7:2)
uelox: celer (47:5)
uergit: cursat (66:4)
uerno: glesco (101:48)
uerum est: constat (7:1)
uesperi: occiduo (51:3)

uestem: pannum (101:60)
uestimenta: stragula (44:6)
uias: calles (92:4)
uini: bachi (78:1)
uirescere: frondescere (3:4)
uirtute: rigore (43:1)
uirtute: (24:4). *See* aliqua
uisum: lumen (65:3)
uitae: fati (74:2)
undas: cerula (17:1)
unguibus: stimulis (35:1)

uociferantes: arsantes (57:5)
uociferet: garriat (60:3)
uoco: clamo (vp:10)
uocor: nuncupor (1:2)
uolantis: uolitantis (29:4)
uolitet: aethera tranet (47:6)
uolito: trano per aethera (41:3)
urenti: flagranti (15:4)
uti: fungi (93:2)
utor: fungor (18:5)
utor: uescor (56:9)

Appendix C

The Old English Glosses

æ⟨blæce⟩: pallida (101:52)

æspringum: *see* circe

and: *see* circe

asigan: succumbere (53:9)

assirisce: seres (32:4)

beoð: conspicimur (8:4)

botraca: testudo (101:37)

brunba⟨su⟩: ostriger (99:1)

cambas: cristas (25:5)

ceuwð: ruminat (66:6)

cinum: rimis (21:2)

circe forsceop ða wif þet hi of þem ⟨æspringum⟩ gewiton in sæ 7 wurdon to hundum (95:T)

clyþan: cataplasma (46:8)

cnosle: prolem (46:5)

cynnes: gentis (46:5)

dæl: *see* limes

denn *uel* fereldu: lustra (65:6)

fereldu: *see* denn

feðriað: plumescunt (41:1)

finnum: squamis (16:2)

forsceop: *see* circe

fylle: lapsu (62:2)

ge: bino (95:5)

ge wole: pestemque (56:8)

⟨g⟩earwe: millefolium (49:T)

gecweden: *see* Scilla

gecyrnode: serratas (25:5)

geryflodre: rugoso (39:1)

geþoht: mentis (VP:28)

geþu⟨f⟩: uirescens (44:1)

gewalcudum: calamistratis (101:47)

gewiton: *see* circe

goldwyrt: solsequium (51:T)

gyrre: *see* ic

haswre: *see* ic

hel⟨mum⟩: coronis (91:6)

hi: *see* circe

hindergenga: retrograda (36:3)

hit: rubescit (94:1)

hit wunað: constet (85:2)

hi⟨wung⟩: error (VP:27)

hor⟨sc⟩: properantior (101:36)

hroðrunge: *see* ic

hundum: *see* circe

hwearft: errat (53:6)

hyda: tergora (31:3)

ic gyrre mid haswre hroðrunge: Garrio...rauco cum murmure (21:5)

ic þy: trudo (35:4)

ican: rubetae (33:5)

in: *see* circe

is: *see* Scilla

kene: belliger (56:2)

lim: cola (Prol:23)

limes dæl: commata (Prol:23)

mid: *see* ic

mote: atomo (101:67)

mugan: aceruos (65:4)

næssas: cautes (92:1)

Nycticorax: Romuleis scribor biblis sed uoce pelasga (34:6)

of: *see* circe

of: sole (5:3)

of wolcspinle: calamistro (101:47)

on: fronde (94:1)

on: aruis (94:2)

on: certamine (101:39)
reocende: halans (101:13)
sæ: see circe
sæhund: *see* Scilla
Scilla ðet is sæhund gecweden: De Scilla
   (95:T)
seolcen: *see* swa
sinewea⟨lt⟩: sperula (101:58)
sint: replentur (12:2)
staðum: ripis (56:1)
su⟨n⟩derboren: nothas (29:2)
suðernes: zephiri (101:35)
swa: sic (6:4)
swa seolcen ðræd: ceu serica pensa
   (101:59)
swe⟨tnysse⟩: see þa
syfeda: furfurae (67:T)
to: *see* circe
toaset: conpressis (80:8)
tunsinwyrt: elleboro (99:T)
tyrninge: uertigine (44:3)
ða: *see* circe
þa: quae (101:81)
þa swe⟨tnysse⟩: hoc nectar (78:7)
þem: *see* circe
ðet: *see* Scilla

þet: *see* circe
þræd: *see* swa
þwancgas: calciamenta (31:3)
þy: *see* ic
undeð: pandit (55:2)
unsmeþust: asperrima (21:4)
unsoðe: irrita (40:1)
upli⟨can⟩: caelestis (91:5)
wælwyrt: ebulo (94:T)
wa: Sed sopor et somnus ieiunia longa
   tulerunt (46:2)
wambe: uentris (54:3)
wearwe [*sic*]: *see* ⟨g⟩earwe
webb: telas (12:1)
wegan: trutina (50:T)
weolcscille: conquilio (99:2)
wif: *see* circe
wo⟨h⟩: uaga (65:6)
wolcspinle: *see* of
wole: *see* ge
wunað: *see* hit
wurdon: *see* circe
wynn (rune): Dilicias epulas regum
   luxusque ciborum (39:3)
7: *see* circe

Appendix D

Index to the Interpretative and Encyclopedic Glosses

metrorum. *See* octo
Minois (27:5)
Minotaurus (27:5)
miraculum (3:4)
mirmicaleon (18:T)
mono enim graece pes latine (Prol:77)
monoceron (60:10)
monoscemi (Prol:77)
mors (87:4)
mortales (101:T)
Moyses? [damaged] (VP:17)
mundi. *See* creatione
mundum (3:3)
mundus (76:2; 101:4)
munuscula (85:4)
muricae (17:1)
Musarum (VP:13)
mustella (82:T)

natura (4:T; 34:1; 43:4; 47:1; 101:7;
    101:19)
naturae. *See* donum
nectar (VP:11)
negator (101:82)
Neptunus (95:T)
nicticorax (34:T)
Nilo flumine (33:6)
niue (67:7)
niuem (67:3)
nomen. *See* proprium
nomen artis (Prol:119)
nomen auis (59:1)
nomen montis (8:1)
nomen paludis inferni (53:8)
nothus (27:3)
nox (4:3)

occasus (58:2)
octo principalia genera metrorum
    (Prol:59)
October (46:T)
onocratulus (59:2)
ops. *See* Isidorus
ops (1:T)

orbatus (63:10)
orbus (63:10)
organum (13:T)
oriens (58:2)
ostrea (36:T)
ouium (17:2)

palmite (99:3)
paludis. *See* nomen
Parcae (44:5; 89:5)
Parnasso (VP:13)
Parnassus (VP:13)
peccatores (18:3)
pedes. *See* septies
penna (29:5)
pentimemeris (Prol:23)
persona (88:2)
pes. *See* mono
pignus (1:2)
pincerni (78:4)
piper (39:T)
piscis. *See* genus
plaustrum (53:2)
Pliades (8:T)
poeta (28:1)
poetae (7:3)
princeps (Prol:40)
principilia genera metrorum. *See* octo
prologum (Prol:17)
proprium nomen holeris (101:14)
puer. *See* Ganimedis
pugio (61:T)
pulcherrimus puer. *See* Ganimedis
pulpa (14:4)
purpura (17:T)
pyrate. *See* cacuma duplex

Q (29:2)

ramosus (44:1)
reges (Prol:40)
Roma (100:1)

salamandra (15:T)

X (29:2)
Y (29:2)

Z (29:2)
Zinzugia (Prol:58)

Appendix E

Index of Sources used by the Glossator
of Royal 12.c.xxiii

Bibliography

MANUSCRIPTS

See Chapter 1.

REFERENCE WORKS

Bosworth, J. and T.N. Toller, eds. *An Anglo-Saxon Dictionary.* 1898; repr. Oxford: Oxford University Press, 1976.

Cappelli, Adriano, ed. *Dizionario di abbreviature latine ed italiane.* 6th ed., Milan: Ulrico Hoepli, 1961.

Clark Hall, J.R. and H.D. Meritt, eds. *A Concise Anglo-Saxon Dictionary.* 1960; Medieval Academy Reprints for Teaching. Toronto: University of Toronto Press, 1984.

Du Cange, Charles Du Fresne. *Glossarium mediae et infimae latinitatis.* 10 vols. Paris: Librairie des Sciences et des Arts, 1840-1850.

Frank, Roberta and Angus Cameron. *A Plan for the Dictionary of Old English.* Toronto: University of Toronto Press, 1973.

Glare, P.G.W., ed. *Oxford Latin Dictionary.* Oxford: Oxford University Press, 1982.

Gneuss, Helmut. "A Preliminary List of Manuscripts Written or Owned in England up to 1100." *Anglo-Saxon England* 9 (1981): 1-60.

Healey, Antonette diPaolo and Richard L. Venezky, compilers. *A Microfiche Concordance to Old English.* Publications of the Dictionary of Old English. Toronto: Dictionary of Old English, 1980.

Ker, Neil R. *Catalogue of Manuscripts Containing Anglo-Saxon.* Oxford: Oxford University Press, 1957.

——. *Medieval Libraries of Great Britain.* 2nd ed., London: Royal Historical Society, 1964.

Latham, Ronald E. *Revised Medieval Latin Word List from British and Irish Sources.* London: Oxford University Press for The British Academy, 1965.

——. *Dictionary of Medieval Latin from British Sources* [Fascicule 1: A-B, Fascicule 2: C]. London: Oxford University Press for The British Academy, 1975-.

Lewis, Charlton T. and Charles Short, eds. *A Latin Dictionary.* Oxford: Clarendon Press, 1879.

Liddell, H.G. and Robert Scott, eds. *A Greek-English Lexicon.* New edition revised by Henry S. Jones. Oxford: Clarendon Press, 1940.

The Oxford English Dictionary. 12 vols. and supplement. Oxford: Oxford University
    Press, 1933.
Temple, Elzbieta. *Anglo-Saxon Manuscripts 900-1066.* London: Harvey-Miller,
    1976.
Thesaurus linguae latinae. Leipzig: Teubner, 1925-1934.
Thompson, Edward M. *Catalogue of Ancient Manuscripts in the British Museum.*
    Vol. 2. London: British Museum, 1884.
Warner, George F. and Julius P. Gilson. *Catalogue of Western Manuscripts in the
    Old Royal and King's Collections in the British Museum.* Vol. 2: *Royal
    Manuscripts 12.A.I to 20.E.X and App. 1-89.* London: British Museum, 1921.
Warwick, Henrietta Holm, ed. *A Vergil Concordance.* Minneapolis: University of
    Minnesota Press, 1975.

PRIMARY SOURCES

Ælfric. *Aelfrics Grammatik und Glossar.* Ed. Julius Zupitza. 2nd ed., Berlin:
    Weidmannsche Buchhandlung, 1966.
Alcuin. *Carmina.* Ed. Ernst Dümmler. MGH: Poet. Lat. 1: 160-351. 1881.
——. *De orthographia.* In Keil 7: 295-312.
——. *Grammatica.* PL 101: 849-902.
Aldhelm. *Enigmata.* Ed. Fr. Glorie. CCSL 133: 359-540. Turnhout: Brepols, 1968.
The Riddles of Aldhelm. Trans. James Hall Pitman. Yale Studies in English 67. New
    Haven: Yale University Press, 1925.
——. *Aldhelm's "De laudibus Virginitatis"; with Latin and Old English Glosses.
    Manuscript 1650 of the Royal Library in Brussels* [Facsimile]. Introduction by
    George van Langenhove. Bruges: Saint Catherine Press, 1941.
——. *De Metris et Enigmatibus ac Pedum Regulis* (also known as the *Epistola ad
    Acircium*). Ed. Rudolf Ehwald. MGH: Auct. Ant. 15: 35-207. 1919.
——. *Aldhelmi Opera Omnia.* Ed. Rudolf Ehwald. MGH: Auct. Ant. 15. 1919.
——. *Aldhelm: The Poetic Works.* Trans. Michael Lapidge and James L. Rosier.
    Cambridge and Dover, New Hampshire: D.S. Brewer, 1985.
——. *Aldhelm: The Prose Works.* Trans. Michael Lapidge and Michael Herren.
    Cambridge: D.S. Brewer; Totowa, N.J.: Rowman and Littlefield, 1979.
Arator. *Aratoris subdiaconi de actibus Apostolorum.* Ed. A.P. McKinlay. CSEL 72.
    1951.
Aratus, Solensis. *Germanici Caesaris Aratea cum Scholiis.* Ed. Alfred Breysig, 1867;
    repr. Hildesheim: Olms, 1967.
Augustinus. *De catechizandis rudibus.* Ed. I.B. Bauer. CCSL 46: 121-178.
——. *De ciuitate Dei.* Ed. Bernard Dombart and Alphonse Kalb. CCSL 47, 48. 1955.
——. *De doctrina christiana.* Ed. Joseph Martin. CCSL 32: 1-167. 1962.
——. *De trinitate libri XV.* Ed. W.J. Mountain and Fr. Glorie. CCSL 50. 1968.
——. *Enarrationes in Psalmos I-L.* Ed. Eligius Dekkers and Johannes Fraipont.
    CCSL 38-40. 1956.
Beda Venerabilis. *De arte metrica.* Ed. C.B. Kendall. CCSL 123A: 82-141. 1975.

——. *De orthographia.* Ed. Charles W. Jones. CCSL 123A: 7-57. 1975.

——. *De schematibus et tropis.* Ed. C.B. Kendall. CCSL 123A: 142-171. 1975.

Biblia sacra cum glossa ordinaria, primum quidem a Strabo Fuldensis collecta. 7 vols. Paris: Franciscus Fevardentium, 1590.

Biblia Sacra iuxta Vulgatam versionem. Ed. Robert Weber. Stuttgart: Deutsche Bibelgesellschaft, 1983.

Boniface. *Epistolae.* Ed. Michael Tangl. MGH: Epist. Sel. 1. 1916.

Burnam, John Martin, ed. *Commentaire anonyme sur Prudence d'après le manuscrit 413 de Valenciennes.* Paris: A. Picard, 1910.

Carmody, Francis J., ed. *Physiologus Latinus.* Paris:Droz, 1939.

Cassiodorus. *Expositio in Psalterium.* PL 70: 25-1056.

——. *De schematibus in Commentarium Cassiodori in Psalmos occurrentibus.* PL 70: 1269-1280.

Diomedes. *Ars grammatica libri III.* In Keil 1: 299-529.

Dobbie, Elliott van Kirk, ed. *The Anglo-Saxon Minor Poems.* The Anglo-Saxon Poetic Records 6. New York: Columbia University Press, 1942.

Donatus. *Ars grammatica.* In Keil 4: 367-402.

——. *De Partibus Orationis Ars Minor.* In Keil 4: 353-366.

Ehwald, Rudolf. *See* Aldhelm.

Eusebius. *Enigmata.* Ed. Maria de Marco. CCSL 133: 209-271. 1968.

Garmonsway, George Norman, ed. *Ælfric's Colloquy.* Rev. ed., Exeter: Exeter University Press, 1978.

Glorie, Fr., ed. *Variae Collectiones aenigmatum merovingicae aetatis.* CCSL 133A: 1968.

Goetz, Georg. *Corpus glossariorum latinorum a Gustavo Loewe inchoatum.* 7 vols. Leipzig: Teubner, 1888-1923.

Goossens, Louis, ed. *The Old English Glosses of MS Brussels Royal Library 1650 (Aldhelm's De laudibus virginitatis).* Verhandelingen van de Koninklijke Academie voor Wetenschapen, Letteren en Schone Kunsten van België, Klasse der Letteren 74. Brussels, 1974.

Gregory. *Moralia in Job.* PL 75: 509-1162, 76: 9-782.

——. *Moralia in Job.* Ed. M. Adriaen. CCSL 143, 143A, 143B.

Hagen, Hermann, ed. *Scholia Bernensia ad Vergili Bucolica atque Georgica.* 1867; repr. Hildesheim: Olms, 1967.

Herren, Michael W., ed. *The Hisperica Famina I: The A-Text.* Studies and Texts 31. Toronto: Pontifical Institute of Mediaeval Studies, 1974.

Holder, Alfred. "Die Bouloneser Angelsächsischen Glossen zu Prudentius", *Germania. Vierteljahrsschrift für Deutsche Alterthumskunde,* pp. 385-403. Wien: Verlag von Carl Gerold's Sohn, 1878.

Iohannes Scottus. *Annotationes in Marcianum.* Ed. Cora Lutz. Cambridge, Mass.: Mediaeval Academy of America, 1939.

Isidore of Seville. *Traité de la Nature.* Ed. Jacques Fontaine. Bibliothèque de l'École des hautes études hispaniques 28. Bordeaux: Feret, 1960.

——. *De proprietate sermonum uel rerum.* Ed. Myra L. Uhlfelder. Papers and Monographs 15. Rome: American Academy in Rome, 1954.

——. *Isidori Hispalensis episcopi etymologiarum siue originum libri XX.* Ed. W.M. Lindsay. 1911; repr. Oxford: Clarendon Press, 1957.

——. *Etimologias.* Edicion Bilingüe. Ed. José Or os Reta and Manuel A. Marcos Casquero. 2 vols. Madrid: Biblioteca de Autores Cristianos, 1983.

Julian of Toledo. *Liber prognosticorum futuri saeculi.* Ed. J.N. Hillgarth. CCSL 115: 11-126. 1976.

Juvencus. *Evangeliorum libri quattuor.* Ed. Johannes Huemer. CSEL 24. 1891.

Keil, Heinrich. *Grammatici Latini.* 8 vols. 1857-1880; repr. Hildesheim: Olms, 1961.

Kindschi, L. *The Latin-Old English Glossaries in Plantin-Moretus MS. 32 and BM MS. Add. 32246.* PhD dissertation. Stanford University, 1955.

Krapp, G.P. and E.V.K. Dobbie, eds. *The Exeter Book.* The Anglo-Saxon Poetic Records 3. New York: Columbia University Press, 1936.

Lindsay, Wallace M. *The Corpus, Epinal, Erfurt and Leyden Glossaries.* London: Publications of the Philological Society 8, 1921.

——. *The Corpus Glossary; with an Anglo-Saxon Index* by Helen McM. Buckhurst. Cambridge: Cambridge University Press, 1921.

Logeman, H., "New Aldhelm Glosses." *Anglia* 13 (1891): 26-41.

Malius Theodorus. *De Metris.* In Keil 6: 581-601.

Marius Servius Honoratus Grammaticus. *De Centum Metris.* In Keil 6: 456-472.

Martianus Capella. *Martianus Capella.* Ed. Adolfus Dick; addenda Jean Préaux. 1925; repr. Stuttgart: Teubner, 1969.

McCann, Justin trans. *The Rule of Saint Benedict.* London, 1952.

Meritt, Herbert D. "Old English Aldhelm Glosses." *Modern Language Notes* 67 (1952): 553-554.

——. "Old English Glosses, Mostly Dry Point." *Journal of English and Germanic Philology* 60 (1961): 441-450.

——. *Some of the Hardest Glosses in Old English.* Stanford: Stanford University Press, 1968.

——. *Old English Glosses: A Collection.* 1945; repr. New York: Kraus 1971.

——. *The Old English Prudentius Glosses at Boulogne-sur-Mer.* Stanford Studies in Language and Literature 16. Stanford, 1959.

Napier, Arthur S., ed. *Old English Glosses Chiefly Unpublished.* Anecdota Oxoniensa. Medieval and Modern Series 11. Oxford: Clarendon Press, 1900.

Oliphant, Robert T. *The Harley Latin-Old English Glossary edited from British Museum MS Harley 3376.* Janua linguarum; Studia memoriae Nicolae van Wijk dedicata, Series practica 20. The Hague: Mouton, 1967.

Page, R.I., ed. "Anglo-Saxon Scratched Glosss in a Corpus Christi College, Cambridge Manuscript." In *Otium et Negotium: Studies in Onomatology and Library Science presented to Olof von Feilitzen,* ed. F. Sandgren, pp. 209-215. Acta Bibliothecae Regiae Stockholmiensis 16. Stockholm: P.A. Norstedt and Soner, 1973.

Pheifer, J.D. *Old English Glosses in the Epinal-Erfurt Glossary.* Oxford: Oxford University Press, 1974.

Pompeius. *Commentum artis Donati.* In Keil 5: 95-312.

Priscianus. *Institutionum grammaticarum libri XVIII.* In Keil 2, and 3: 1-384.

Prudentius. *See* Holder and Meritt.

Remigius of Auxerre. *Remigii Autissiodorensis Commentum in Martianum Capellam.* Ed. Cora Lutz. 2 vols. Leiden: Brill, 1965.

Rypins, Stanley, ed. *Three Old English Prose Texts in* MS. *Cotton Vitellius A xv.* EETS 161. London: Published for EETS by Oxford University Press, 1924.

Saeculi Noni Auctoris in Boetii Consolationem Philosophiae Commentarius. Ed. Edmund T. Silk. Rome: American Academy in Rome, 1935 [tentatively ascribed to Joannes Scottus].

Sedulius. *Sedulii opera omnia.* Ed. Johannes Huemer. CSEL 10. 1885.

Servius. *Servianorum in Vergilii carmina commentariorum.* Ed. E.K. Rand et al. Harvard edition. Special Publications 1. Lancaster, Pa: American Philological Association, 1946.

Sisam, Celia and Kenneth Sisam, eds. *The Salisbury Psalter.* EETS 242. London: Published for EETS by Oxford University Press, 1959.

Smith, A.H., ed. *Three Northumbrian Poems: Caedmon's Hymn, Bede's Death Song and the Leiden Riddle.* 2nd ed. London: Methuen, 1968.

Steinmeyer, Elias and Eduard Sievers. *Die althochdeutschen Glossen.* 5 vols. Berlin: Weidmannsche Buchhandlung, 1879-1922.

Stryker, William G. *The Latin-Old English Glossary in* MS. *Cotton Cleopatra AIII.* PhD dissertation. Stanford University, 1951.

Symphosius. *Enigmata.* Ed. Fr. Glorie. CCSL 133A: 611-723. 1968.

Tatwine. *Enigmata.* Ed. Maria de Marco. CCSL 133: 165-208. 1968.

Tupper, Frederick. *The Riddles of the Exeter Book.* 1910; repr. Darmstadt: Wissenschaftliche Buchgesellschaft, 1968.

Vergil. *The Aeneid.* Ed. R.D. Williams. 2 vols. London: Macmillan; New York: St. Martin's Press, 1972-1973.

——. *Bucolica et Georgica.* Ed. T.E. Page. London: Macmillan, 1898.

Williams, Mary Jane. *The Riddles of Tatwine and Eusebius.* PhD dissertation. University of Michigan, Ann Arbor, 1974.

Williamson, Craig. *The Old English Riddles of the Exeter Book.* Chapel Hill: North Carolina University Press, 1977.

Wright, Thomas and R.P. Wülcker. *Anglo-Saxon and Old English Vocabularies.* 2nd ed., 2 vols. London: Trübner, 1884.

Zupitza, J. "Altenglische Glossen", *Zeitschrift für deutsches Altertum und deutsche Literatur* 33 (1889): 237-242.

——. *See also* Ælfric.

SECONDARY SOURCES

Bierbaumer, Peter. *Der botanische Wortschatz in altenglischen Glossen.* 3. Teil. Der botanische Wortschatz des Altenglischen. Frankfurt am Main, 1979.

Bishop, T.A.M. *English Caroline Minuscule.* Oxford: Oxford University Press, 1971.

Bishop, T.A.M. "Notes on Cambridge Manuscripts." *Transactions of the Cambridge Bibliographic Society* 1 (1949-53): 432-440; 2 (1954-58): 185-199, 323-336; 3 (1959-63): 93-95, 412-423; 4 (1964-68): 70-76, 246-252, 396-400.

Blair, Peter H. *The World of Bede.* London: Secker and Warburg, 1970.

———. *An Introduction to Anglo-Saxon England.* 2nd ed. Cambridge: Cambridge University Press, 1977.

Bolton, W.F. *A History of Anglo-Latin Literature I: 597-740.* Princeton: Princeton University Press, 1967.

———. "Pre-Conquest Anglo-Latin: Perspectives and Prospects." *Comparative Literature* 23 (1971): 151-166.

Boyer, Blanche B. "Insular Contribution to Medieval Literary Tradition on the Continent" [Part 1]. *Classical Philology* 42 (1947): 209-222.

Bradley, Henry. "Remarks on the Corpus Glossary." *Classical Quarterly* 13 (1919): 89-108.

Brown, T.J. "An Historical Introduction to the Use of Classical Latin Authors in the British Isles from the Fifth to the Eleventh Century." In *La cultura antica nell'occidente latino dal VII all'XI secolo,* 18-24 aprile 1974, pp. 238-299. Settimane di studio del centro italiano di studi sul'alto medioevo 22. Spoleto, 1975 for 1974.

Bullough, D.A. "The Educational Tradition in England from Alfred to Ælfric: Teaching *utriusque linguae.*" In *La scuola nell'occidente latino dell'alto medioevo,* 15-21 aprile 1971, 2: 453-494. Settimane di studio del centro italiano di studi sull'alto medioevo 19. Spoleto, 1972.

Butt, John J. "The Ninth-Century Library at St. Gall." St. Gall and the Middle Ages. *Cuyahoga Review* 1.1 (Spring 1983): 73-76.

Byrne, Mary. *The Tradition of the Nun in Medieval England.* Washington DC: The Catholic University of America Press, 1932.

Cameron, M.L. "Aldhelm as Naturalist: A Re-examination of Some of his Enigmata." *Peritia* 4 (1985): 117-133.

Campbell, J.J. "Learned Rhetoric in Old English Poetry." *Modern Philology* 63 (1966): 189-201.

———. "Knowledge of Rhetorical Figures in Anglo-Saxon England." *Journal of English and Germanic Philology* 66(1967): 1-20.

Cross, James E. "The Literate Anglo-Saxon: On Sources and Disseminations." *Proceedings of the British Academy* 58 (1972): 67-100.

———. *Latin Themes in Old English Poetry.* Bristol: J.W. Arrowsmith, 1962.

Derolez, René. "Zu den Brüsseler Aldhelmglossen." *Anglia* 74 (1956): 153-180.

———. "Aldhelmus Glosatus III." *English Studies* 40 (1959): 129-134.

———. "Aldhelmus Glosatus IV: Some Hapax Legomena among the Old English Aldhelm Glosses." *Studia Germanica Gandensia* 2 (1960): 81-95.

———. "Anglo-Saxon Literature—Attic or Asiatic? Old English Poetry and its Latin Background." In G.A. Bonnard, *English Studies Today,* pp. 93-105, Bern, 1961; repr. in *Essential Articles for the Study of Old English,* ed. Jess B. Bessinger and Stanley Kahrl, pp. 46-63. Hamden, CT: Archon Books, 1968.

———. Review of *The Harley Latin-Old English Glossary*, ed. R.T. Oliphant. *English Studies* 51 (1970): 149-151.

Draak, M. "Construe-Marks in Hiberno-Latin Manuscripts." *Mededelingen der Koninklijke Nederlandse Akademie van Wetenschappen, afd. Letterkunde* [Nieuwe Reeks] 20 (1957): 261-282.

Dumville, David. "English Libraries Before 1066: Use and Abuse of the Manuscript Evidence." In *Insular Latin Studies*, ed. Michael Herren, pp. 153-178. Papers in Mediaeval Studies. Toronto: Pontifical Institute of Mediaeval Studies, 1981.

Erhardt-Siebold, Erika von. *Die lateinischen Rätsel der Angelsachsen: Ein Beitrag zur Kulturgeschichte Altenglands*. Heidelberg: Carl Winter, 1925.

———. "Aldhelm in Possession of the Secrets of Sericulture." *Anglia* 60 (1936): 384-389.

Garmonsway, G. "The Development of the Colloquy." In *The Anglo-Saxons: Studies in some Aspects of their History and Culture, presented to Bruce Dickins*, ed. Peter Clemoes, pp. 248-261. London: Bowes and Bowes, 1959.

Gneuss, Helmut. "The Origin of Standard Old English and Æthelwold's School at Winchester." *Anglo-Saxon England* 1 (1972): 63-83.

Gough, J.V. "Some Old English Glosses." *Anglia* 92 (1974): 273-290.

Greenfield, Stanley B. and Fred C. Robinson, eds. *A Bibliography of Publications on Old English Literature to the End of 1972*. Toronto: University of Toronto Press, 1980.

Grosjean, Paul. "Confusa Caligo." *Celtica* 3 (1956): 35-85.

Hellmann, Siegmund. *Sedulius Scottus*. Quellen und Untersuchungen zur lateinischen Philologie des Mittelalters 1. Munich: C.H. Beck, 1906.

Herren, Michael. "Hisperic Latin—'Luxuriant Culture-Fungus of Decay'." *Traditio* 30 (1974): 411-419.

Holtz, Louis. "La Typologie des Manuscrits Grammaticaux Latins." *Revue d'Histoire des Textes* 7 (1977): 147-269.

Howe, Nicholas. "Aldhelm's Enigmata and Isidorian Etymology." *Anglo-Saxon England* 14 (1985): 37-60.

Jones, P.F. "The Gregorian Mission and English Education." *Speculum* 3 (1928): 335-348.

Kerlouegan, François. "Une Mode Stylistique dans la Prose Latine des Pays Celtiques." *Études Celtiques* 13 (1972): 275-297.

Knowles, David. *The Monastic Order in England*. Cambridge: Cambridge University Press, 1963.

Korhammer, Michael. "Mittelalterliche Konstruktionshilfen und Altenglische Wortstellung." *Scriptorium* 34 (1980): 18-58.

Lagorio, Valerie M. "Aldhelm's Aenigmata in Codex Vaticanus Palatinus latinus 1719." *Manuscripta* 15 (1971): 23-27.

Laistner, M.L.W. *Thought and Letters in Western Europe AD 500-900*. New rev. ed. Ithaca: Cornell University Press, 1957.

Lapidge, Michael. "The Hermeneutic Style in 10th Century Anglo-Latin Literature." Anglo-Saxon England 4 (1975): 67-111.

———. "Aldhelm's Latin Poetry and Old English Verse." *Comparative Literature* 31 (1979): 209-231.

———. "St. Dunstan's Latin Poetry." *Anglia* 98(1980): 101-106.

———. "The Present State of Anglo-Latin Studies." In *Insular Latin Studies*, ed. Michael Herren, pp. 45-82. Papers in Mediaeval Studies. Toronto: Pontifical Institute of Mediaeval Studies, 1980.

———. "Beowulf, Aldhelm, the *Liber Monstrorum* and Wessex." *Studi medievali* [3rd ser.] 23 (1982): 151-192.

———. "The Study of Latin Texts in Late Anglo-Saxon England: (1) The Evidence of Latin Glosses." In *Latin and the Vernacular Languages in Early Medieval Britain*, ed. Nicholas P. Brooks, pp. 99-140. Leicester: Leicester University Press, 1982.

Law, Vivien. "The Latin and Old English Glosses in the Ars Tatuini." *Anglo-Saxon England* 6 (1977): 77-90.

Leclercq, Jean, OSB. *The Love of Learning and the Desire for God: A Study of Monastic Culture*, translated by Catharine Misrahi. New York: Fordham University Press, 1961.

Levison, William. *England and the Continent in the Eighth Century.* Oxford: Oxford University Press, 1946.

Mady, Z. "An VIIIth Century Aldhelm Fragment in Hungary." *Acta Antiqua Academiae Scientiarum Hungaricae* 13 (1965): 441-453.

Manitius, Max. *Geschichte der lateinischen Literatur des Mittelalters.* 3 vols. Munich: C.H. Beck, 1911-1931.

Marenbon, John. "Les Sources du Vocabulaire d'Aldhelm." *Archivum Latinitatis Medii Aevi* [*Bulletin du Cange*] 41 (1977-1978): 75-90.

Martin, B.K. "Aspects of Winter in Latin and Old English Poetry." *Journal of English and Germanic Philology* 68 (1969): 375-390.

Meritt, Herbert D. *Fact and Lore About Old English Words.* Stanford: Stanford University Press, 1954.

Mustanoja, Tauno F. "Notes on Some Old English Glosses in Aldhelm's De Laudibus Virginitatis." *Neuphilologische Mitteilungen* 51 (1950): 49-61.

O'Keeffe, Katherine O'Brien. "The Text of Aldhelm's Enigma no. c in Oxford, Bodleian Library, Rawlinson C. 697 and Exeter Riddle 40." *Anglo-Saxon England* 14 (1985): 61-74.

O'Keeffe, Katherine O'Brien and Alan R.P. Journet, "Numerical Taxonomy and the Analysis of Manuscript Relationships." *Manuscripta* 27(1983): 131-145.

Page, Ray I. "The Study of Latin Texts in Late Anglo-Saxon England: (2) The Evidence of English Glosses." In *Latin and the Vernacular Languages in Early Medieval Britain*, ed. Nicholas P. Brooks, pp. 141-165. Leicester: Leicester University Press, 1982.

———. "More Aldhelm Glosses from CCCC 326." *English Studies* 56 (1975): 481-490.

Parkes, M.B. "The Manuscript of the Leiden Riddle." *Anglo-Saxon England* 1 (1972): 207-217.

Pollard, G. "Some Anglo-Saxon Bookbindings." *The Book Collector* 24 (1975): 130-159.

Rella, F.A. "Continental Manuscripts Acquired for English Centers in the 10th and early 11th Centuries: A Preliminary Checklist." *Anglia* 98 (1980): 107-116.

Rigg, A. George and G.R. Wieland. "A Canterbury Classbook of the Mid-Eleventh Century (the 'Cambridge Songs' Manuscript)." *Anglo-Saxon England* 4 (1975): 113-130.

Robinson, Fred C. "Syntactical Glosses in Latin Manuscripts of Anglo-Saxon Provenance." *Speculum* 48 (1973): 443-475.

Ross, Alan S.C. "Notes on the Method of Glossing Employed in the Lindisfarne Gospels." *Transactions of the Philological Society* (1933): 108-119.

Scott, Peter Dale. "Rhetorical and Symbolic Ambiguity: The Riddles of Symphosius and Aldhelm." In *Saints, Scholars and Heroes. Studies in Medieval Culture in Honor of Charles W. Jones*, ed. Margot King and Wesley M. Stevens, 1: 116-144. 2 vols. Minnesota: Hill Monastic Library, 1979.

Whitbread, L. "The Old English Poem Aldhelm," *English Studies* 57 (1976): 193-197.

———. "The Liber Monstrorum and Beowulf." *Mediaeval Studies* 36 (1974): 434-471.

Whitman, F.H. "The Christian Background to Two Riddle Motifs." *Studia Neophilologica* 41 (1969): 93-98.

———. "Medieval Riddling: Factors Underlying Its Development." *Neuphilologische Mitteilungen* 71 (1970): 177-185.

Wieland, Gernot R. *The Latin Glosses on Arator and Prudentius in Cambridge University Library, MS Gg.5.35*. Studies and Texts 61. Toronto: Pontifical Institute of Mediaeval Studies, 1983.

———. "The Glossed Manuscript: Classbook or Library Book?" *Anglo-Saxon England* 14 (1985): 153-174.

Williamson, Craig. *A Feast of Creatures: Anglo-Saxon Riddle-Songs*. Philadelphia: University of Pennsylvania Press, 1982.

Winterbottom, Michael, ed. *Three Lives of English Saints*. Toronto Medieval Latin Texts. Toronto: Pontifical Institute of Mediaeval Studies, 1972.

———. "Aldhelm's Prose Style and Its Origins." *Anglo-Saxon England* 6 (1977): 39-76.

General Index

DATE DUE

HIGHSMITH   # 45220